The sense of early modern writing

Manchester University Press

The sense of early modern writing

Rhetoric, poetics, aesthetics

Mark Robson

Manchester University Press

Manchester and New York

distributed exclusively in the USA by Palgrave

Copyright © Mark Robson 2006

The right of Mark Robson to be identified as the author of this work has been asserted by him in accordance with the Copyright, Designs and Patents Act 1988.

Published by Manchester University Press
Oxford Road, Manchester M13 9NR, UK
and Room 400, 175 Fifth Avenue, New York, NY 10010, USA
www.manchesteruniversitypress.co.uk

Distributed exclusively in the USA by
Palgrave, 175 Fifth Avenue, New York,
NY 10010, USA

Distributed exclusively in Canada by
UBC Press, University of British Columbia, 2029 West Mall,
Vancouver, BC, Canada V6T 1Z2

British Library Cataloguing-in-Publication Data
A catalogue record for this book is available from the British Library

Library of Congress Cataloging-in-Publication Data applied for

ISBN   0 7190 6946 7 *hardback*
EAN   978 0 7190 6946 8

First published 2006

15 14 13 12 11 10 09 08 07 06   10 9 8 7 6 5 4 3 2 1

Typeset
by SNP Best-set Typesetter Ltd, Hong Kong
Printed in Great Britain
by Bell & Bain Ltd, Glasgow

Contents

List of illustrations   vi

Acknowledgements   vii

1 Introduction: the sense of early modern writing   1

Part I Sense's reading

2 Rhetoric, in more than one sense   15

3 Is there an early modern aesthetic?   39

4 Poetry's defences   60

Part II Reading's senses

5 To sign: *Sir Thomas More*   91

6 Swansongs   120

7 To hear with eyes   146

8 Blind faith   169

9 Epilogue   200

Select bibliography   203

Index   221

List of illustrations

1 Odinet Godran, 'Expositio Mortis Thomae
   Mori', f.4r.   175
   Permission British Library, MS Add. 28786.

2 Antoine Caron, 'The Arrest and Supplication of Sir
   Thomas More (1478–1535)'.   179
   Musée de Blois, Blois, France, Lauros/Giraudon/
   Bridgeman Art Gallery.

Acknowledgements

Because this work has arisen from several other projects over several years, the debts that I have accrued are many and various. The bulk of the work for this book took place in Leeds and Nottingham. I have been fortunate in my colleagues, and thanks must also go to students at Leeds, Manchester and, especially, Nottingham, who have borne being experimented on with generosity and good humour. Those who will find traces of their influence and friendship here (however indirectly) include: David Alderson, Barry Atkins, Patricia Badir, Ron Carter, Helen Freshwater, Sarah Grandage, Matt Green, Richard Kirkland, John McLeod, John McRae, Caz Masel, Jo Morra, Louise Mullaney, Matthew Pateman, Antony Rowland, Nicola Royan, Julie Sanders, Marq Smith and Peter Stockwell.

More direct help came from those (often also friends) who have read parts of the book in this or earlier forms: Paul Hammond, Thomas Healy, Peter Howarth, John Joughin, David Lindley, James Loxley, Simon Malpas, Nigel Mapp, Nicholas Royle and Matthew Steggle. Thanks.

The staffs of the following libraries deserve special mention: the Brotherton Library, Leeds; the John Rylands Libraries, Manchester; the Hallward Library, Nottingham; the British Library, London and Boston Spa; and the Bodleian Library, Oxford.

Financial assistance came from the School of English, University of Leeds, as well as the School of English Studies and the Research Committee, University of Nottingham. I am grateful to all those who made this funding possible.

Much of the material that appears here has been tried out at conferences and seminars. My thanks go to the organisers and audiences whose encouragement (and disagreement) prompted me to further thought. Several sections of this book, often in dramatically different versions, have appeared previously. Most of Chapter 3 appears in *The New Aestheticism*, edited by John J. Joughin and Simon Malpas (Manchester and New York: Manchester University Press, 2003), pp. 119–30. Sections of Chapter 6 may be found in *English Manuscript Studies, 1100–1700* 9 (2000): 238–56. A shorter version of Chapter 7 was published in *Early Modern Literary Studies* 7.1 (2001). I am grateful to the editors and to the readers who shaped the material in these earlier incarnations. Some of the material in Chapters 5 and 8 derives from my unpublished doctoral thesis, 'Posthumous Representations of Thomas More: Critical Readings' (University of Leeds, 1996). Particular thanks go to David Lindley for his exemplary supervision of this thesis.

All at MUP deserve a measure of thanks. Matthew Frost turns editing into a form of friendship. Kate Fox brought some much needed sanity to the process. As readers, James Loxley and Nick Royle, by unmasking themselves, made it possible to improve some sections immeasurably. Those who remained anonymous are also thanked.

This book is dedicated to Elodie.

1

Introduction: the sense of early modern writing

I

What does it mean to call a book *The sense of early modern writing*? What is revealed, concealed, confirmed or exposed in such a gesture? What, we might ask, is the rhetorical force of such a title?

First of all, and simply put, the title is a recognition of the importance of an attention to sense in reading early modern texts. That is, of course, a little too simply put. When I talk about the significance of sense, I am really trying to name two things. So I do not simply mean to say that a sense of 'sense' is crucial for an understanding of early modern culture, although I do think that that is true. My title is also an attempt precisely to mark another significance. In emphasising sense, I want to draw together three areas from which sense is made: rhetoric, poetics and aesthetics. Coming to terms with rhetoric, poetics and aesthetics, I believe, is essential for understanding not only early modern writing but also a certain influential narrative of modernity.[1] This notion of modernity is not a purely literary one, and my discussion has nothing to say about artistic ideas of modernism. Rather, the narrative I have in mind is best thought of as a philosophical one, and in particular is associated with the inheritance of a post-Kantian European philosophical tradition. It would also be possible to start this story a little further back, perhaps with Descartes, but attempts to offer a definitive 'origin' for modernity, philosophical or otherwise, would not add much to my discussion. I will follow the post-Kantian route because that has been, and continues to be, of the greatest influence in the determination of concepts such as the aesthetic, the work of art or the concept of history.[2] *The sense of early modern writing*, then, is concerned both with rhetoric, poetics and aesthetics as they are to be found in early modern texts, and equally with the thought that allows us to make sense of the early modern as a conceptual category.

Having said that, this study is neither 'philosophical' nor 'historical' (and not even 'historicist' in its ultimate aims).[3] In pursuing an avowedly theoretical investigation of these topics I am putting my work at odds with much recent scholarship on the early modern period. For example, David Kastan writes in *Shakespeare After Theory*, a book that he claims is 'about reading Shakespeare historically', that: 'Shakespeare's plays are always situated in and saturated by history. History marks the texts as they are set forth, and the texts continue to absorb new histories as they are performed and read'. Ultimately, however, he wishes to 'restore Shakespeare's artistry to the earliest conditions of its realization and intelligibility'.[4] My concern is much more with the 'new histories' generated, and that will continue to be generated, by reading. There are places, then, in which I make a deliberate if not always explicit gesture towards anachronism. As such, *The sense of early modern writing* is opposed to a view such as that of Brian Vickers, who laments the turn towards 'theory driven' readings, claiming that: 'anachronism distorts the past to suit the whims of the present'.[5] The desire for an 'undistorted' sense of the past implies the possibility of being secure in the knowledge of what such a 'pure' history would look like, but it also renders inert the performative dimensions of texts that allow for the generation of what Kastan calls new histories.[6] By what right, we might want to ask, might one claim either to have an undistorted access to the past, or to have been able to calculate all that such a past might become?

It is hard not to be struck by Jonathan Goldberg's recent comment on the state of early modern studies: 'the demise of "theory" – or, better, the demise of its promise, especially in early modern studies – has prompted moves "after theory", which is also to say, before theory. New historicism, insofar as it is still practiced, is virtually indistinguishable from old historicism; early modern cultural studies divide the world into prefabricated binarisms and think themselves liberatory in so doing. In Shakespeare studies, postmodernity has passed; conservatism has returned.'[7]

Certainly Goldberg could adduce plenty of evidence for this somewhat gloomy diagnosis, and he is entirely right about the dominant tone of early modern studies at the present time. The sigh of relief that theoretically informed studies seem to be on the wane can audibly be heard emanating from some quarters. It is also true that the reflex references to the figures of 'high' theory that littered the footnotes of those whose true interests clearly lay elsewhere (to Derrida, Barthes, Foucault, Lacan, Althusser and others – and nearly always to the anthologised essays) have been tidied away. But this has, I think, been replaced by a much deeper – if less widespread – engagement with theoretical texts and the tradition of European thought from which they emerged among some of those working in this area. What is intriguing is that these engagements often go under the name of 'philosophy', or are centred upon more local debates such as 'ethics' or 'aesthetics' or 'modernity', rather than announcing themselves as avowedly theoretical projects. Thus the references will as often be to Nietzsche, Kierkegaard or Hegel as to the French and German thought of the twentieth century. Much of this work is only just emerging, and is largely to be found at conferences rather than in print. Most reassuringly of all, there has as yet been no attempt to offer a label, -ism or 'school' badge to describe such work. It is with such work that I would wish to express a solidarity, but not in order to institute another disciplinary area. *The sense of early modern writing* is not primarily a sustained dialogue with contemporary criticism, in part because of the reluctance of early modern studies to pay anything like serious attention to theoretical issues, and in part because I have a more positive urge towards demonstrating both the applicability and the fecundity of a theoretically-based approach. My desire to make this book readable for those who have not immersed themselves in the critical developments of the last twenty years or so has led to a more implicit approach to critical debate.

What I am concerned with here might best be understood under the misleadingly simple heading of 'reading'. In the final footnote, little more than a sketch, for his essay 'Shakespeare's Ear', Joel Fineman intimates a path to be followed, insisting on remembering 'the rhetorical question'. He comments: 'people don't want to read nowadays, substituting thematic reaction for reading'.[8] Such thematisation is particularly tempting for historicist studies, and we need to remember, alongside the rhetorical question (which I take to be the question of rhetoric itself), the caution advised by Paul de Man. Explaining his 'failure' to write a literary historical work, de Man tells us 'I began to read Rousseau seriously in preparation for a historical reflection on Romanticism and found myself unable to progress beyond local difficulties of interpretation'.[9] Local difficulties such as those encountered by de Man are precisely what should trouble attempts to offer a global view (or world picture) of a given period and its literatures, and I make no attempt to do so here.[10] These local difficulties are not without significance and the stakes for such readings are high. It does matter that the readings given here are more than simply idiosyncratic, and I have been led by another of de Man's comments: 'What makes a reading more or less true is simply the predictability, the necessity of its occurrence, regardless of the reader or of the author's wishes.'[11] This necessity is what operates as a guard-rail against the charge made by Vickers that theoretically informed readings are a matter of subjective preference and imposition. As far as has been consciously possible, I don't believe that the readings offered here are products of my whim. On the contrary, part of the concern of this book is to discern the outline of an ethics of reading, which is a matter to which I will return at the end of this introduction.

There are, of course, few things less simple than reading. While some, even recent, books that claim to address reading are more properly thought of as source studies, the topic of reading as both a theoretical and historical phenomenon is attracting increased attention.[12] Early modern studies by Sherman, Sharpe, Kintgen and others have laid some of the groundwork for a better understanding of reading in a historicising mode.[13] But they are still to be fruitfully combined with theoretical work by de Man, J. Hillis Miller, and others.[14] *The sense of early modern writing* is not an attempt to bring these two areas of investigation together in an explicit way, but it indicates some of the forms that such an encounter might take. In part why I believe that this encounter is necessary lies in my agreement with Michael Syrotinski that 'it is precisely the incursions of "reading", in the strong theoretical sense of the term, into "sensual experience", that disarticulate the categories to which the senses have traditionally been assigned'.[15]

Where reading meets aesthetics, rhetoric and poetics is in a concern with cognition. Aesthetics, rather than being representative of any etiolated idea of 'taste' in the judgement of art, is here intended in the sense in which Kant uses it. For Kant, aesthetics is a way into the perception, knowledge and judgement of objects, and these objects are not confined to the 'artificial', that is, to art. Much of Kant's Third Critique is concerned with nature. Indeed, to many readers who are looking for a theory of art and its appreciation, the *Critique of Judgment* is far *too* concerned with nature, and is excessively recalcitrant in yielding the tools of art criticism. This is because for Kant the stakes of the aesthetic are far higher than a philosophy of art, still less art criticism. Indeed, it is better to think in terms less of aesthetics than of *aisthesis*. This broader category addresses both the ways in which we make sense of the world, and the utility of the senses in this process of making sense. Art does not stand outside of these processes. Indeed, art and in particular literature have often been best described as revealing and being powerful ways in which we make sense of the world. But that does not separate them from that world. As Margreta de Grazia notes: 'language is a material medium to be experienced like the rest of the material world through the senses'.[16] Reading must, then, as she puts it, look *at* rather than see *through* early modern texts. Seeing texts as objects also reminds us of their construction, that they are made, and this is a recognition marked in the idea of the poet as maker (in Sidney and Jonson, for example), from the Greek *poiein*. As many critics have noted, 'art' in the early modern period was close to the Greek *techne*, applicable both to the arts as we now think of them and to the mechanical crafts. It is in this sense that we need to think of rhetoric as an 'art' of persuasion.[17] This is one reason for wishing to understand how this art relates to what we now call the arts.

There is another reason why the decision to begin this book with a brief discussion of the aesthetic might appear in need of explanation. The aesthetic as a category has been through a period of renunciation, but is now returning to the critical forefront.[18] This resurgence of explicit interest does not, however, mean that the problems posed to aesthetics by thinking from a variety of perspectives suddenly disappear. Most significantly here, rhetoric itself presents certain problems. As Cynthia Chase has proposed:

The rhetorical character of language, the primacy of rhetorical 'force' and figure (that is, of *language*) in any art, constrains us to think 'art' from the standpoint of language rather than the inverse. The conflict in rhetoric precludes our understanding literature essentially as art, that is, as the harmonious interpenetration of content and form. Rhetoric thus makes a problem out of art or the aesthetic, insofar as the notion of the aesthetic is predicated upon the possibility of fusion or continuity of form and substance, being and doing. Their *dis*continuity – the forcing, in both senses, of their connection – especially troubles interpretation where it appears as an incompatibility between what a text implicitly says about language and figuration and its own figural structures and effects.[19]

What I will be arguing in this book is that, while accepting Chase's delineation of the problems that rhetoric poses to aesthetics, it is only through an attention to aesthetics and rhetoric together that it is possible to draw out the importance of this relation, as her work demonstrates. Rhetoric attains an importance for modernity because of its supposedly antagonistic position with respect to aesthetics; as such it is not so much opposed to as implicated within aesthetics. Equally, what is at stake in aesthetics becomes apparent only once rhetoric is factored back into the equation.

In thinking about how we make sense (of the world, of art, of each other, and so on), it is inevitable that this book is also concerned with the senses. Sense, of course, is not a new topic, but it has not been treated quite as it will be here.[20] One option would be to pursue the use of the word 'sense', to trace its complexity, drawing out the ways in which 'sense' makes sense. Such a path has already been opened up by William Empson.[21] What, then, am I doing with the senses? If texts actualise the senses in their attempts to make sense – in other words, if we always experience a text through a particular sense such as sight or hearing – then we also phenomenalise a body in or behind the text.[22] The most common version of this is the idea of an author's 'voice' (which I read in Chapter 5). What this book does is to draw together an awareness of the ways in which meaning is generated through the senses with an emphasis on the rhetorical (that is, linguistic) dimensions of the texts themselves. If, for example, a text tells us to be wary of trusting what we see, or if it tells us that speech may be a form of poison, then how do we continue to read using sight or hearing?

II

While *The sense of early modern writing* touches upon many large issues, my primary purpose here is much less ambitious than these statements might lead one to believe. There is no attempt here to give a conspectus of thought in the early modern period on questions of sense and cognition. Neither, as I have already suggested, is this a stepping stone in a historical narrative, a piece of a jigsaw that would allow us to place the early modern period among a series of interlocking but period-specific arguments that would allow such a picture to be put together. Instead, this book demonstrates the necessity of reading, but of a reading that is always local, located, limited – always aware, that is, of its limitations. To claim to have read a few texts, in the end, is not as small a claim as it might at first appear. In the current historicist climate, reading has, like rhetoric, become somehow unfashionable except as a topic for excavation. As such, this book might also be thought of as a metacritical exercise. To paraphrase Frank Kermode, if literature is thought of as one of the ways in which we make sense of the world, then criticism is best conceived as how we make sense of the ways we make sense of the world.

Each example that is used in this book is supposed to indicate the ways in which these ideas might be carried forward into other readings. There is no last word to be had on these subjects. Thus, when I discuss one of Shakespeare's texts, I am not attempting to give an overview of Shakespeare's works, but neither do I wish to assert that Shakespeare's work represents an 'age'. Despite the necessary inclusivity of my title, this is not an attempt to give an account of the whole of the interest of the early modern period's writers in questions of sense. At times the examples chosen may seem a bit obvious (including Shakespeare and Sidney), at others wilfully obscure (including Hester Pulter and Ro:Ba:). The discussion will make frequent reference to non-literary as well as literary materials, often in an attempt to provide a minimal degree of historical reconstruction necessary to allow a text to be understood. But I have tended to privilege those aspects of a text that seem to go beyond the limits of such period-specific contexts. What I am trying to do is to present a sense of the unfamiliar aspects of all too familiar texts, and at the same time to state the necessity of moving beyond the familiar narratives when we approach unfamiliar texts. Too often, the extension of the canon has been precisely that: the incorporation of 'new' texts into what rapidly become rather comfortable narratives. As several critics have noted, the increased attention given to apparently undervalued documents does tend to legitimate that attention through an appeal to what such documents can tell us about commonly discussed material, most obviously Shakespeare.

My initial consideration of rhetoric, poetics and aesthetics informs the organisation of the book, since what becomes apparent is the need to think about the relationship of sense as meaning to phenomenal aspects of texts, to how meaning is sensed, and thus to particular senses such as sight and hearing. Part I of the book, 'Sense's reading', contains three chapters that together form an elaboration of the connections between rhetoric, aesthetics and literature. Frequent recourse is made to rhetorical treatises, but equally frequently there are discussions of material that comes from periods other than the early modern, both earlier and later. Part II of the book, 'Reading's senses', offers four chapters, each of which focuses on either an aspect of the body related to the sense of reading (such as hands, voice, eyes and ears) or on the deliberate disavowal of the body and its senses.

If we are to understand early modern texts as something other than museum exhibits or as sacral objects, if we are to recognise the force of these texts without domesticating them as versions of what we think we already know, then we must be attentive not only to how we continue to make sense of them, but also to how they make sense, and make us sense. *The sense of early modern writing* is a first step in that process.

Notes

1 Discussions of early modern rhetoric are numerous, and those new to the field would need to begin with J. Bender and D. E. Wellbery (eds), *The Ends of Rhetoric: History, Theory, Practice* (Stanford: Stanford University Press, 1990); T. M. Conley, *Rhetoric in the European Tradition* (London: Longman, 1990); V. Kahn, *Rhetoric, Prudence and Skepticism in the Renaissance* (Ithaca: Cornell University Press, 1985); R. A. Lanham, *The Motives of Eloquence: Literary Rhetoric in the Renaissance* (New Haven: Yale University Press, 1994); R. McDonald, *Shakespeare and the Arts of Language* (Oxford: Oxford

University Press, 2001); P. Mack (ed.), *Renaissance Rhetoric* (Basingstoke: Macmillan, 1994); P. Parker, *Literary Fat Ladies: Rhetoric, Gender, Property* (London: Methuen, 1987); N. Rhodes, *The Power of Eloquence and English Renaissance Literature* (London: Harvester Wheatsheaf, 1992); D. Summers, *The Judgement of Sense: Renaissance Naturalism and the Rise of Aesthetics* (Cambridge: Cambridge University Press, 1987); B. Vickers, *Classical Rhetoric in English Poetry* (London: Macmillan, 1970) and *In Defence of Rhetoric* (Oxford: Clarendon Press, 1988).

2 On Kant's philosophy of history, see P. D. Fenves, *A Peculiar Fate: Metaphysics and World-History in Kant* (Ithaca: Cornell University Press, 1991). Although it is with Kant that most commentators begin, obviously the influence of Hegel should not be ignored. See T. Bahti, *Allegories of History: Literary Historiography after Hegel* (Baltimore: Johns Hopkins University Press, 1992).

3 As Linda Charnes observes: 'Too many scholars of Renaissance culture read, in the important injunction to "always historicize", an injunction to *only* historicize.' *Notorious Identity: Materializing the Subject in Shakespeare* (Cambridge, MA: Harvard University Press, 1995), p. 15 (her emphasis).

4 Kastan, *Shakespeare After Theory* (London: Routledge, 1999), pp. 15–16.

5 Vickers, *Shakespeare, Co-Author: A Historical Study of Five Collaborative Plays* (Oxford: Oxford University Press, 2002), p. 541.

6 In speaking of performativity, I am aware of the connections to the work of critics such as Quentin Skinner and David Norbrook, but my position is much closer to that of Derrida and de Man.

7 Goldberg, *Shakespeare's Hand* (Minneapolis: University of Minnesota Press, 2003), pp. ix–x.

8 Fineman, *The Subjectivity Effect in Western Literary Tradition: Toward the Release of Shakespeare's Will* (Cambridge, MA: MIT, 1991), p. 231, n. 5.

9 de Man, *Allegories of Reading: Figural Language in Rousseau, Nietzsche, Rilke, and Proust* (New Haven: Yale University Press, 1979), p. ix. As he later comments: 'Except for some passing allusions, *Allegories of Reading* is in no way a book about romanticism or its inheritance.' See *The Rhetoric of Romanticism* (New York: Columbia University Press, 1984), p. vii.

10 In talking about notions of 'world' in the context of early modern studies, there is always the risk of raising in a reader the fear that this book would be broaching yet again the plausibility of a 'world picture', whether Tillyard's or otherwise. While it is hard to be fully convinced by either Tillyard or the more absolute denials of his work, what is

aimed at here is something closer in spirit to the work of Jean-Luc Nancy. Nancy's *The Sense of the World* offers the single most rigorous and compelling meditation on exactly what is at stake in the notions of 'sense' and of 'world'. It is possible to register the significance of this work here in only the most cursory of ways, in ways far from adequate to the rigour imposed by Nancy's own text, or to the stricture of accounting for the fact that 'there is no longer any sense of the world'. *The Sense of the World*, trans. J. S. Librett (Minneapolis: University of Minnesota Press, 1997), p. 4. Nancy has continued this elaboration of 'sense' in, for example, *A Finite Thinking*, ed. S. Sparks (Stanford: Stanford University Press, 2003), especially in the title essay.

11 See de Man, *Critical Writings 1953–1978*, ed. L. Waters (Minneapolis: University of Minnesota Press, 1989), p. 221. The most sustained account of de Man's sense of reading is R. Gasché, *The Wild Card of Reading: On Paul de Man* (Cambridge, MA: Harvard University Press, 1998).

12 An example of a source study masquerading as a book on reading would be R. S. Miola, *Shakespeare's Reading* (Oxford: Oxford University Press, 2000).

13 See W. H. Sherman, *The Politics of Reading and Writing in the English Renaissance* (Amherst: University of Massachusetts Press, 1995); K. Sharpe, *Reading Revolutions: The Politics of Reading in Early Modern England* (New Haven: Yale University Press, 2000); E. R. Kintgen, *Reading in Tudor England* (Pittsburgh: University of Pittsburgh Press, 1996); chapters 7 to 10 of *A History of Reading in the West*, ed. G. Cavallo and R. Chartier (Cambridge: Polity, 1999); *Reading, Society and Politics in Early Modern England*, ed. K. Sharpe and S. Zwicker (Cambridge: Cambridge University Press, 2003).

14 I am thinking of J. H. Miller, *The Ethics of Reading* (New York: Columbia University Press, 1987); the essays in *Readers and Reading*, ed. A. Bennett (London: Longman, 1995), and *Sensual Reading: New Approaches to Reading and Its Relations to the Senses*, ed. M. Syrotinski and I. Maclachlan (London: Associated University Presses, 2001).

15 See Syrotinski's 'Introduction: Hors d'œuvre', in *Sensual Reading*, pp. 7–12.

16 M. de Grazia, 'Shakespeare and the craft of language', in *The Cambridge Companion to Shakespeare*, ed. M. de Grazia and S. Wells (Cambridge: Cambridge University Press, 2001), pp. 49–64, 52. See also de Grazia and P. Stallybrass, 'The Materiality of the Shakespearean Text', *Shakespeare Quarterly* 44 (1993): 1–29.

17 This notion persists into the later German thought. Thus Alexander Gottlieb Baumgarten, the 'founder' of the modern idea of aesthetics, writes in his *Reflections on Poetry* (1735), §68: 'the poet is like a maker or a creator. So the poem ought to be like a world. Hence by analogy whatever is evident to the philosophers concerning the real world, the same ought to be thought of a poem'. Cited in H. Caygill, *Art of Judgement* (Oxford: Basil Blackwell, 1989), p. 157.

18 See, for example, J.-L. Nancy, *The Muses*, trans. P. Kamuf (Stanford: Stanford University Press, 1996); W. Welsch, *Undoing Aesthetics*, trans. A. Inkpin (London: Sage, 1997); C. Menke, *The Sovereignty of Art: Aesthetic Negativity in Adorno and Derrida*, trans. N. Solomon (Cambridge, MA: MIT, 1998); E. Scarry, *On Beauty and Being Just* (London: Duckworth, 2000); *From an Aesthetic Point of View: Philosophy, Art and the Senses*, ed. P. Osborne (London: Serpent's Tail, 2000); J. Rancière, *The Politics of Aesthetics: The Distribution of the Sensible*, trans. G. Rockhill (London: Continuum, 2005); M. Redfield, *The Politics of Aesthetics: Nationalism, Gender, Romanticism* (Stanford: Stanford University Press, 2003); and *The New Aestheticism*, ed. J. J. Joughin and S. Malpas (Manchester and New York: Manchester University Press, 2003).

19 Chase, *Decomposing Figures: Rhetorical Readings in the Romantic Tradition* (Baltimore: Johns Hopkins University Press, 1986), p. 4. The passage cited includes a footnote to Lacoue-Labarthe's essay 'Le détour', on Nietzsche and rhetoric, now translated in *The Subject of Philosophy*, ed. T. Tresize (Minneapolis: Minnesota University Press, 1993), pp. 14–36. The relevant passage is on p. 31.

20 See *The Varieties of Sensory Experience. A Sourcebook in the Anthropology of the Senses*, ed. D. Howes (Toronto: University of Toronto Press, 1991); C. Classen, *Worlds of Sense: Exploring the Senses in History and across Cultures* (London: Routledge, 1993); and S. Stewart, *Poetry and the Fate of the Senses* (Chicago: University of Chicago Press, 2002).

21 See Empson, *The Structure of Complex Words* (Harmondsworth: Penguin, 1995), especially chapters 12–15. Most relevant to this discussion is Chapter 13 'Sense in *Measure for Measure*'.

22 The 'body' has attracted a great deal of recent interest in early modern studies. See, for example, L. Enterline, *The Rhetoric of the Body from Ovid to Shakespeare* (Cambridge: Cambridge University Press, 2000); J. G. Harris, *Foreign Bodies and the Body Politic: Discourses of Social Pathology in Early Modern England* (Cambridge: Cambridge University Press, 1998); D. Hillman and C. Mazzio (eds), *The Body in Parts: Fantasies of Corporeality in Early Modern Europe* (London:

Routledge, 1997); M. C. Schoenfeldt, *Bodies and Selves in Early Modern England: Physiology and Inwardness in Spenser, Shakespeare, Herbert, and Milton* (Cambridge: Cambridge University Press, 1999); S. Scholz, *Body Narratives: Writing the Nation and Fashioning the Subject in Early Modern England* (Basingstoke: Macmillan, 2000).

Part I
Sense's reading

2

Rhetoric, in more than one sense

I

In a work ascribed to Ben Jonson, we find the following suggestion: 'Language most shows a man: speak, that I may see thee.' Such a statement has an aphoristic quality, a sense of a truth revealed, or at least glimpsed. This invitation to speak is itself concerned with revelation, with an opening to sight through language. But this aphorism trembles between the senses. Language as speech calls upon the ear, but the voice that it calls forth is to be seen with the eye, or perhaps with the mind's eye. What this hints at is a visible language, that is, not speech but writing. Equally, there is a curious relation between language and the one who would speak. The notion of 'showing' implies that there is something to be shown, that there is already something that lies behind the linguistic utterance. But there is also the implication that unless the person speaks, he cannot be seen truly, or perhaps at all.[1] Let us follow the thread of this thought as it unwinds:

> Language most shows a man: speak, that I may see thee. It springs out of the most retired and inmost parts of us, and is the image of the parent of it, the mind. No glass renders a man's form or likeness so true as his speech. Nay, it is likened to a man . . .[2]

The first half of the second sentence seems to solve some of the mystery, but our certainty falters as the sentence unfolds. There is an 'inmost' part – what we might want to think of as that within which passes show – but instead of language revealing that inmost part itself, it becomes an image of it. In other words, as readers of Shakespeare's sonnets will quickly recognise, language becomes the 'child', a 'reproduction' rather than the thing itself, and the 'parent' to this child is not the whole person but only the mind. This explains, of course, why it cannot be seen without linguistic articulation. Language thus becomes a kind of telepathic medium, which allows the mind's eye of the one who hears to see the (image of the) mind of the one who speaks. But the metaphor of the glass or mirror that follows in the next line adds a further level of mediation. Speech is something external to the man, a reflection or imitation of the mind, a like-ness. This similitude leads to a further step; language itself is a kind of man, an effigy or substitute body, and Jonson goes on in this passage to elaborate the linguistic corpus.

This may seem to be stretching a point, but the status of language in this text is a far from trivial matter. A little earlier in the *Discoveries* we find:

> Speech is the only benefit man hath to express his excellency of mind above other creatures. It is the instrument of society. Therefore Mercury, who is the president of language, is called *deorum hominumque interpres* ['The interpreter of gods and men']. In all speech, words and sense are as the body and the soul. The sense is as the life and soul of language, without which all words are dead. Sense is wrought out of experience, the knowledge of human life and actions, or of the liberal arts, which the Greeks called Εγχυχλο παιδειαν ['General education']. Words are the people's, yet there is a choice of them to be made; for *verborum delectus origo est eloquentiae* ['The choice of words is the beginning of eloquence'].[3]

Even without tackling the 'content' as such (to which I will return later), there is much to note about this passage. Firstly, there is the problem of saying whose ideas these are. Although this is in many ways Jonson's text, *Discoveries* is, as its full title makes clear, a compendium of commonplaces largely drawn from Jonson's reading. In this case, as the fragments of Latin and Greek suggest, the ideas may be found in Virgil, Quintilian and Cicero, just as the first quotation leads back to Vives. And the Cicero may be traced further back to a lost text by Julius Caesar, *De Analogia*, as Jonson's own marginal note indicates. Yet it is this very lack of what we would now call (in a thoroughly post-romantic fashion) 'originality' that makes these passages of particular interest here. Such distancing from the authority of an authorial presence is part of the attraction of the aphorism, of a truth that stands independently of the one who gives voice to it. As it is put in the *Discover-*

ies: 'Truth lies open to all; it is no man's several.'[4] So while I agree with Richard Dutton that although there is no sense of a systematic logic to the *Discoveries* nonetheless 'Jonson forges an identity, or a speaking voice, for himself out of pre-existing materials', I would perhaps place more emphasis on that word 'forges' than Dutton may have intended.[5] Indeed, Dutton persuasively suggests that:

> at times Jonson wanted to believe that the 'sense' of a poem could be divorced from the linguistic structure in which it was embedded, but at other times he saw the impossibility of this. . . . Indeed (the central point around which he constantly revolves, though he never confronts it openly) language itself may be inherently unreliable and unpredictable: there is only the custom of the tribe, its consensual usage, to prevent its being so. And how far can you trust those?[6]

Though Jonson may have expressed his preference for a plainness and eloquence that sought to minimise such instability, passages such as those above demonstrate the problems that creep in to even the most simple and conventional statements of principle.

Jonson's struggle to control the effects of language, which may also be seen for example in his comments on the proper use of metaphor in the *Discoveries*, is indicative of a wider debate about the nature of language and its relation to meaning or sense. The central distinction is between, on the one hand, a version of Cratylism in which words are seen to have a natural affinity with the objects that they designate and, on the other, an Aristotelianism proposing human convention as the only guarantee of meaning (although such a distinction is both oversimplified and complicated since both positions could be adopted within the same text in this period).[7] Such distinctions have to rely, of course, upon the perception of the object, of the word and of the relation between them, and this returns us to the observation that I made above about the sensory dimensions of linguistic utterance. First, though, I would like to offer a few comments on another connection that should be made with Jonson's statements. The passages that I've quoted above come from sections of the *Discoveries* that have a pedagogical impulse, and it has been speculated that these may have come from Jonson's preparatory notes for some lectures on rhetoric at Gresham College, London.[8] The status of rhetoric thus seems to deserve a few comments at this point, before we come back to this question of the relation between rhetoric and the senses.

II

As is well known, rhetorical training was central to the humanist educational system. Stemming in large part from the texts and example of Erasmus, early modern rhetorical instruction worked to recover and disseminate ideas from classical texts, and thus those who received such training were made familiar with works by Aristotle, Quintilian, Cicero and others.[9] This does not mean that early modern understandings of rhetoric were simply repetitions of the classical texts, of course, just as there is not an unbroken continuity between early modern and medieval rhetorical thought, and there is much debate in the period (such as that inspired by Peter Ramus, for example) on the need to reform rhetoric.[10] Such texts remained at the heart of educational practice, however. The central features of this training emphasise the classical division of rhetoric into *inventio* (the rules for the 'discovery' of subject matter); *dispositio* (which gave the rules for the arrangement of this subject matter); and *elocutio* (the rules governing the presentation or performance of the discourse). This was combined with a division of discourse into three different kinds of oration: *deliberative* (or legislative, Aristotle calls it political; usually used to exhort or dissuade); *forensic* (or judicial; usually used to accuse or defend); and *epideictic* (or panegyric; for commemoration, praise or blame, frequently with a ceremonial element).[11] These divisions were also matched in pedagogical practice with an emphasis on argumentation in formal terms, such that students were encouraged to pursue a dialectical approach that stressed the capacity to argue both sides of a case, what is generally referred to as argument *in utramque partem*. In the first English rhetorical text addressed to the general reader, Thomas Wilson offers the following definition: 'Rhetorique is an Arte to set foorth by utteraunce of words, matter at large, or (as *Cicero* doth say) it is a learned, or rather an artificiall declaration of the mynd, in the handling of any cause, called in contention, that may through reason largely be discussed.'[12] As in the passages from Jonson, language is related back to a 'declaration of the mynd'. Conventional in his adoption of a formulation originated by Cicero but also given in Horace and Quintilian, for Wilson the ultimate purpose of the oration is expressed as the 'affective triad': to teach (*docere*), to delight (*delectare*), and to persuade (*movere*).[13]

Rhetoric, in both the early modern period and the classical texts from which it took its most powerful ideas, tended to be seen as either neutral or double, that is, as suspect as well as to be lauded.[14] The tradition of prejudice against rhetoric goes back at least as far as Plato, and is often found to be most clearly expressed in his *Gorgias*. Precisely because it is an art of persuasion, there is always the suspicion that this is rhetoric's only concern. In other words, there is no necessity for the rhetorician to be interested in truth, only in what will prove persuasive.[15] In the *Gorgias*, a clear distinction is made between a form of persuasion that is designed to ensure that the individual survives and thrives, the aim of which is to allow one to live as long as possible (see 511b–c), and the art of dialogue or dialectic, in which truth is pursued even at the expense of life itself (see 448d–e and 471d–e). The 'platonic' critique of rhetoric, then, is part of a strategy to elevate philosophy, since philosophy arrogates for itself the access to truth that it denies to rhetoric.[16] Revising this view somewhat, in the *Phaedrus* we still find in Plato an insistence that if the rhetorician is to persuade in a positive way, it is necessary that he know the truth of his subject, and not merely be in a position to express an opinion.[17] The truth of a discourse comes not from its expression but from a prior 'content', with the assumption that the truth of this prior knowledge would be achieved through dialogue or dialectic. Thus knowledge of rhetoric alone is not sufficient. Such an observation is repeated in the early modern period by writers such as Sir Thomas Elyot who, in *The Boke named the Governour* (1531), proposed that 'they which do only teach rhetoric – which is the science whereby is taught an artificial form of speaking wherein is the power to persuade, move, and delight – or by that science only do speak or write without any adminiculation of other sciences ought to be named rhetoricians, declamators, artificial speakers (named in Greek *logodedali*), or any other name than orators.'[18] Elyot thus has a similar view of rhetoric to that of Wilson, but he assigns to it a different value.

There is a suspicion that the continuation of rhetorical training stems from a need to recognise its threat. All were taught how to do it, but perhaps only so they might learn how to recognise its usage by others. Certainly there is a problem in identifying the status of rhetoric in a culture that has been trained both to use it and to be suspicious of it. We might come to feel that it is only possible to *see* rhetoric if you can also *see through* it. It is such a negative attitude that seems to underpin the later attempts to turn rhetoric back into a form of unpersuasive ornament, and thus into a merely decorative poetics. The obvious, though far from isolated, examples here would be Kant and Hegel, and the diminution of rhetoric that we might for convenience call 'romantic' acts as an unavoidable stumbling block in our attempts to recover a full sense of rhetoric's status in the early modern period.

III

In Kant's *Critique of Judgment*, as Rodolphe Gasché has pointed out, there is a distinct division in his handling of the question of rhetoric.[19] What has become most well known is Kant's negative attitude to rhetoric. While there is a clear preference for poetry over rhetoric on the grounds that rhetoric is more bound to precepts and examples than poetry, what emerges clearly is the distinction between rhetoric as a vivifying force (as in Cicero), and rhetoric as an *ars oratoria*, as a force of persuasion. Prepared to concede to rhetoric its positive function in making the concepts of reason entertaining, Kant has nothing positive to say about the persuasive aspect of rhetoric. Such persuasion draws upon the ability to sway the emotions that it shares with poetry, but is, Kant argues, designed to sway the mind, stripping it of its autonomy. As such, rhetoric always partakes of deception. In this, Kant to some extent echoes a certain reading of Plato.[20]

Those looking for the 'romantic' rejection of rhetoric would do well to turn to a comment such as the following from Hegel's *Aesthetics*, in which he discusses sentence-construction in poetry: 'To this field there belong the so-called "figures of speech", so far that is, as they are related to clothing thoughts in words. But their use easily leads to rhetoric and declamation (in the bad sense of these words). The individual vitality of a poem is destroyed if these word forms substitute a universal mode of expression, constructed on rules, for the peculiar outpouring of feeling and passion.'[21] This idea of language as a form of clothing is not only an element of the romantic dismissal of rhetoric, it is also common in the early modern period, and will reappear at moments throughout this book. Hegel stresses poetic construction according to rules as damaging to the vitality of a poem, and goes on to argue that if the form of expression of a poem and the effect that it wishes to achieve are seen to be its most important aspects, then: 'this is the place where rhetoric and declamation . . . are developed in a way destructive of poetry's inner life, because the circumspection which shapes the poem is revealed as *intentional*, and a self-conscious and regulated art impairs the true effect which must appear to be and be unintentional and artless'. He complains that even Virgil and Horace sound 'artificial, deliberately manufactured', and that if rhetorical tropes and tricks are employed too fully (as in the French classical style) language becomes 'decorative'.[22]

What Hegel seems to be alluding to here is a version of linguistic construction that revivifies the classical notion of the poet as maker. Again, we find this expressed in conventional form in Jonson's *Discoveries* (although it is also to be found in Sidney, as we shall see). Answering the question 'What is a poet?', Jonson notes:

> A poet is that which by the Greeks is called χατ' ἐξοχήν, ὁ Ποιητής, a maker or a feigner [*par excellence*]; his art, an art of imitation or feigning, expressing the life of man in fit measure, numbers, and harmony, according to Aristotle: from the word ποιεῖν, which signifies to make or feign. Hence he is called a poet, not he which writeth in measure only, but that feigneth and formeth a fable, and writes things like the truth. For the fable and fiction is (as it were) the form and soul of any poetical work or poem.[23]

As he goes on to say, in distinguishing between a poem and poesy, 'A poem, as I have told you, is the work of the poet, the end and fruit of his labour and study. Poesy is his skill or craft of making; the very fiction itself, the reason or form of the work.'[24] While in the Aristotelian tradition stemming from the first book of the *Poetics* this emphasis on imitation and making elevates the role of the poet, it is precisely this connection that raises the suspicion that this artifice, feigning and manufacturing remains (to borrow a word that is so often applied to rhetoric, and which we have already seen used by Wilson and Elyot) merely 'artificial'. This is the doubleness inherent in the idea of poetry as making: there is always the possibility that poetry's proximity to the mechanical arts could be seen to make poetry itself mechanical. From the perspective of a romantic aesthetic, which to some extent still underwrites any modern aesthetic, art must be kept at a safe distance from artifice. Hegel concludes this section: 'Truly poetic expression refrains both from purely declamatory rhetoric and also from pompous and witty playing with words.'[25] Excerpting passages in this way does little service to the complexity of Hegel's thought on art and poetry, of course, and it would be necessary to look more carefully at the whole of the *Aesthetics* and the discussions elsewhere in his work (for example in the *Phenomenology of Spirit* and the *Encyclopedia*).[26] But, partial though these statements are in the context of Hegel's work, in terms of the post-romantic attitude towards rhetoric, they have a suitably exemplary character.

The notion that art must appear artless is, however, not as new as this might make it sound. The Renaissance idea of *sprezzatura* had the same end in sight, but courtly manuals such as Castiglione's *Il Cortegiano* make explicit the degree to which this artlessness is itself the product of work and practice.[27] In the early modern dictum which could be found in Aristotle, Ovid and Longinus, *ars est celare artem*, 'the art is to conceal art'. In English texts, this idea is repeatedly presented in, for example, both Sidney's *A Defence of Poetry* and Puttenham's *Arte of English Poesy*. Sidney complains of the kind of courtiers who use art to show art rather than to conceal it, arguing that in this they 'flieth from nature, and indeed abuseth art'.[28] Similarly Puttenham suggests that the courtier may be 'a dissembler only in the subtilties of his arte: that is, when he is most artificiall, so to disguise and cloake it as it may not appeare, nor seeme to proceede from him by any studie or trade of rules, but to be his naturall'.[29] Hegel's clothing is also Puttenham's cloak. Both of these ideas rest upon a fundamental distinction between form and content, but such a distinction itself has a metaphorical dimension. As I. A. Richards notes, this a distinctly unhelpful way of thinking, and he describes the form/content opposition as a 'wretchedly inconvenient' metaphor, adding: 'So is that other which makes language a dress which thought puts on.'[30] This set of distinctions takes on another aspect in the later reception of the philosophical tradition which underpins it, in which the relation between language and truth becomes a central aspect of the post-romantic inheritance. As Lacoue-

Labarthe has pointed out, in Martin Heidegger's attempt to come to terms both with the German tradition represented by Kant, Schiller and Hegel and the wider Western tradition of which it is a part, a crux of that reading is the distinction between *phusis* and *techne*, between Nature and Art, between Ancient and Modern, and thus between two conceptions of the political ramifications of the relation of poetry to truth.[31] This is the shadow that falls across any discussion of the role of mimesis in the definition of art, and while this book does not take on these problematics directly, I hope that readers will be able to discern the outlines of an implicit engagement.[32]

Indeed, further difficulties occur even within the philosophical manifestation of this 'history' of rhetoric's decline. As I have already suggested, Kant is often seen to embody the strongest example of the Enlightenment critique of rhetoric in favour of a transparent immediacy of language. It is in Kant that we find clear expression both of the traditional charges against rhetoric that had been made from Plato onwards, and of the romantic thought about art that will make rhetoric a supposed irrelevance to the literary arts.[33] Yet, in 'Hypotyposis', the essay that is reprinted as the conclusion to his recent book on Kant's aesthetics, Gasché offers the following suggestion:

> Considering the philosophically innovative use of imagination in Kant, the question arises as to whether Kant's development of this notion is not indebted to a tradition other than the explicitly philosophical one, namely, to the rhetorical tradition. The aesthetic theory developed by Alexander Gottlieb Baumgarten in the eighteenth century has been linked to a revival of rhetoric. . . . Indeed, aesthetic theory – and this is still true of Kant – is primarily a poetics, one that is to a large extent a rhetoric.[34]

What Gasché proposes here is not the narrative with which we have become familiar. The more conventional story would propose that aesthetics displaces rhetoric, decisively, that rhetoric falls away as aesthetics rises. Indeed, this is where Gasché's essay begins. Noting Kant's explicit rejection of the art of oratory, Gasché proposes, nonetheless, that in the *Critique of Judgment* there is a philosophical appropriation of rhetoric that is part of a recognition of rhetoric's essential relation to beautiful art.[35] This becomes apparent, for Gasché, in Kant's adoption of the term *hypotyposis* at a crucial point in the Third Critique. In §59, 'On Beauty as the Symbol of Morality', Kant attempts to draw together the beautiful and the good, having made a clear separation between the two in his earlier discussion:

> All *hypotyposis* (exhibition, *subiecto ad adspectum* [submission to inspection, itself echoing Aristotle's notion of putting 'before the eyes']) consists in making ⟨a concept⟩ sensible, and is either *schematic* or *symbolic*. In schematic hypotyposis there is a concept that the understanding has formed, and the intuition corresponding to it is given a priori. In symbolic hypotyposis there is a concept which only reason can think and to which no sensible intuition can be adequate, and this concept is supplied with an intuition that judgment treats in a way merely analogous to the procedure it follows in schematizing; i.e., the treatment agrees with this procedure merely in the rule followed rather than in terms of the intuition itself, and hence merely in terms of the form of the reflection rather than its content.[36]

As de Man proposes in his reading of this passage in 'The Epistemology of Metaphor', 'Hypotyposis makes present to the senses something which is not within their reach, not just because it does not happen to be there but because it consists, in whole or in part, of elements too abstract for sensory representation'.[37] (De Man goes on to make the fascinating suggestion that the figure which is closest to *hypotyposis* is that of *prosopopeia*, which will be discussed in Chapter 3). Central to this passage from Kant, as de Man points out, is the ability to make a rigid distinction between schemata and symbols.

Kant's own examples are illuminating. When he comes to show how his conception of the symbolic works he proposes that 'a monarchy ruled according to its own constitutional laws would be presented as an animate body, but a monarchy ruled by individual absolute will would be presented as a mere machine (such as a hand mill): but in either case the presentation is only *symbolic*'.[38] We understand that there is no direct correlation between a hand mill and a despotic state, but we can also understand that there is a similarity between the ways in which we perceive and judge these two things. Indirectly, we arrive at the concept, and this indirection characterises symbolic hypotyposes.

It is worth pausing for a moment to consider the history of rhetorical thought on the particular figure that Kant employs. *Hypotyposis* was, of course, drawn from a rhetorical tradition that was concerned with its effect, and this figure goes elsewhere under the name of *enargeia*, which itself bleeds into *ekphrasis* and *energeia*.[39] When the English rhetorician George Puttenham comes to describe the term, he offers the following account of what he calls 'HYPOTYPOSIS; *or, the counterfait representation*':

> The matter and occasion leadeth us many times to describe and set foorth many things in such sort as it should appeare they were truly before our eyes, though they were not present, which to do it requireth cunning: for nothing can be kindly counterfait or represented in his absence, but by great discretion in the doer. And if the things we covet to describe be not naturall or not veritable, than yet the same axeth more cunning to do it, because to faine a thing that never was nor is like to be, proceedeth of a greater wit and sharper invention than to describe things that be true.[40]

Puttenham effectively describes a form of phenomenalisation, in which an object that no longer has (or has never had) material existence is made to appear. Rhetoric, through the figural resources of *hypotyposis* that Puttenham describes, is capable of *counterfeiting* presence, and this is not simply another way of describing the mimetic faculty of representing nature. In the *Arte of Poesie*, *hypotyposis* attains its strength because it may be used to bring the objects of invention, those things that are strictly absent, into presence. Such figuration implies an invention that matches that of literature itself, it opens up figuration as fiction, as a form of making that again takes us back to *poiesis*.

Hypotyposis, then, is an example of the creative, or perhaps it is better to say inventive power of rhetoric.[41] But this potency is explicitly a matter of presenting something to the senses. In Puttenham's definition, this power of putting a thing 'before our eyes' raises several initial questions. Such questions are set in train by virtue of the figurative nature of the description of figures. The idea of putting something before our eyes is itself a figure, since what is actually being defined is not perception but imagination. As we have already suggested, there is no present 'object' that the eyes could see. If we want to think about the operation of language here in terms of referentiality, then the figure can only be said to refer to an object recalled from memory. This is a thing only seen by the 'mind's eye'. Or at least, that is the case if we are thinking of oratory. In writing, however, we are led towards a substitution.

A written text is translated into a visual image, but the written text is itself a visual stimulus. While poets such as George Herbert will make this visual aspect of the text explicit in poems such as 'The Altar' or 'Easter Wings', we need to preserve the distinction between 'looking at' a text and reading. But the real point to be carried forward here is that even in the most anti-rhetorical texts (such as that of Kant), a rhetorical dimension appears that cannot be limited to, or in some cases even attributed to, authorial intention. As such, it is necessary to be extremely cautious in moving too quickly from linguistic structures to knowledge, even – or especially – in texts that propose that such a move should be unproblematic.

How, then, is this early modern account of *hypotyposis* and of sense taken up by the later aesthetic tradition? It is *hypotyposis*, as a form of presentation (*Darstellung*) that amounts to 'throwing before the eye' (*subjectio ad adspectum*), making vivid as well as making visible, that allows Kant to account for the ways in which objects that we judge to be beautiful 'arouse sensations in us that are somehow analogous to the consciousness we have in a mental state produced by moral judgments'.[42] Yet we must be clear what the function of the rhetorical term is in Kant's text. As Gasché remarks: 'In contrast to the rhetorical use of the term "hypotyposis", whose restricted application to the lively painting of a variety of scenes of aesthetic or moral interest is still quite broad, Kant's very new and original use of the term narrows hypotyposis down to the production of the reality of our concepts, and with it the life of the mind and its powers. Hypotyposis is thus best called a transcendental presentation.'[43] As a transcendental presentation, Kant's sense of *hypotyposis* goes beyond accounting for an object as such. As we find in the *Critique of Pure Reason*, Kant entitles transcendental 'all cognition that deals not so much with objects as rather with our way of cognizing objects in general insofar as that way of cognizing is to be possible a priori'.[44] Transcendental presentation is thus concerned with the conditions of possibility of presentation, and is occupied with the modes of cognition appropriate to presentation rather than with any empirical presentation (or object) as such.[45] What Puttenham calls the capacity to 'set foorth' 'before our eyes' in his description of *hypotyposis* might lead us to think about the linguistic resources that make such a presentation possible. Following Kant, however, it becomes clear that this also opens up the more fundamental question of the possibility of cognition itself.[46]

It should by now be apparent that any historicism that is predicated upon the phenomenalisation of historical phenomena within the text, such that these become readable as objects capable of being known, must encounter the figural and thus rhetorical dimension of this phenomenalisation. It is this figurality that threatens to dissolve the solidity of the knowledge that the text appears to promise. Such a promissory structure is itself that which forms the relation between language and meaning, and it is not, therefore, one figure among many; it cannot be substituted for a more 'reliable' figure. Meaning is promised by language, but this promise is a performative which always runs the risk of misfire. Crucially, this speech act does not offer the knowledge that would be needed to tell the difference between its failure and its success. In part, the problem of the relationship of secure cognition to the promise as performative is a problem of temporality, deferral and decision.[47]

IV

It is time to return to the content of the second Jonson passage that I quoted earlier. Speech not only expresses the mind of an individual, it is also the 'instrument of society' and words are said to belong to the people. But more intriguing for my discussion is the suggestion that 'sense' is a kind of life or soul that vivifies language. Language becomes a body, as we saw in the first passage, but in this case it is – in the absence of sense – akin to a dead body, perhaps to an effigy or mechanical body. But how are we to think, here, of sense? In Jonson's own text we find more than one possible answer – the appropriate subject matter or plots for different genres; an emphasis on the 'best' thoughts, in line with the Aristotelian insistence that the ultimate purpose of the poet is to give a pattern of living well and happily – but much boils down to a notion of 'matter'. While the early modern sense of matter could broadly equate to content or to the issue being discussed, it also leads us to think about the materiality of sensation. Not least due to the role that he accords to language, in Jonson's text it is quite clear that sense must itself be sensed. What we might want to ask, then, is what the role of the reader is in this process of *making* sense, seeing this idea of making as one which allows us to extend the making of the poet into the territory of reading as a form of poetics (or poesy), and in which the reader also contributes to the feigning of sense. In other words, how does the sense of the writer or speaker, that which is in his mind, become the sense of the utterance that the reader or hearer sees in his mind's eye? And are these senses the same?

One perspective on this question of sense and sensation is provided by a philosophical attempt to sum up and counter contemporary ideas. In *Leviathan* (1651), following his previous discussions in *Human Nature* and *De Corpore Politico* (together comprising *The Elements of Law*, 1640), Thomas Hobbes begins with the chapter 'Of Sense'. Sense must be tackled first, he claims, 'For there is no conception in a man's mind which hath not at first, totally or by parts, been begotten upon the organs of sense.'[48] 'Begotten upon' may at first seem to be an odd locution, but it is key both to understanding Hobbes's notion of how the senses work and to recognising the view that he is opposing. (It also echoes the idea of the image as child that Jonson invokes.) The view that Hobbes sets himself against is important because, as in the case of the Jonson 'commonplaces', it represents a prevailing conception of the question at hand. Hobbes begins by thinking about the objects that cause sense impressions, placing a great deal of emphasis on the notion of 'pressure':

> The cause of sense is the external body, or object, which presseth the organ proper to each sense, either immediately, as in the taste and touch, or mediately, as in seeing, hearing, and smelling; which pressure, by the mediation of nerves and other strings and membranes of the body, continued inwards to the brain and heart, causeth there a resistance, or counter-pressure, or endeavour of the heart to deliver itself; which endeavour, because *outward*, seemeth to be some matter without. And this *seeming*, or *fancy*, is that which men call *sense*; and consisteth, as to the eye, in a *light* or *colour figured*; to the ear, in a *sound*; to the nostril, in an *odour*; to the tongue and palate, in a *savour*; and to the rest of the body, in *heat*, *cold*, *hardness*, *softness*, and such other qualities as we discern by *feeling*. All which qualities called *sensible* are in the object that causeth them but so many several motions of the matter, by which it presseth our organs diversely. Neither in us that are pressed are they anything else but divers motions (for motion produceth nothing but motion).

All senses, to some extent, become a form of touch. There is a connection between Jonson's 'matter' and that of Hobbes, since both lead us to the sensation of sense (and vice versa). Characteristically, Hobbes uses mechanical, materialist notions such as pressure and motion to explain the senses, just as in the more overtly political later sections of *Leviathan* he will define liberty as a freedom of motion. But this materialism does not quite explain the ways in which we perceive and interpret the impressions that these objects produce, and he continues by refining this sense of pressure:

> their appearance to us is fancy, the same waking that dreaming. And as pressing, rubbing, or striking the eye, makes us fancy a light, and pressing the ear, produceth a din, so do the bodies also we see, or hear, produce the same by their strong, though unobserved action. For if those colours and sounds were in the bodies, or objects, that cause them, they could not be severed from them, as by glasses, and in echoes by reflection, we see they are, where we know the thing we see is in one place, the appearance in another. And though at some certain distance the real and very object seem invested with the fancy it begets in us, yet still the object is one thing, the image or fancy is another. So that sense in all cases, is nothing else but original fancy, caused (as I have said) by the pressure, that is, by the motion, of external things upon our eyes, ears, and other organs thereunto ordained.

It would be possible to translate this without too much difficulty into an analogy with Jonson's view of language. The separation of the image from the object tells us something about the nature of the object, but in largely negative terms. So although the objects produce an impression by their effect upon an organ of perception, we should not think of our perception as a quality of the object itself. The notion of 'appearance' or 'fancy' marks the difference between object and perception. Fancy is equivalent to the Greek 'phantasma'. While this may not appear too controversial to us even if we would express such ideas in other terms, such a position is, as Hobbes goes on to explain, not the orthodox one in the period. For those being educated within the philosophical establishments to be found in early modern universities, quite the opposite would have been taught:

> the philosophy-schools, through all the universities of Christendom, grounded upon certain texts of *Aristotle*, teach another doctrine,

and say, for the cause of *vision*, that the thing sendeth forth on every side a *visible species* (in English, a *visible show*, *apparition*, or *aspect*, or *a being seen*), the receiving whereof into the eye is *seeing*. And for the cause of *hearing*, that the thing heard sendeth forth an *audible species*, that is, an *audible aspect*, or *audible being seen*, which entering at the ear maketh *hearing*. Nay for the cause of *understanding* also, they say the thing understood sendeth forth *intelligible species*, that is, an *intelligible being seen*, which coming into the understanding makes us understand.[49]

The interaction between object perceived and perceiver depends upon this 'sending forth' meeting an appropriate sense organ. What Hobbes is referring to here is the by now familiar debate between two conceptions of vision, that which sees sight as a matter of intromission, and that which sees it as extramissive.[50] These represented the two main strands of thinking about vision stemming from Greek thought. The debate hinges on whether we see the eye taking in that which comes from outside, that is, objects are illuminated by the sun and the rays bounce off the object and meet our eyes (intromission) or whether seeing is itself a process of sending rays out into the world which then bounce off objects (extramission). As Philip Armstrong puts it: 'The Atomists [such as Lucretius] insisted that perception arises when *eidola* enter the senses from outside. They attributed sight to those images streaming off objects which impinged upon the eye. The Platonists, on the other hand, postulated a visual fire with the capacity to flash out from the eyes.'[51] Kepler was the main source for the shift towards favouring intromission in the early modern period, and was the source for Descartes's work on the *Dioptrics* in the 1630s. But even in Descartes, Armstrong points out, there is a residue of extramission in his image of the blind man who 'sees' with the aid of two sticks, thus metaphorically placing sight in the hands.[52] This interference of extramission and intramission again opens up a sense of the synaesthetic dimension of a single sense, in this case, sight.

What I want to note in the passage from Hobbes here is also the oddness of the phrasing. For Hobbes to translate 'visible species' into 'a being seen' is straightforward enough. But we might wish to pause longer over the equivalent 'audible being seen' and 'intelligible being seen'. There is a kind of synaesthesia implied here, as in Armstrong's reading of Descartes, and this idea of the senses combining, crossing and interfering with each other will become increasingly significant in the course of this book. Equally, I want to note the separation made between seeing, hearing and understanding. Hobbes seems to suggest that it is possible to see or hear without understanding, that intelligibility is additional (I am tempted to say in a Derridean mode 'supplementary') to perceptibility.

But we still need to go back to an earlier question. How does this work in terms of reading? In attempting to take Hobbes's insights into sensation back onto more literary terrain, we would do best to look at one of the poetic treatments of this topic. Again, the reading here will be brief and somewhat schematic, sketching out the ground for the more detailed readings of other texts that follow in subsequent chapters. George Chapman's 1595 poem *Ovids Banquet of Sence* combines several aspects of interest to us here.[53] The volume in which it first appears begins by pondering on its title page '*Quis leget haec?*' – who will read this? – and the question is intended not so much as a gesture of self-effacement as an attack on more fashionable treatments of Ovidian materials such as Shakespeare's *Venus and Adonis*. This disdain for popular taste continues into the Dedication, where Chapman defends his poetic strategies. He stresses in particular the problems of a common insistence on clarity, arguing that the suggestion that 'Poesie should be as perviall as Oratorie, and plainnes her speciall ornament, were the plaine way to barbarisme'.[54] 'Perviall' is a peculiarly pointed way to express this, since it is a word (derived from 'pervious' and meaning 'clear', or 'easy to see through') that the *OED* suggests has only ever been used by Chapman, here and in his translation of the *Iliad*. So 'perviall' is itself impervious to the popular. It is hard to think that Chapman would have endorsed Jonson's suggestion that 'Words are the people's'. He continues to pursue the visual metaphor as the Dedication proceeds:

> That, *Enargia*, or cleerenes of representation, requird in absolute Poems is not the perspicuous delivery of a lowe invention; but high, and harty invention exprest in most significant, and unaffected phrase; it serves not a skilfull Painters turne, to draw the figure of a face onely to make knowne who it represents; but he must lymn, give luster, shaddow, and heightening; which though ignorants will esteeme spic'd, and too curious, yet such as have the judiciall perspective, will see it hath, motion, spirit and life.[55]

As is common, poetry is related to painting, but the emphasis is upon a rhetorical dimension, indicated by the invocation of *enargeia*. The vivid appeal to the senses and particularly the visual immediacy that this figure designates, like its cognates *hypotyposis* and *prosopopeia*, is a form of mimetic rendering that works to give life to sense. A form of phenomenalisation or animation, its most obvious impact is in personification, anthropomorphism, animism, and so on. *Enargeia*'s functioning is worth considering here, since it has a curious analogy with Hobbes's description of the functioning of the senses.

While the figure is discussed by Aristotle, it is Quintilian who gives it the most sustained treatment in the classical tradition. Quintilian notes that 'oratory fails of its full effect, and does not assert itself as it should, if its appeal is merely to the hearing, and if the judge merely feels that the facts on which he has to give his decision are being narrated to him, and not displayed in their living truth to the eyes of the mind'.[56] Where Chapman talks of the 'judiciall perspective', Quintilian also invokes judgement. Here again, also, is the synaesthetic principle in which the spoken word produces images. But, as in Jonson's notion of language showing the man, the process is more complex. The speaker must employ his visual imagination to create an image in his own mind (Φαντάσιαι, what we saw earlier as phantasma or fancy), and it is this image which is then rendered into words (10.7.15). Hobbes's sense of the importance of fancy in the sensing of objects is also seen to be at the origin of vivid oratory (and by extension poetry). We might also want to think of this in terms of *Darstellung*, or throwing 'before the eyes', to borrow Aristotle's term for vividness. All of this must proceed, in Jonson's terms, from the original 'matter', that is, the sense that a speaker or writer initially wishes to convey. The process is thus one of presentation as much as representation, since the layers of mediation (from 'matter' to image to words to image) render any simple notion of mimetic representation deeply unsatisfactory.[57]

Equally, we should not forget another crossing of the senses that we find in the quotation from Chapman. Those who are ignorant, he suggests, may find the painter's embellishment of the plain image 'spic'd'. Whether he is thinking here of taste or of smell – and there is no strict division, of course, between them – Chapman here moves us from hearing to sight to another sense. Such a movement from one sense to another in the Dedication is appropriate for the text that follows. The poem itself, as its title indicates, uses the conventional topos of the banquet of sense to explore an episode from Ovid which hinges on his perception of his beloved Corynna. Encountering her while bathing, he is initially enchanted by the sound of her singing. Then he smells the scents that she uses in her bath. Next he sees her naked body, but this only makes him wish to taste her kiss, which he does. Finally, he attempts to touch her, and this is where the narrative is interrupted by the arrival of other women. Chapman produces a perverse descent down the Neoplatonic ladder of love, such as we find in Castiglione, moving from a disembodied ideal to the desire to touch a physical body.

But this movement from the idea to the physical manifestation is not simply a piece of anti-platonic moralising (although it certainly has more than a touch of that to it). What Chapman's text makes us aware of is the fundamentally anti-platonic impulse of much rhetorical thought. Or, rather, of the paradox that confronts any attempt to make visible the 'fancy' that exists within the mind of the writer or speaker in the mind of the reader or hearer. The movement from mind to mind demands a mediating force, such as language, but a language that must itself (if it is to work) take on a material, perceptible form. The sense (meaning) of a linguistic utterance must activate a sense (such as sight) that allows its sense to be sensed. What Hobbes calls motion we have also seen as animation, and it is the role of rhetoric to make such a living embodiment of thought both possible and effective. Abstraction moves in the direction (in French, as Derrida reminds us, *sens*) of matter, it has to take its place in the world, and as Quintilian puts it, it will only have an impact on that world if it strives to attain a 'living truth'.[58]

Notes

1 I should note that, as is well known, texts from this period have a habit of envisaging a 'he' as the active participant in discourse, whether as writer, subject or reader. It would not be appropriate to insist on a 'he or she' formulation that would be entirely alien to writers of this period, although I have endeavoured as far as possible to adopt this usage in my own commentary.

2 Jonson, *Timber, or, Discoveries, Made upon men and matter, as they have flowed out of his daily readings, or had their reflux to his peculiar notion of the times*, in *The Oxford Authors: Ben Jonson*, ed. I. Donaldson (Oxford: Oxford University Press, 1985), pp. 521–94, 574.

3 Jonson, *Discoveries*, pp. 570–1. I discuss this notion of the political status of speech and of the relation between human speech and non-human animals in Chapter 5.

4 Jonson, *Discoveries*, p. 525.

5 R. Dutton, *Ben Jonson, Authority, Criticism* (Basingstoke: Macmillan, 1996), p. 10.

6 Dutton, *Ben Jonson*, p. 125. See also the following pages.

7 See the discussion in J. H. Anderson, *Words That Matter: Linguistic Perception in Renaissance English* (Stanford: Stanford University Press, 1996).

8 See Donaldson's introductory note to the *Discoveries* on p. 735.

9 For an introduction to these works, see *The Cambridge History of Literary Criticism, Volume 1: Classical Criticism*, ed. G. A. Kennedy (Cambridge: Cambridge University Press, 1993). For an account of the extent to which Erasmus himself produced and controlled this reputation for European influence, see L. Jardine, *Erasmus, Man of Letters* (Princeton: Princeton University Press, 1993).

10 On the Ramists, see W. J. Ong, *Ramus, Method, and the Decay of Dialogue* (Cambridge, MA: Harvard University Press, 1958).

11 See Aristotle, *Rhetorics*, in *The Complete Works of Aristotle*, ed. J. Barnes, 2 vols (Princeton: Princeton University Press, 1984), 2: 1358a.

12 T. Wilson, *The Arte of Rhetorique* (London: 1553), p. 1.

13 Wilson, *The Arte of Rhetorique*, p. 2.

14 See W. A. Rebhorn, *The Emperor of Men's Minds: Literature and the Renaissance Discourse of Rhetoric* (Ithaca: Cornell University Press, 1995) and the texts collected in *Renaissance Debates on Rhetoric*, ed. and trans. Rebhorn (Ithaca: Cornell University Press, 2000).

15 Plato, *Gorgias*, in Plato, *The Collected Dialogues of Plato, Including the Letters*, ed. E. Hamilton and H. Cairns (Princeton: Princeton University Press, 1989), 459b–c, p. 242.

16 P. G. Platt, 'Shakespeare and Rhetorical Culture', in *A Companion to Shakespeare*, ed. D. S. Kastan (Oxford: Blackwell, 1999), pp. 277–96.

17 See *Phaedrus* in *The Collected Dialogues of Plato*, 277b5–c6.

18 Elyot, in *English Renaissance Literary Criticism*, ed. B. Vickers (Oxford: Clarendon Press, 1999), pp. 63–4. On Kant's style in the

context of *logodedali*, see J.-L. Nancy, *Le Discours de la syncope: 1. Logodaedalus* (Paris: Aubier-Flammarion, 1976).

19 See R. Gasché's essay 'Hypotyposis', in *The Idea of Form: Rethinking Kant's Aesthetics* (Stanford: Stanford University Press, 2003), pp. 202–18.

20 As Caygill notes, however, in §vii of the *First Introduction* to the Third Critique, Kant follows Baumgarten, and thus borrows a rhetorical schema: 'Imagination is inventive, it takes up the manifold of intuition, while understanding disposes it into a synthetic unity, and judgement presents the concept, adapting it to a form in which it may be exhibited in intuition.' It is easy to see how this maps on to the division of *inventio*, *dispositio* and *elocutio*. See H. Caygill, *Art of Judgement* (Oxford: Blackwell, 1989), p. 316. Also, see p. 359, where Caygill also reads this schema in the ordering of the sections from §49. Equally, Friedrich Schiller is both praised for having a style influenced by Quintilian, and criticised because he is not like Quintilian. See the Introduction to Schiller, *On the Aesthetic Education of Man*, trans. and intro. E. M. Wilkinson and L. A. Willoughby (Oxford: Clarendon Press, 1967), p. cxxxvii.

21 G. W. F. Hegel, *Aesthetics: Lectures on Fine Art*, trans. T. M. Knox, 2 vols (Oxford: Clarendon Press, 1998), 2: 1008.

22 Hegel, *Aesthetics*, 2: 1010. For similar sentiments, see A. Schopenhauer, *Parerga and Paralipomena: Short Philosophical Essays*, trans. E. F. J. Payne, 2 vols (Oxford: Clarendon Press, 2000), 2: 525: 'in the arts of speech we must guard against all unnecessary rhetorical refinement, all useless amplifications, and generally all superfluity of expression; thus we must aspire to *chastity* of style'.

23 Jonson, *Discoveries*, p. 582.

24 Jonson, *Discoveries*, p. 583.

25 Hegel, *Aesthetics*, 2: 1011. Here, of course, Hegel sounds closer to Samuel Johnson's lament for the 'fatal Cleopatra' of the 'quibble' for which Shakespeare apparently sacrificed so much. See *Dr Johnson on Shakespeare*, ed. W. K. Wimsatt (Harmondsworth: Penguin, 1969), p. 68.

26 See Hegel, *Phenomenology of Spirit*, trans. A. V. Miller (Oxford: Oxford University Press, 1977), pp. 424–53; and *Hegel's Philosophy of Mind*, trans. W. Wallace and A. V. Miller (Oxford: Clarendon Press, 1971), pp. 293–7.

27 See B. Castiglione, *The Book of the Courtier*, trans. G. Bull (Harmondsworth: Penguin, 1986), especially p. 67.

28 Sidney, *A Defence of Poetry*, ed. J. A. van Dorsten (Oxford: Oxford University Press, 1991), p. 72.

29 G. Puttenham, *The Arte of English Poesie*, ed. G. D. Willcock and A. Walker (Cambridge: Cambridge University Press, 1970), p. 302.

30 I. A. Richards, *The Philosophy of Rhetoric* [1936] (Oxford: Oxford University Press, 1965), p. 12. On p. 5, Richards has just cited Berkeley on his preference for 'bare notions' and 'naked undisguised ideas' over the 'dress and encumbrance of words'.

31 P. Lacoue-Labarthe, *Poétique de l'histoire* (Paris: Galilée, 2002), Ch. 1.

32 I will hold over a more explicit commentary for a project in progress, tentatively entitled *Figures of Hamlet: Readings in the Politics of Tragedy*.

33 See, for example, the discussion in J. Bender and D. E. Wellbery, 'Rhetoricality: On the Modernist Return of Rhetoric', in Bender and Wellbery (eds), *The Ends of Rhetoric: History, Theory, Practice* (Stanford: Stanford University Press, 1990), pp. 3–39, 14–22.

34 Gasché, *The Idea of Form*, p. 218.

35 An illustration of how this might be conceived in romantic thought may be found in the famous (indeed totemic) text, the so-called 'Oldest Programme for a System of German Idealism', which states: 'I am now convinced that the highest act of reason, by encompassing all ideas, is an aesthetic act, and that *truth and goodness* are only siblings in *beauty*.' See *Classic and Romantic German Aesthetics*, ed. J. M. Bernstein (Cambridge: Cambridge University Press, 2003), pp. 185–7. The fragment is here attributed to Hölderlin, although as Bernstein notes it is most likely the product of a collaboration between Hölderlin, Schelling and Hegel, which complicates the 'I' in the quoted sentence.

36 Kant, *Critique of Judgment*, trans. W. S. Pluhar (Indianapolis: Hackett, 1987), §59, p. 226. < > indicates Pluhar's insertion.

37 P. de Man, *Aesthetic Ideology*, ed. and intro. A. Warminski (Minneapolis: University of Minnesota Press, 1996), p. 46.

38 Kant, *Critique of Judgment*, §59, p. 227.

39 Where my use of particular rhetorical terms is not clearly informed by a source under discussion, helpful definitions may be found in R. A. Lanham, *A Handlist of Rhetorical Terms*, 2nd edn (Berkeley: University of California Press, 1991).

40 Puttenham, *The Arte of English Poesie*, p. 238.

41 On the ramifications of 'invention' as a term, see Derrida, 'Psyche: Inventions of the Other', in *Reading de Man Reading*, ed. L. Waters and W. Godzich (Minneapolis: University of Minnesota Press, 1989), pp. 25–65; Gasché, *Inventions of Difference: On Jacques Derrida* (Cambridge, MA: Harvard University Press, 1994); and Attridge, *The Singularity of Literature* (London: Routledge, 2004), Chs 3 and 4.

42 Kant, *Critique of Judgment*, p. 230.
43 Gasché, *The Idea of Form*, p. 210.
44 Kant, *Critique of Pure Reason*, trans. W. S. Pluhar (Indianapolis: Hackett, 1996), A 12/B 25.
45 Behind this lies Kant's notion of the imagination, a topic that is beyond the scope of this discussion. For indications of just why I do not wish to broach this here, see Gasché, *The Idea of Form*, Ch. 2; G. Banham, *Kant and the Ends of Aesthetics* (Basingstoke: Macmillan, 2000), Ch. 2 and his 'Apocalyptic Imagination', in *Kant after Derrida*, ed. P. Rothfield (Manchester: Clinamen, 2003), pp. 66–79; J.-L. Nancy, *A Finite Thinking*, ed. S. Sparks (Stanford: Stanford University Press, 2003), Chs 10 and 11; and M. Heidegger, *Kant and the Problem of Metaphysics*, trans. R. Taft, 5th edn (Bloomington and Indianapolis: Indiana University Press, 1997), especially Pt 3.
46 While this is not the place to do so, this idea might be extended through a reading of Bernstein's introduction to *Classic and Romantic German Aesthetics*, and in particular his discussion of the power of the imagination in a specifically German idealist mode, in which he stresses its need for artistic incompletion.
47 On the promise and temporality, see my 'Shakespeare's Words of the Future: Promising *Richard III*, *Textual Practice* 19.1 (2005): 13–30.
48 T. Hobbes, *Leviathan, with selected variants from the Latin edition of 1668*, ed. E. Curley (Indianapolis: Hackett, 1994), p. 6. See also the later chapter 'Of Speech'. On Hobbes's relation to rhetoric, see Q. Skinner, *Reason and Rhetoric in the Philosophy of Hobbes* (Cambridge: Cambridge University Press, 1996).
49 All passages from Hobbes, *Leviathan*, pp. 6–7. The reference to 'certain texts' of Aristotle is vague enough to be impossible to identify with any assurance, although *De Anima*, *De Sensu* and the *Metaphysics* would seem the most obvious candidates. On the complexities of identifying Aristotle's 'position' on these matters, see S. Everson, *Aristotle on Perception* (Oxford: Clarendon Press, 1999).
50 Vision has been a much-discussed topic in recent years, so I will not go over this ground in any detail here. See, among many examples, C. Pye, *The Regal Phantasm: Shakespeare and the Politics of Spectacle* (London: Routledge, 1990); D. C. Lindberg, *Theories of Vision from Al-Kindi to Kepler* (Chicago: University of Chicago Press, 1976); D. M. Levin, *The Philosopher's Gaze: Modernity in the Shadows of Enlightenment* (Berkeley: University of California Press, 1999); Levin (ed.), *Modernity and the Hegemony of Vision* (Berkeley: University of California Press, 1993).
51 Armstrong, *Shakespeare's Visual Regime: Tragedy, Psychoanalysis and the Gaze* (Basingstoke: Palgrave, 2000), p. 177.

52 Armstrong, *Shakespeare's Visual Regime*, p. 178.

53 All quotations will be from G. Chapman, *Plays and Poems*, ed. J. Hudston, original spelling edition (Harmondsworth: Penguin, 1998).

54 Chapman, p. 239.

55 Chapman, p. 239. On *enargeia* in the period see also J. B. Altman, '"Preposterous Conclusions": Eros, *Enargia*, and the Composition of *Othello*', *Representations* 18 (1987), 129–57; T. Cave, '*Enargia*: Erasmus and the Rhetoric of Presence in the Sixteenth Century', *L'Esprit Créateur* 16: 4 (1976), 5–19; L. Galyon, 'Puttenham's *Enargeia* and *Energeia*: New Twists for Old Terms', *Philological Quarterly* 60: 1 (1981), 29–40.

56 *The Institutio Oratoria of Quintilian*, trans. H. E. Butler, 4 vols (London: William Heinemann, 1953), 8.3.62.

57 Interesting in this context is the comment of T. S. Eliot who, in his essay on 'The Metaphysical Poets', states: 'In Chapman especially there is a direct sensuous apprehension of thought, or a recreation of thought into feeling.' See *Selected Essays* (London: Faber & Faber, 1999), p. 286.

58 Derrida plays on the multiple sense of *sens* (to refer to meaning, to the senses, and to direction) in many places, especially in the essays in *Writing and Difference*, trans. A. Bass (London: Routledge, 1978).

3

Is there an early modern aesthetic?

I

In the previous chapter I concluded with the notion of a 'living' truth, that is, of a truth that came about or could be sensed through the animating interactions with language that were the domain of rhetoric. As such, my discussion was focused upon the visions of rhetoric to be found in early modern texts, as well as in some of the classical texts that underpinned without entirely circumscribing these definitions, and in the romantic texts that seemed to complicate attempts to 'see' rhetoric clearly in its early modern manifestations. In this chapter, I want to pursue a parallel path that will instead take as its focus the conceptualisation of the early modern itself, again combining commentary on both early modern and later texts. Having arrived at a desire for 'living' truth in the earlier discussion, here I want to circle around the notion of a truth that is already consigned to a past, and is thus mourned as always already lost. In part, this is a matter of the truth of the early modern itself as a critical category. This *critical* sense is vital, as I hope to demonstrate. Attempting to take account of the 'truth' of the aesthetic, and in trying to articulate the relation of the aesthetic to rhetoric (and poetics), I am immediately confronted by the imposition of a question:

Is there an early modern aesthetic?

Any question that begins with an 'is', of course, is a question about presence, about temporal and spatial location. As such, any critic might feel uneasy about bringing together the early modern with a present tense. It seems to be the case that before I can begin to answer this question, one that appears to be about the aesthetic, it may be necessary to answer a series of other questions, questions about the relations between past and present. So, it may be better, if a little more clumsy, to ask:

What does one call the space currently occupied by aesthetics before aesthetics emerges?

In shifting the emphasis from the temporal dimension to the spatial one, this reformulation of my initial question conjures up a division of intellectual categories that already implies the existence of the aesthetic. In other words, it assumes the legitimacy of a projection of the idea of the aesthetic on to a period prior to the emergence of the aesthetic as a distinct category. Is such an assumption reasonable? In order to assess this, I must first look more closely at the term *early modern*, at the place of the aesthetic within later, primarily romantic, thought, and at the notions of modernity that make a question about the presence of the aesthetic necessary in the first place.

Formulation of the idea of the early modern can be taken as an exemplary moment in the permeation of a 'new' historicism through literary studies since the early 1980s, most obviously through the twin historicisms of cultural materialism and cultural poetics.[1] The periodising title *early modern* is part of a movement away from notions such as 'the English Renaissance' or from 'the Tudor period', although such names are retained by some of historicism's adherents, and it is hard to think that they will ever be entirely erased.[2] From the perspective of a rather jaundiced hindsight, however, the emergence of the phrase *early modern* seems to mark a strategic attempt to delineate what otherwise appears to be a depressingly familiar ramification of what I suppose we must now term 'old' historicism. Far from inhibiting its success, this sense of déja vu with respect to new historicism has done nothing to diminish the institutional effectiveness of either the term or the critical mode with which it is associated. One marker of this effectiveness is the resistance that the term is beginning to generate.[3] As this resistance indicates, it is not an exaggeration to say that historicism, new or old, is the dominant critical mode within literary studies at the present time.

Institutionally successful as it may have been, one area that has always created concern about the new historicist project lies in its treatment of aesthetics. 'Cultural poetics', which prior to the wide-spread adoption of new historicism was Stephen Greenblatt's pre-ferred term for his form of criticism, makes clear the expansion of 'poetics' into a domain that is no longer strictly associated with 'poetry' (however widely conceived).[4] Aesthetics has been expanded as a term within new historicist discourse to encompass any form of symbolic interaction that is susceptible to (literary-) critical analysis. As Catherine Gallagher and Greenblatt have argued:

> In the analysis of the larger cultural field, canonical works of art are brought into relation not only with works judged as minor, but also with texts that are not by anyone's standard literary. The conjunction can produce almost surrealist wonder at the revelation of an unan-ticipated aesthetic dimension in objects without pretensions to the aesthetic.[5]

This sense of wonder is crucial to Greenblatt's project (in collabo-ration with Gallagher or not), and this ready acknowledgement of an affective dimension to his critical work is partly what has made it such an attractive mode to many.[6] The compelling quality of the word 'wonder' is noted by Philip Fisher:

> English preserves the connection between intellectual curiosity ('I wonder if . . .') and the pleasure of amazement, that is, wonder taken in the aesthetic sense of admiration, delight in the qualities of a thing. Admiration in its root *mira* is, of course, the Latin word for wonder and also the root word for miracle.[7]

Fisher helpfully points out the dialectical senses of wonder, that it is both a response to the qualities of a thing itself – a sense that something *is* wondrous – and an affective experience for the per-ceiver of the thing. We are already back in the territory of the doubled senses of sense, that is, in the relation between meaning and the processes by which meaning might be perceived or generated.

We should pause over the final phrase in the passage from Gal-lagher and Greenblatt, in which they identify: 'the revelation of an unanticipated aesthetic dimension in objects without pretensions to the aesthetic'. The key ideas here are 'revelation', 'anticipation' and 'pretension'. The logic seems to be, if we were to risk para-phrase, that the critic finds something beautiful or affecting in an unexpected place. The fact that the conjunction is one created by the critic we may, as Gallagher and Greenblatt do, pass over without comment for now. But it is more complicated than this. 'Revelation', even if we ignore its religiosity, carries overtones of truth, of unveiling, and is thus evoking the Greek notion of truth as *aletheia*. Revelation suggests that something true has been dis- or un-covered about the object. The notion of 'anticipation' proposes, however, that the force of this revelation is produced by the preconception of the critic, and is thus not (or at least not only) an aspect of the object. Surprise and wonder are produced by the misalignment of expectation and experience. So far we might read this as thoroughly and straightforwardly dialectical. The question of 'pretension' takes a further step, inviting us to think about the 'intention' behind the making of the object. This intention is grammatically masked by attributing the pretension to the object rather than to its creator. What is implied here is a functioning concept or category of the aesthetic that the (maker of the) object could have drawn upon or aimed at, and that this concept or category was at least broadly similar to the 'unanticipated aesthetic dimension' recognised by the critic. This is further complicated when the discussion deals with texts and objects from the early modern period. As I will show, the aesthetic, as a recognisable category, does not emerge until the eighteenth century. Thus, it would be literally impossible for *any* object, whether canonical or not, literary or not, to have been made in the early modern period with the *pretension* to be aesthetic. Since the aesthetic did not itself exist as a category, the best that this can tell us is that we are returned to my initial question. Is there an early modern aesthetic, and if so, how might it best be conceived?

Part of the problem in dealing with passages such as the one quoted above from *Practicing New Historicism* is in the nature of the new historicist project. Eschewing theoretical formulations, new historicism favours an attention to 'particularity' over what is considered to be the universalising impulse of more explicitly delineated critical projects. Thus the readings of 'social energies' produced, encompassing objects and practices that are not bounded by an aesthetics that takes art as its focus, deliberately offer no systematic place for the aesthetic.[8] Part of the reasoning behind this is a desire to avoid falling back into a conservative notion of the 'special' quality of art in which, as Gallagher and Greenblatt put it: 'The rest of human life can only gaze longingly at the condition of the art object, which is the manifestation of unalienated labour, the perfect articulation and realization of human energy.'[9] Certainly the forms of aesthetic idealism that they take as their target here do not seem to offer a fruitful avenue for enquiry. But does a more narrow conception of the aesthetic than that offered by new historicism necessarily entail such a vision of unity, lack of alienation and perfection? Part of the purpose of this chapter is to suggest that this form of idealism was always an illusion, but that its illusory nature does not mean that it may easily be dismissed.

Tellingly, in *Practicing New Historicism*, one of the main impulses behind the authors' approach comes not from within early modern culture, but instead from the German Idealist thinker Johann Gottfried Herder.[10] Thus it locates itself within the ambit of German romanticism or Idealism and its inheritances, seeking to read the early modern in terms of an aesthetic that is post-Kantian (although not Kantian) rather than being itself early modern. Indeed, new historicist discourse frequently foregrounds its relation to present concerns, but tends to be selective about what those concerns are. A general, if far from generous, sense of this rubric might be discerned in Harold Bloom's aligning of new historicists (in several places in his work) with what he calls the 'School of Resentment'.[11] There is an inevitable filtering of the early modern by the modern. While it would not be possible simply to avoid the impact of a modern notion of aesthetics on contemporary critical practices, it is worth giving further consideration both to the relationship between modernity and early modernity, and to the role of the aesthetic within modernity itself. It will then be possible to look to an early modern text on the role and functions of art, Sidney's *A Defence of Poetry*, in order to begin to address more fully my opening questions.[12]

Let's take an example of how this has informed recent criticism. Hugh Grady has been one of the most consistently interested critics of recent years in the modernity of the early modern, and in a series of books he has focused his work on Shakespeare.[13] As Grady has pointed out, however, the term *early modern* has itself been employed with a certain degree of ambivalence:

Widespread use of the term *early modern* expresses much of the ambiguity [around the question of Shakespeare's modernity] by positing both continuity and difference: the era is part of modernity but it's 'early' modernity. While Stephen Greenblatt has called for something like a revival of Burckhardt's idea of Renaissance modernity, critics such as Catherine Belsey and Jonathan Dollimore have followed T. S. Eliot, making of the Renaissance a premodern transitional age in which discourses from an earlier medieval mentality overlap newer ones from the Age of Absolutism and an embryonic modernity.[14]

Leaning more towards what he identifies as Greenblatt's view, Grady suggests that rather than seeing Shakespeare (who here almost seems to stand in for the early modern *tout court*) as caught between a residual medieval position and a modern humanistic one (a view which he sees particularly in Belsey's work), it is possible 'that Shakespeare was working from a mentality that was specific to his own phase of early modernity'.[15] One aspect of the problem is that the term *early modern* is a slippery and ill-defined one for the most part, especially in its relation to the modern, and consequently in different contexts '*modern* and *early modern* overlap and compete with each other'.[16] When Grady comes to discuss his sense of Shakespeare's modernity in this essay, he provides a conventional set of characteristics which he wishes to call modern: instrumental reason, power, and autonomous subjectivity. Any philosophical notion of aesthetics becomes submerged in talk of the effects of a 'postmodern' aesthetic of discontinuity, and Shakespeare emerges as 'distant enough from modernity to be its critic, implicated in its logic and dynamics enough to speak to us of its unfulfilled possibilities'.[17] The aesthetic here, then, is almost entirely negative. It is seen to be part of a modernity that it is not significant in shaping in conceptual terms, and its role for Grady is as a marker of critical distance and a reminder of *unfulfilled* possibilities. What of the possibilities that were fulfilled? They are seemingly not Grady's primary concern. The early modern (as Shakespeare) is not modern, but it remains modern enough to be recognisable in its differences from modernity. The term 'early' thus operates as a marker of these differences. This sense of the familiarity of the early modern is plausible enough, since anything that was *absolutely* different would be unrecognisable. It seems clear, though, that Grady's ambivalence to the term *early modern* hinges on a concept of the early modern that is itself ambivalent. Further, what lies behind this is a more deep-seated ambivalence towards modernity itself. Grady's attempt to find a 'mentality' specific to the early modern period, rather than one defined as between the modern and the medieval, should suggest that we look more closely at what lies within both modern and early modern aesthetic discourses.

II

To repeat: *What does one call the space currently occupied by aesthetics before aesthetics emerges?* Let me recall what prompted me to consider such a question in the first place. In part, I was motivated by a series of concerns about definitions of modernity that necessarily impact upon the emergence of the idea of the early modern. In *The Fate of Art*, Jay Bernstein offers what seems in many respects to be a compelling delineation of modernity, which he sees as beginning with the Kantian critical project, remarking that: 'it is Kant's third *Critique* that attempts to generate, to carve out and constitute, the domain of the aesthetic in its wholly modern signification'.[18] We have to begin with this 'wholly modern' signification.[19] Outlining Kant's attempt to separate the categories in the process of delimiting pure and practical reason, and thus to establish a division of art from truth and goodness that persists in the notion of autonomous art, Bernstein notes the crucial role that aesthetics plays in the articulation of Kant's critical philosophy as a whole. Indeed, the question of philosophical aesthetics is the question of philosophy as system. For Kant, as for Hegel, the role of the aesthetic is crucial to the elaboration of a systematic critical project, that is, for the possibility of the closure of this thought as system. The aesthetic, then, is not something to be added to philosophy, nor is it simply one branch of philosophy among others. It is, rather, that which allows for a crucial step in philosophy's project of completing itself. We might say that a philosophy without aesthetics is not a philosophy, and certainly not a critical philosophy. Equally, we must not think of aesthetics in terms of a category that is separated or separable from this philosophical context, that is, from a context which always conceptualises the aesthetic in relation to (in Kantian terms) theoretical and practical reason.[20]

Reason, then, always provides the framework for the discussion of aesthetics. The context for this post-romantic 'story' of aesthetics is usefully reconstructed by Andrew Bowie, following Gadamer. In a trajectory which stretches from Kant and Baumgarten through German Idealism to Nietzsche and Schopenhauer, Bowie suggests that the crucial aspect of the story of aesthetics is 'the relationship between competing claims to truth' but that, as Gadamer indicates, 'one cannot presuppose that the nature of the division between philosophy and art can be truly defined by philosophy'.[21] In freeing art from instrumental social functions, German Idealism stresses the role of the imagination in going beyond particular rules of and for art: 'Instead of being conceived of principally in terms of mimesis, representation, or entertainment, art begins to be conceived of in terms of its ability to reveal the world in ways that may not be possible without art.'[22] Terms such as mimesis and representation are central to early modern debates about art and to the classical tradition from which these debates are derived, as we have already seen in the previous chapter, and it will be necessary to return to these ideas later. The central thing to note at this point is the insistence on the connection between art and truth.

The truth offered or revealed by art is the point from which Bernstein begins. The categorial separation of domains in Kant's critical philosophy does not in itself, suggests Bernstein, offer any real problems to those who believe in a notion of enlightened modernity, but it must be related to the parallel move to use aesthetic judgement to prove the underlying unity of reason. This far less successful Kantian move, argues Bernstein, opens the space in which it is possible to read the emergence of the critique of enlightened modernity, since the fragmentation of reason that the categorial separation reveals may be seen to mirror the fragmentation of modernity itself. This establishes a line of critical thought that we might for convenience's sake call Hegelian. From this recognition of the failure of Kant's move in the *Critique of Judgment*, and its consequences for the idea of the autonomous artwork in modernity, Bernstein puts forward his notion of 'aesthetic alienation'.[23] In this alienated form, aesthetics suffers mourning for its separation from reason and morality, and the 'fate' of art of Bernstein's title refers to this alienation from truth. Having stressed the importance of a sense of mourning to modernity, Bernstein reads in the third *Critique* what he calls a 'memorial aesthetics', in which pain is brought together with the experience of or production of pleasure. Bernstein cites Kant's own example in the third *Critique* of the possibility of feeling some pleasure in a painful experience, which is that of the mourning widow who simultaneously remembers both her loss and the worth of her dead husband. It is tempting to read the widow as an allegorical figure for the position of the philosopher who wishes to preserve both the critical and systemic ambitions of a critical philosophy.

For Bernstein, the loss of the systematic unity of Kant's critical project is not to be read as a purely negative fall from a rational grace, since the critical element of the project need not be abandoned. To those who would wish to save Kant from his troublingly aporetic reading of the third *Critique*, Bernstein proposes that: 'Resistance to the memorialization of aesthetics on the grounds that it destroys the universality of Kant's critical system through the introduction of an essentially aporetic moment, a non-recuperable indeterminacy at the core of determinate reason, is nonetheless misplaced since it ignores the fact that his metaphysics was aporetic from the beginning', adding that 'to ignore the moments of limit and opacity in the critical system is to render it uncritical'.[24] Resistance is, then, misplaced if it is motivated by a desire to preserve an illusory integrity, since the unity for which it offers to stand guard can only be sustained by ignoring the *critical* integrity of the critical system. In other words, to be critical is more important, ultimately, than to be systematic, and clearly any system could only be produced by the integrity of a critical approach. One way to think through this might be to say that the critical aspect of Kant's project is doubled or enfolded, in that it acts as a form of resistance to its systemic ambitions.

It seems pertinent to consider further what relationship Grady's ambivalent periodisation bears to Bernstein's Habermasian characterisation of modernity, and thus to turn again to the question embedded in my title: is there an early modern 'aesthetic'? One of the problems for a historicist attempt to answer this question is that the spectre of anachronism is involved here, not least because it is well accepted that the term 'aesthetics' itself is first used by Baumgarten in 1735, and that the system of the arts to which it refers emerges in the eighteenth century.[25] The emergence of aesthetics in this period marks an attempt to make a decisive shift away from discourses of art that focus upon rules and prescriptions, in other words, aesthetics emerges as that which is not poetics or rhetoric. As Cynthia Chase has argued: 'The rise of aesthetics happens concurrently with the fall of rhetoric: it is the institutionalized discipline of "Rhetoric" that is displaced by aesthetics, and it is the power of "rhetoric" that is castigated in the literature and the politics which in this respect it may be right to call "romantic".'[26] Rhetoric is not then just replaced, it is explicitly abjected in romanticism, and again we have already seen an indication of this in the passages from Hegel and others that I drew upon in the previous chapter. It is this negative valuation of rhetoric within the post-romantic tradition that we must think beyond if we are to encounter that which occupies the space of aesthetics in the pre-romantic period, and yet it must not simply be assumed that this is possible. In part this is because any notion of a sudden division of pre- and post-romantic thought is dubious as well as hard to define, but it is also because any rational inquiry must proceed according to categories, concepts and procedures fully imbricated with this romantic inheritance.

III

Certainly, 'aesthetics' in the post-Kantian terms with which we are familiar did not exist in the sixteenth and seventeenth centuries in England, and the matter of aesthetics must be traced in a submerged form in discussions of poetics and rhetoric in this period, as well as reconstituted from what is frequently a very self-reflexive literary culture.[27]

There is an analogy to be drawn between the line of inquiry that I am following here and the problem posed by attempts to use psychoanalysis in reading early modern culture. Greenblatt, for example, suggests that 'psychoanalysis is the historical outcome of certain characteristic Renaissance strategies'. He further proposes that: 'psychoanalytic interpretation seems to follow upon rather than to explain Renaissance texts . . . psychoanalytic interpretation is causally belated, even as it is causally linked: hence the curious effect of a discourse that functions *as if* the psychological categories it invokes were not only simultaneous with but even prior to and themselves causes of the very phenomena of which in actual fact they were the results'.[28] It should be noted, however, that historicism can differentiate itself from psychoanalysis only by reference to psychoanalysis. In this sense it always comes after psychoanalysis, and cannot (itself belatedly) be rigorously separated from it. The structure of this problem is thus similar to that which confronts attempts to use the category of the aesthetic in discussions of early modern artworks.

It is necessary to relate this to what we have been calling the romantic attitude to rhetoric, since the treatment of rhetoric identified by Chase inevitably raises the question of what precisely is being abjected. Alongside reading the often prescriptive 'how to' manuals of poetics and rhetoric, it is important in attempting to assess early modern discourses on art to look to the various prefaces, epistles, dedications and other paratexts that frame both literary and non-literary texts, as well as to read those moments in the texts themselves in which their own textuality becomes an explicit matter of concern.[29] Metatheatricality has long been a topic of critical interest in the study of Renaissance drama, and there are similarly metapoetic and metarhetorical elements to be found in verse and prose. My use of terms beginning with 'meta-' is, of course, purely strategic. It is by no means certain that it would be possible to distinguish clearly between a language that was poetic/rhetorical and a language that would be able to comment upon poetics/rhetoric from a 'safe' distance. The problem faced parallels the comments by Derrida and others concerning the difficult notion of metalanguage. Because commentary on language typically takes place within language, such commentary must, to the extent that it is language, itself be subject to that commentary. Metalanguage is thus impossibly inside and outside, both that which is commented upon and that which makes commentary possible. In effect, there is no metalanguage, which is another way of saying that there is only metalanguage.[30]

Of course, in constituting this reflexivity, much of this material reflects a classical inheritance, which often follows and disrupts the 'Aristotelian' division between poetics and rhetoric. As has already been suggested, the question of poetics is opened up in Aristotle's work through an emphasis on mimesis, and all of the poetic forms that he discusses are treated as 'modes of imitation', including not just poetry (in the linguistic sense) but also music, specifically flute-playing and lyre-playing.[31] In this, Aristotle is picking up on the discussion in Book X of Plato's *Republic*, in which the poet also appears as an imitator.[32] Here it is part of an argument about the relationship between appearance, reality and truth, and art is thought of in terms of other forms of making (that is, as *poiesis*). Again, it is the relationship of art to truth that is central to the debate. The notably negative conception of poetry in this section of the *Republic* condemns poets, like all imitators, to a position at 'the third remove from truth', arguing that 'the imitator knows nothing worth mentioning of the things he imitates, but that imitation is a form of play, not to be taken seriously, and that those who attempt tragic poetry, whether in iambics or heroic verse, are all altogether imitators'.[33] This indicates an antagonism that was already well enough established for Socrates to comment 'that there is from of old a quarrel between poetry and philosophy'.[34]

Poetry in the Aristotelian sense includes everything that we have come to call literature. Against this emphasis on mimesis in the definition of poetics, in rhetoric, for Aristotle, 'The modes of persuasion are the only true constituents of the art: everything else is mere accessory'.[35] Rather than being a second-order representation of a first-order reality (or in Plato's terms a third-order imitation of a second-order reality that is itself a weak model of the Form), the rhetorical dimension of linguistic works have a direct impact on the world in working upon the listener or reader. Since both poetics and rhetoric are primarily arts of language, however, there are points at which Aristotle's categories intersect and, as Clark Hulse argues, ' "poetics" never exists in isolation, and is always overlapping, contesting, combining, and separating from the other arts, especially the arts of rhetoric, music, philosophy, theology and even geometry. It is precisely in those zones of interaction that theorists are best able to work out the important issues of poetics, concerning the nature, function, and forms of literature'.[36] It is for this reason that Hulse employs the term 'aesthetics', in order to mark the co-implication of poetics with other domains of artistic production and inquiry, in particular those which are non-linguistic. Yet this does seem to leave aesthetics as a largely strategic category in which all discourse on art (broadly conceived) might be contained. As such, it fails to occupy a systemic position similar to that envisaged in the Kantian critical project.

This mimetic inheritance can be read a little differently. Translation of *mimesis* as 'representation' rather than 'imitation' offers a way out of the problem posed by the apparent secondariness of literature, but we need to remember that in the early modern period imitation does not itself have the negative connotations that we have inherited from romantic thought. As Thomas M. Greene comments: 'The imitation of models was a precept and an activity which during that era embraced not only literature but pedagogy, grammar, rhetoric, esthetics, the visual arts, music, historiography, politics, and philosophy. It was central and pervasive.'[37] Linguistic arts are frequently related to the other arts, even in attempts to define poetry itself. Yet as Terence Cave points out, this relation of a writer to past authors is far more than just a matter of source material: 'Imitation theory is more complex in that it recognizes the extent to which the production of any discourse is conditioned by pre-existing instances of discourse; the writer is always a rewriter, the problem then being to differentiate and authenticate the rewriting. This is executed not by the addition of something wholly new, but by the dismembering and reconstruction of what has already been written.'[38] This helps us to understand a little better the practice of a writer such as Jonson in the construction of the *Discoveries*, and accords with Dutton's account of the formation of a distinctive position from within apparently unoriginal materials. As Sir Philip Sidney proposes in *A Defence of Poetry*, perhaps the most famous of English Renaissance treatises on art:

> Poesy is . . . an art of imitation, for so Aristotle termeth it in the word μίμησις [*mimesis*] – that is to say, a representing, counterfeiting, or figuring forth – to speak metaphorically, a speaking picture – with this end, to teach and delight.[39]

Here we see a positive valuation of imitation, but one that is valued in particular because it has a specific purpose, to teach and to delight, echoing the insistence of Wilson and others on the importance of *docere* and *delectare* (see above p. 19). The figure of the 'speaking picture' recognises that the figures and images of poetry are already metaphorically crossing from language into another realm (and this is, of course, what metaphor means, 'to carry across'). It also recognises the intersection of poesy and rhetoric. For Sidney, both pleasure and moral content must be present. The teaching invoked here is what Brian Vickers has called the ethical-rhetorical function of early modern literature, and Sidney recognises that this lesson is unlikely to be successful if the mode of instruction is unpalatable.[40] This is in part why, for Sidney, poetry is to be preferred to historical writing, or indeed philosophy. Literature, according to this definition, fails to recognise a clear distinction between poetics and rhetoric, partaking of both in its attempts to delight as it persuades. There is seemingly no purity or autonomy to poetics, in that it always attempts to act within the world. But what is the nature of this action? What is it that literature as poetry teaches?

The eminence of poetry, for Sidney as for Jonson, comes from the idea that the poet is a maker. Picking up on the Greek word ποιεῖν as the root of poetics, Sidney uses this to suggest that poetry cannot be relegated to the status of mere copying.[41] Noting the reliance of the astronomer, the geometrician and arithmetician, philosophers both natural and moral, the lawyer and historian, and others, on objects and rules (including in this the world and nature), Sidney argues that:

> Only the poet, disdaining to be tied to any such subjection, lifted up with the vigour of his own invention, doth grow in effect another nature, in making things either better than nature bringeth forth, or, quite anew, forms such as never were in nature, as the Heroes, Demigods, Cyclops, Chimeras, Furies, and such like: so as he goeth hand in hand with nature, not enclosed within the narrow warrant of her gifts, but freely ranging only within the zodiac of his own wit. Nature never set forth the earth in so rich tapestry as divers poets have done; neither with so pleasant rivers, fruitful trees, sweet-smelling flowers, nor whatsoever else may make the too much loved earth more lovely. Her world is brazen, the poets only deliver a golden.[42]

Here, then, is a treatise on poetics that emphasises the possibility of going beyond rules and prescriptions. Instead of a comparison between nature and art in which the representation is able to go in only one direction, from nature to art, nature is held up to the richness of art and is found wanting. There is a line of argument in the platonic inheritance that would accept this reversal of the relationship of art to nature while retaining a sense of art as a secondary manifestation. Here it could be argued that art offers access to the Forms that is equivalent to that offered by objects in nature (that is, to sense experience), and is thus not tertiary compared to a secondary reality, but is still no better than secondary. Despite this secondarity, Sidney asserts the possibility of moving beyond sense perception, beyond the world, beyond 'subjection', beyond history (conceived of as the constraint of saying 'what really happened'). What might be read as irresponsibility in the face of history is revealed to be in the service of a higher notion of truth. Such a truthful element, which might be seen as a moment of utopian invention, carries with it (like all utopias) the negative recognition that the world of the senses from which it is freeing itself is imperfect, or fallen. Such a recognition would certainly accord with Sidney's Protestantism.[43] But from the perspective of our discussion, this movement beyond history may be read as an attempt to offer a truly historical cognition of the world.

In this allusion to a truth beyond a mimetic relation to the world, Sidney is also able to combat charges that poets are liars. Sidney argues that 'though he [the poet] recount things not true, yet because he telleth them not for true, he lieth not' (p. 53). The truth lies in the moral example, not in the fiction through which it is conveyed, and the emphasis is again on persuasion, since as he notes earlier in the *Defence*: 'a feigned example hath as much force to teach as a true example' (p. 36). This is precisely the ground of the platonic complaint against the persuasive aspects of rhetoric, of course. The truth of the true example has no moral validity beyond that of the truth which may appear through a fiction, but this does not entail upon the writer any necessity to claim that the fiction is itself true. This insight is not the subject of *unalloyed* joy, however. Only poetry can deliver a vision of the golden world, but the pleasure that this produces cannot free itself entirely from the painful tarnish of its brazen counterpart. Brass is, of course, an alloy, a combination of elements that could only mistakenly be associated with purity. The poet may be able to offer a glimpse of this purity, but his status as maker firmly places his work within the world of objects. Poetry, as defined here by Sidney, is co-extensive with the world but opens the space for critical engagement with that world. Its speaking pictures, as mirrors up to nature, open a space for reflection.

IV

In this context of debates around the term *early modern*, everything apparently hinges on the word 'modern'. But it is worth pausing over the term 'early'. As in Grady's use of it, the word 'early' is effectively empty in itself, acting as a marker of division, partition and ordering. 'Early' implies both a cut and a continuity. It shares some of the characteristics of the French verb *partager*, in that it implies both a sharing and a sharing out.[44] Early modernity is both a distinct periodic division (even if the place of division is itself largely indistinct), and at the same time clearly a share of the modern. As my repeated use of 'both' indicates, *early* is thus itself divided by its attachment to *modern*. It is neither cleanly inside nor outside of modernity, nor is it separable from the non-modern space (the 'medieval') that it is intended to demarcate. 'Early' is thus parasite and host, dependent for its own definition upon a modernity that it qualifies and modifies (in the grammatical sense). 'Early' opens up a futural space for the modernity that has already happened. If we cannot, in good faith, call the sixteenth and seventeenth centuries part of modernity itself, then the use of early modernity does not offer a more secure identification. The term 'early' acts to displace the problem that it was intended to solve. What, then, does this do to the idea of an early modern aesthetic?

If we simply abandon the modern sense of aesthetics on the grounds of some notion of fidelity to periodised chronology, can the concept of the early modern be retained, or must it similarly be jettisoned? The Habermasian view of modernity that Bernstein elaborates makes clear the centrality of the aesthetic to its definition, however alienated that aesthetic may be, and indeed aesthetics is crucial to post-Kantian accounts of philosophical modernity *as* modernity. The consequences for those attached to the term *early modern* would seem to be that, without the elaboration of an effective role for what we would now call aesthetics, the *early* modern will cease to bear any relation to modernity that might afford genuinely critical purchase. The force of the term *early modern* threatens to dissipate along with the aesthetic, revealing itself as an indefinable concept, without any referent in the world (and there are several possible ways in which 'world' might be conceived here).[45] In other words, the narrativisation of modernity that the term *early modern* implies would reveal that the sense of the word 'modern' would have to remain open, perhaps even empty. Furthermore, the concept of the early modern would also appear to have no necessary relation to the concept and narrative of history upon which historicism

depends. What seems on the verge of appearing, then, is a historicism with no securely knowable connection to history. If historicism does not provide a reliable conceptual scheme, then, how are
we to think about the relationship between literature, aesthetics
and history?

One answer would seem to be offered by a return to rhetoric
and poetics, here conceived precisely in terms of their combination
of persuasion and force with pleasure. Rhetoric opens the relation
of text to world, recognising that language as art (the arts of language) can only be gifted autonomy through a violent separation.
This is fundamental to early modern notions of poetics that stress
an ethical-rhetorical dimension to art. It is this dimension that
promises art's connections to truth and cognition. Early modern
discourse on the aesthetic domain itself exhibits an awareness of
the inter-relation of pleasure and pain, and this is activated through
the dual recognition that (as part of the world) it always occupies
a fallen, secondary position with respect to a transcendent realm,
and simultaneously that any glimpse of that realm is only possible
through an act of invention, imagination or desire (what Hobbes
calls 'fancy' or Quintilian might describe as 'phantasma'). As an
act, art does not fall outside that which is available to sense
perception, but it is not simply bounded by it. Indeed, it is this
doubled or enfolded act of (re)cognition that art makes possible,
both in spite of and because of its secondarity (as mimesis or representation). Kantian modernity, precisely located in this violent
separation and in the mourning that ensues, is a doubling of the
recognition that the interaction of poetics and rhetoric ensures.
Prior to the Kantian critical philosophy is not a happily unified
realm in which aesthetics might be observed in harmony with pure
and practical reason, and this is what spurs Kant on, but the
mourning that Bernstein posits is itself an enfolded version of the
pleasure and pain that art produces through and as (rhetorical)
force. Such a force offers the pleasurable pain of reflective thought
(of thought as reflection). Rhetoric and poetics, at the points at
which they intersect, always seem to be aware of their loss (the
golden world of unity). Modernity's sense of loss is thus a doubling, a double mourning; we have lost the unity of reason, but
have also lost the rhetorical/poetical discourse that allowed us to
recognise that such unity was always already lost. The recognition of this loss can only come about through a questioning of

aesthetics itself; it cannot simply be thought from a position
securely 'outside' it. Art as poetics, even before the rise of aesthetics, was always already alienated. This is what an early modern
'aesthetic', in the form of rhetoric and poetics, can tell us.

Notes

1 For definitions of new historicism see, among many possible sources,
   H. A. Veeser (ed.), *The New Historicism* (London and New York:
   Routledge, 1989); R. Wilson and R. Dutton (eds), *New Historicism
   and Renaissance Drama* (Harlow: Longman, 1992); Greenblatt's
   introduction to *The Power of Forms in the English Renaissance*, ed.
   S. Greenblatt (Norman, OK: Pilgrim, 1982); L. A. Montrose,
   'Renaissance Literary Studies and the Subject of History', *English
   Literary Renaissance* 16 (1986), 5–12; J. Pieters, *Moments of Nego-
   tiation: The New Historicism of Stephen Greenblatt* (Amsterdam:
   Amsterdam University Press, 2001); and Pieters (ed.), *Critical Self-
   Fashioning: Stephen Greenblatt and the New Historicism* (New
   York: Peter Lang, 1999).
2 On the term itself, see, among many other texts that might be cited
   here, D. Aers, 'A Whisper in the Ear of the Early Modernists; or,
   Reflections on Literary Critics Writing the "History of the Subject"',
   in Aers (ed.), *Culture and History 1350–1600* (Detroit: Wayne State
   University Press, 1992); H. Dubrow, 'The Term *Early Modern*',
   PMLA 109 (1994), 1025–6.
3 See, for example, L. Charnes, 'We were never Early Modern', in
   Philosophical Shakespeares, ed. J. J. Joughin (London and New York:
   Routledge, 2000), pp. 51–67. Charnes is following the argument of
   B. Latour, *We Have Never Been Modern*, trans. C. Porter
   (Cambridge, MA: Harvard University Press, 1993).
4 See Greenblatt's essay, 'Towards a Poetics of Culture', in *Learning to
   Curse: Essays in Early Modern Culture* (London and New York:
   Routledge, 1990), pp. 146–60.
5 C. Gallagher and S. Greenblatt, *Practicing New Historicism* (Chicago:
   University of Chicago Press, 2000), p. 10.
6 See, for example, Greenblatt's essay, 'Resonance and Wonder', in
   Learning to Curse, pp. 161–83 and his *Marvellous Possessions: The
   Wonder of the New World* (Oxford: Clarendon Press, 1991). For a
   brief analysis of 'wonder' in Greenblatt's work, see C. Colebrook,
   *New Literary Histories: New Historicism and Contemporary
   Criticism* (Manchester: Manchester University Press, 1997), esp.
   pp. 214–19.

7 Fisher, *Wonder, the Rainbow, and the Aesthetics of Rare Experiences* (Cambridge, MA: Harvard University Press, 1998), p. 11.

8 Social energy becomes a key term in Greenblatt's work in his *Shakespearean Negotiations: The Circulation of Social Energy in Renaissance England* (Oxford: Clarendon Press, 1988).

9 Gallagher and Greenblatt, *Practicing New Historicism*, p. 11.

10 Gallagher and Greenblatt, *Practicing New Historicism*, pp. 5–8, 13. For a sense of Herder's place within the German romantic/Idealist context, see D. O. Dahlstrom, 'The Aesthetic Holism of Hamann, Herder, and Schiller', in *The Cambridge Companion to German Idealism*, ed. K. Ameriks (Cambridge: Cambridge University Press, 2000), pp. 76–94.

11 For a typically polemical passage, see the Prologue to his *How to Read and Why* (London: Fourth Estate, 2000). Also typically, when Gallagher and Greenblatt respond to Bloom he is not even named (never mind cited) in the text, his name appearing only in the index.

12 It may be objected that I have not given a very nuanced account of the new historicism, nor of Greenblatt's work in particular. I concede this, and hope that you will allow me to refer you to my *Stephen Greenblatt* (London: Routledge, 2007).

13 See Grady, *The Modernist Shakespeare: Critical Texts in a Material World* (Oxford: Oxford University Press, 1991); *Shakespeare's Universal Wolf: Studies in Early Modern Reification* (Oxford: Oxford University Press, 1996); *Shakespeare, Machiavelli and Montaigne: Power and Subjectivity from Richard II to Hamlet* (Oxford: Oxford University Press, 2003); and, as editor, *Shakespeare and Modernity: Early Modern to Millennium* (London: Routledge, 2000).

14 H. Grady, 'Renewing Modernity: Changing Contexts and Contents of a Nearly Invisible Concept', *Shakespeare Quarterly* 50 (1999), 268–84, 272. The cited passage ends with a note to Greenblatt, *Renaissance Self-Fashioning: From More to Shakespeare* (Chicago: University of Chicago Press, 1980); C. Belsey, *The Subject of Tragedy: Identity and Difference in Renaissance Drama* (London: Methuen, 1985); and J. Dollimore, *Radical Tragedy: Religion, Ideology, and Power in the Drama of Shakespeare and his Contemporaries*, 2nd edn (Hemel Hempstead: Harvester Wheatsheaf, 1989).

15 Grady, 'Renewing Modernity', p. 276.

16 Grady, 'Renewing Modernity', p. 278.

17 Grady, 'Renewing Modernity', p. 284.

18 J. M. Bernstein, *The Fate of Art: Aesthetic Alienation from Kant to Derrida and Adorno* (Cambridge: Polity, 1992), p. 5.

19 Bernstein's view offers a way through what is, of course, a complex area. Those interested in definitions of philosophical modernity

should perhaps begin with J. Habermas, *The Philosophical Discourse of Modernity*, trans. F. Lawrence (Cambridge: Polity, 1987); H. Lefebvre, *Introduction to Modernity*, trans. J. Moore (London: Verso, 1995); and D. Kolb, *The Critique of Pure Modernity: Hegel, Heidegger, and After* (Chicago: University of Chicago Press, 1986).

20 For an elaboration of this sketch, which suggests that this concern for aesthetics characterises what is called continental philosophy, see P. Osborne (ed.), *From an Aesthetic Point of View* (London: Serpent's Tail, 2000).

21 A. Bowie, 'German Idealism and the arts', in *The Cambridge Companion to German Idealism*, pp. 239–57, 242.

22 Bowie, 'German Idealism and the arts', p. 243.

23 Bernstein, *The Fate of Art*, pp. 4–5.

24 Bernstein, *The Fate of Art*, p. 64. Kant's example is to be found in the opening paragraph of §54 of the *Critique of Judgment*.

25 On the relation between spectrality and anachronism, see Derrida, *Specters of Marx: the State of the Debt, the Work of Mourning, and the New International*, trans. P. Kamuf (London: Routledge, 1994).

26 Chase, 'Literary Theory as the Criticism of Aesthetics: De Man, Blanchot, and Romantic "Allegories of Cognition"', in *Critical Encounters: Reference and Responsibility in Deconstructive Writing*, ed. C. Caruth and D. Esch (New York: Rutgers University Press, 1995), pp. 42–91, 44.

27 See C. Hulse, 'Tudor Aesthetics', in *The Cambridge Companion to English Literature, 1500–1600*, ed. A. F. Kinney (Cambridge: Cambridge University Press, 2000), pp. 29–63; T. J. Reiss, 'Cartesian Aesthetics', in *The Cambridge History of Literary Criticism: Volume 3 The Renaissance*, ed. G. P. Norton (Cambridge: Cambridge University Press, 1999), pp. 511–21.

28 See Greenblatt, 'Psychoanalysis and Renaissance Culture', in *Learning to Curse*, pp. 131–45, 144, 142.

29 See G. Genette, *Paratexts: Thresholds of Interpretation*, trans. J. E. Lewin (Cambridge: Cambridge University Press, 1997).

30 See J. Culler, *On Deconstruction: Theory and Criticism after Structuralism* (London and New York: Routledge, 1983), p. 199.

31 Aristotle, *Poetics*, in *The Complete Works of Aristotle*, ed. J. Barnes, 2 vols (Princeton: Princeton University Press, 1984), 2: 1447a.

32 Plato, *The Collected Dialogues, including the Letters*, ed. E. Hamilton and H. Cairns (Princeton: Princeton University Press, 1961 [1989]), 596e.

33 Plato, *Republic*, Book X, 602b.

34 Plato, *Republic*, Book X, 607b. A few lines earlier Socrates warns that 'if you grant admission to the honeyed Muse in lyric or epic, pleasure and pain will be lords of your city instead of law' (607a).

35 Aristotle, *Rhetoric*, in *The Complete Works of Aristotle*, 2: 1354a.

36 Hulse, 'Tudor Aesthetics', p. 35.

37 See *The Light in Troy: Imitation and Discovery in Renaissance Poetry* (New Haven: Yale University Press, 1982), p. 1.

38 Cave, *The Cornucopian Text: Problems of Writing in the French Renaissance* (Oxford: Clarendon Press, 1979), p. 76.

39 Sidney, *A Defence of Poetry*, ed. J. A. van Dorsten (Oxford: Oxford University Press, 1991), p. 25.

40 B. Vickers, 'Introduction', *English Renaissance Literary Criticism*, ed. Vickers (Oxford: Oxford University Press, 1999), p. 10.

41 For a text which begins from a similar recognition, see J.-L. Nancy, *Résistance de la poésie* (Bordeaux: William Blake & Co., 1997).

42 Sidney, *A Defence of Poetry*, pp. 23–4.

43 On this, see A. Weiner, *Sir Philip Sidney and the Poetics of Protestantism* (Minneapolis: University of Minnesota Press, 1978).

44 This notion of *partage* has been central to the recent work of both Jean-Luc Nancy and Jacques Rancière. See, for example, Nancy, *The Inoperative Community*, trans. P. Connor and others (Minneapolis, Minnesota University Press, 1991); *La Communauté affrontée* (Paris, Galilée, 2001). See Rancière, *The Politics of Aesthetics: The Distribution of the Sensible*, trans. G. Rockhill (London: Continuum, 2005).

45 See, notably, J.-L. Nancy, *The Sense of the World*, trans. J. S. Librett (Minneapolis: Minnesota University Press, 1997).

4

Poetry's defences

I

In Chapter 3, I argued that it was only through an examination of rhetoric and poetics that we could avoid leaving the crucial systemic place of the aesthetic as an open or empty category. Any articulation of an early modernity, I proposed, found itself imbricated within the systemic ambitions of philosophical modernity. This discussion was guided by an emphasis on the notion of the aesthetic in broad terms, that is, on a generalised sense of art that went beyond modern conceptions of 'literature'. In part, this was led by a historical appreciation of the problems surrounding the identification of a category that we might call literature in the early modern period. But it was also partly the result of an unease concerning the definition of literature *per se*. As we have seen, resort to the classic statements regarding poetics and rhetoric lead us not towards 'literariness', but instead towards a version of *poiesis* as making that subsumes the verbal arts within representation (as in Aristotle), or else towards a view of the work of the poet that treats it with a suspicion that attaches to all mimetic or oratorical acts (as in Plato). This chapter will extend this analysis by asking: What, then, is the place of literature *as literature* in our sense of the early modern? In particular, I will be focusing on conceptualisations of the relation between literature, aesthetics, history and philosophy as a way of tying together both modern theoretical explorations of this question and the answer to be found in Sidney's *A Defence of Poetry*.

The question will thus be approached from two directions in this chapter. First of all, I would like to suggest a framework for investigating the place of literature that will be provided by turning to *what becomes literature*, or perhaps it is as well also to say, *what literature becomes*. This protocol of priority is much more than a matter of syntax, it contains the kernel of the question itself. It might best be understood in terms of the habitual distinction, borrowed from speech act theory, between constative and performative utterances. If what we are looking for is a constative, that is, for a description, then this implies that there is a pre-existing 'something' identifiable as 'literature' (let's hold off for now from calling it an object) that might be susceptible to such description. If, instead, we look for a performative utterance that will produce a definition of literature precisely as an act, then this displaces the matter of priority, and 'literature' comes into being through and as a performative enactment. From this opening discussion of literature and its definition, I will proceed to a reading of Sidney that explicitly raises the formal matter of defence.

II

In *The Literary Absolute*, a work that has been rightly much-lauded in the twenty-five years since its first publication in French, Philippe Lacoue-Labarthe and Jean-Luc Nancy offer a compelling reading of Jena romanticism which suggests that both our conception of literature, and indeed our modern sensibility itself, emerge in response to three concurrent crises. These are listed as a social and moral crisis of the bourgeoisie; the political crisis of the French Revolution; and the crisis represented by the Kantian critical project. The Jena romantics who gather around the *Athenaeum*, say Lacoue-Labarthe and Nancy, participate in these three crises such that 'their project will not be a literary project and will open up not a crisis *in* literature, but a general crisis and critique (social, moral, religious, political: all of these aspects are found in the *Fragments*) for which literature or literary theory will be the privileged locus of expression'.[1] Rather than stemming from anything that could be attributed to individual psychology or to factors that would submit themselves to a historicism, 'the theoretical romanticism of Jena characterized itself as the *critical* question of literature with all the historical and conceptual overdetermination we [Lacoue-Labarthe and Nancy] have just evoked – or perhaps even as the most properly critical (with all the values and limits of the term) formulation of *the* crisis of modern history'.[2]

What I am really talking about here, of course, is literary theory, and in particular a familiar debate about the relative merits of formalism and historicism. The question of literary theory is, among other things, the question of the literariness of literature. It is tempting to propose that any theory's pretence is that it is capable of offering an account of the essence of its object that would be in some sense systematic and not, therefore, reliant upon any particular instance of that object. A theory of literature cannot work for only a single text and maintain any compelling claim as a theory at all, and yet it must begin with a specific text in any attempt to prove its adequacy. Literary theory, then, is produced as the relation between each singular example and the generality that it purports to exemplify. In the present discussion, I make no pretence to offer a definition of the literariness of literature; such an ambition seems prone to miserable failure.[3] Among the many problems posed to such attempts are those encountered by Jacques Derrida in his projected thesis on the 'ideality' of the literary object (which are in part, of course, those offered by any object's ideality). The problems which led to Derrida's abandonment of that work cannot be attributed to a lack of will or invention on his part.[4] On the contrary, what Derrida's and Paul de Man's works have revealed (often in markedly different ways) is that it is not at all clear that literature *is* an object in any meaningful sense, still less that its essence might be susceptible to systematic description.[5] Indeed, it often seems that the literariness of literature has most frequently been identified negatively: literature is not criticism, and in particular not theory; not a science; not history (or any other form of discourse normally described as 'non-fiction'); not morals; not politics; and, like all art, not *life*, and, like all culture, not *nature*. Such distinctions are neither purely arbitrary nor simply false, and under certain conditions are indeed necessary. Yet the consequence of such conceptualisations of literature is that, confronted by the claims of seemingly more pressing and urgent issues, literature, and poetry as its 'highest' form, is often seen to be in need of defence. And this remains the case despite the supposed eminence of works which grant that among the arts, poetry holds the highest place.[6]

There is always a suspicion, however, that to mount a defence of literature might be simply defensive, that indeed it may be a form of resistance, perhaps even a resistance to analysis and to the conceptual and critical frameworks that make analysis possible. As such, it is always possible that poetry's defences are mobilised not by the enemy at the gates but by its fifth column, by a foreign body that has always already made itself at home within poetry, in however uncanny a fashion. It is by no means certain that this apparent resistance is bad thing. This is not the place to open the question of the framing of resistance to and by psychoanalysis – and what I am calling analysis here is not bounded by psycho- analysis – but a comment by Derrida in this regard may prove instructive, since it is clear that resistance must not be seen as simply negative. In his elaboration of a resistance to analysis that also conjures a resistance *of* psychoanalysis, to itself and from its origins, Derrida notes: 'Resistance must be interpreted; it has as much meaning as what it opposes; it is just as charged with meaning and thus just as interpretable as that which it disguises or displaces: in truth, it has *the same meaning*, but dialectically or polemically adverse, if one can say that.'[7] Resistance in the name of poetry might then be seen as an opening to the meaning not just of that resistance but of that which is being resisted. And so a doubled, enfolded sense of resistance appears. Just as poetry does not purely defend itself against that which may be securely located outside it, so these defensive acts may not be simply opposed to poetry as its inartistic guard. Defending poetry may itself be considered an art form; yet it remains possible that poetry is indefensible, as I will suggest at the end of this chapter.

Let us take this sense of resistance (and, as should be clear, resistance is always a matter of *sense*) back towards the definition of literature. Although I have been talking in terms of literary theory, it is clear that this is not a topic that respects disciplinary boundaries. What is clear is that the question 'what is literature?' is *not* a literary one, it falls, and has repeatedly fallen, within the ambit of philosophy.[8] This is not to suggest that literature is a branch of philosophy, nor that it is possible to know what litera- ture 'is' without reading texts that are commonly thought to be 'literary', even if we often have to fall back upon functionalist models of literature for our working definition. Equally, literature is not best thought of (or about) as a set of philosophical examples.

For it is clear that literature raises philosophical questions, and questions for philosophy, without offering philosophical argu-ments. It might also be the case, conversely, that those who read only literary texts do not know what they are reading, in any strong sense.[9] The relationship of reading to cognition cannot be assumed, and this is something that literature's participation in language makes clear even about what is too quickly called 'ordi-nary' language. If we accept that the question of literature is the question of reading, then clearly the challenge that literature poses to other disciplines, whether philosophy or others such as history, sociology or politics, is the challenge of reading itself. Reading does have its histories and politics, and it is susceptible to treat-ment from a sociological perspective, but reading cannot be enfolded within these disciplines. The encounters of history, soci-ology and politics with reading must themselves be open to an act of reading that can only be predicted or programmed with a certain violence. Read in this way, and recognising the foreign body that reading may always turn out to be within any body of thought, reading offers resistance, and vice versa.

III

It is no coincidence, then, that few practices have encountered such a pervasive antagonism as reading. Rather than being an innocent or neutral activity, reading offers a site of contestation, seemingly independent of what is being read. If we follow the lines of Paul de Man's famous argument in 'The Resistance to Theory', we find this problem restated. Reading and resistance are related by de Man such that they mirror each other, becoming versions of the same basic problem which, disconcertingly, appears to be reading itself, since 'the resistance to theory is in fact a resistance to reading, a resistance that is perhaps at its most effective, in con-temporary studies, in the methodologies that call themselves theo-ries of reading but nevertheless avoid the function they claim as their object'.[10] Resistance, which should be seen in this context as a property of all objects in the world, is inseparable from language, and, in particular, language's performative (or rhetorical) dimension. 'The resistance to theory is a resistance to the use of language about language', claims de Man, offering examples from several quarters in which the main form of resistance is to the apparent 'technicity' of theoretical description.[11] Here then is restated the opposition of literature and criticism. But de Man is not naive enough to believe that this resistance may be attributed to the *naïveté* of others, instead locating the source of such resistance in a far more unavoidable place: 'Nothing can overcome the resistance to theory since theory *is* itself this resistance.'[12] Paradoxically, this (self-) resistance is what allows theory to flourish, since, as de Man claims in the following sentence, 'the loftier the aims and the better the methods of literary theory, the less possible it becomes', but he remains unconvinced about whether this flourishing should be seen as a triumph or a fall.[13]

Before moving forward, I should say a little more about what is being understood by the term 'theory' here, since I am not simply talking about a body of discourse that emerges in the 1960s, and am not, therefore, using the term as a euphemism for the various -isms and -ologies that are frequently taken to constitute that discourse. Equally, what I have suggested so far about the relationship of theory to literature might perhaps lead us to believe that the answer lies in philosophical aesthetics, in other words, that the answer might be *to be more philosophical*. Those whose interest is in literary criticism should not be so quick, however, to seek refuge in the apparent security of an alternative discipline. Wlad Godzich, in his 'Foreword' to *The Resistance to Theory*, reminds us of the problems of attempting to view literary theory as a branch of aesthetics, in which literature becomes a mode of art, comparable to sculpture, music or painting, noting:

> It may be useful at this juncture to recall what theory is. Presently we tend to use the term to mean a system of concepts that aims to give a global explanation to an area of knowledge, and we oppose it to praxis by virtue of the fact that it is a form of speculative knowledge. The term obviously has taken on this meaning after Kant . . . Etymologically, the term comes from the Greek verb *theorein*, to look at, to contemplate, to survey. And in Greek, it does not enter into an opposition with praxis – an opposition constructed in Idealist philosophy and eventually used to combat the latter – but rather with *aesthesis*.[14]

What Godzich usefully recalls is that the relationship of theory to aesthetics has always been basically antagonistic, in part since they are produced by and work upon differing epistemological modes.

In this, there is an obvious parallel with what Socrates calls the 'ancient quarrel' between poetry and philosophy. The problem then, as Godzich states it, is the movement from theory (*theoria*) as seeing and telling, in which the linguistic dimension that supplements perception is clearly articulated, to *aisthesis* as sense perception, in which (literary) language becomes a form apprehended as its affect. *Aisthesis* thus becomes *the* form of mediation, displacing language into a secondary position. Yet this displacement of theory involves the fall away from a relation between event and testimony which rested upon deictic articulation. Deixis acts as a form of reference in that it refers to the fact that something (most obviously language itself) has taken place and is taking place, allowing for the identification and distinction of 'then and there' and 'here and now'. In other words, it acts as an index of presence. From this form of (self-) referral all other forms of referral (or what is usually called reference) arise. It is this referral of language to itself *as language* that opens the space for resistance, in that it is possible that 'reference' and event (what we might think of as linguistic performance) may not coincide, and this potential resistance of language to itself grounds the recognition of other forms of resistance. Rather than acting as a witness to sense perception, language becomes itself something to be perceived. This not too far from Jonson or even Quintilian, as we saw in Chapter 2.

IV

The antagonistic element in the prehistory of aesthetics identified by de Man and Godzich may also be seen to mark its development within the more familiar narrative of post-romantic thought. The relocation of aesthetics within the philosophical field remains in this romantic phase a matter of struggle, disavowal and displacement. A charged encounter of the aesthetic and its other occurs again in the romantic narrative, only this time the conflict occurs not with theory but with rhetoric. This confrontation suggests, as I have indicated in earlier chapters, that rhetoric must be denigrated within romantic theory if aesthetics is to achieve its ascendancy. In part, this stems from an insistence in the romantic discourse on art that the artist, and in particular the artist as genius, must not be bound by rules. Such rules were explicitly contrasted to nature and its teachings. Indeed, unlike the scientist, the artistic genius is one who would not be able either to 'learn' how to create true art, nor to communicate to another the process by which that creation took place. Artists may, of course, learn from other artists, but this takes the form of a general sense of inspiration, rather than of any specific teachings that may be abstracted from the artwork. Indeed, the artwork itself is not primarily what is 'known' in aesthetic judgement. Central to the aesthetic discourse that develops in and from Kant, the judgement of art takes on its primary significance in allowing the emergence of a certain form of thinking that moves from intuition and perception to understanding and cognition. In the case of Hegel, and of those who follow such as Schiller, art takes on a supreme importance in its promise of allowing for the coming together of subject and object, for a unification of consciousness and nature. What has been taken from this line of post-romantic thought is the promise that literature, and especially poetry, offered in terms of a *rapprochement* between the mind and the phenomenal world, that cognition and sensation could be restored to a certain unity. Fundamental to this, particularly in the Hegelian version of this inheritance, is a process of internalisation. For de Man, this history of a posited continuity between language and phenomena is the central characteristic of a powerful and pervasive 'aesthetic ideology', and this is seen most clearly in three late essays 'Phenomenality and Materiality in Kant', 'Sign and Symbol in Hegel's *Aesthetics*', and 'Kant's Materialism'.[15]

This history of the romantic discourse of aesthetics is one that, however, throws historical explanation itself into doubt, as de Man's essays make clear. Cynthia Chase observes that, in de Man's readings in his late work, it is the role of literature that is crucial to the modification of the entanglement of theory and aesthetics:

> To conceive theory as the critical encounter of aesthetics and literature is on the one hand to locate it historically, to see its enabling conditions in 'the rise of aesthetics as an independent discipline in the later half of the eighteenth century,' as de Man notes. But it is on the other hand to undercut conceptions of history dependent upon the possibility that literature and literary theory put into doubt (including period concepts, such as 'Romanticism' [and, and I forced to add, the early modern]): the possibility of access to reliable knowledge via the aesthetic totalization claimed by means of texts' narrative or spatial figures.[16]

What Chase argues for, then, is a reading of de Man that both opens up the relation of literature to history (as an encounter between the aesthetic and the literary), and at the same time undermines the possibility of historical explanation that such an encounter might demand (by unsettling the conceptual determination of 'history' itself). One clue to such a problematic relation lies in the reliance of aesthetic discourse on certain tropes and figures for which historical explanation remains inadequate. It is, then, precisely narrative and spatial figures that make historical accounts of the relation of aesthetics to literature both possible and impossible. As we have seen, it remains possible to place the emergence of aesthetics in a historical narrative, and de Man's account frequently gestures back to one of the key intellectual concerns of this book, namely the status of rhetoric. Romanticism is the name to which the pre-eminence of aesthetics has become attached, but the solidity of romanticism as a concept which grants access to secure knowledge is that which is perhaps least secure in romantic thought. As we might expect, it is a matter of language for de Man. The potential for the diremption of the linguistic act and the cognition that the linguistic utterance appears to promise is seen to be a consequence of the romantic disavowal of rhetoric, since this disavowal institutes a degree of blindness to the rhetorical strategies that the romantic texts themselves employ.

One of the problems lies in the insistence on judgement in the romantic conception of aesthetics, and that conception's reliance in turn on sense perception. De Man is absolutely clear in *The Resistance to Theory* that literariness, if it is to be defined rigorously, should not be confused with aesthetic response. If much of the effect of literariness is freed from an aesthetic determination, and located instead in the realm of rhetoric, then the use of language 'can no longer be said to be determined by considerations of truth and falsehood, good and evil, beauty and ugliness, or pleasure and pain'. Such a view is explicitly non-platonic and also profoundly non-Idealist. He continues:

> Whenever this autonomous potential of language can be revealed by analysis, we are dealing with literariness and, in fact, with literature as the place where this negative knowledge about the reliability of linguistic utterance is made available. The ensuing foregrounding of material, phenomenal aspects of the signifier creates a strong illusion of aesthetic seduction at the very moment when the

actual aesthetic function has been, at the very least, suspended. . . .
Literature involves the voiding, rather than the affirmation, of
aesthetic categories.[17]

In stressing the unreliability of language from the perspective of
sense perception and aesthetic judgement, de Man is clearly swerv-
ing away from the aesthetic ideology that rests on the continuity
of the linguistic and the phenomenal. It is the materiality of the
signifier, and the phenomenal aspects of language itself, which are
brought to the fore rather than the materiality and phenomenality
of the objects of the world. It is not clear then how aesthetics can
get a purchase on such forms of materiality and phenomenality,
since they do not depend upon *aisthesis* in the sense of responding
to an object. Literature's status as a non-object poses problems
to aesthetics in its romantic form, if that form is understood
through interiorisation and the promised unity of consciousness
and world.

From this voiding of the categories of aesthetics, it follows that
philosophy does not provide all the answers to the questions posed
by literature. By allowing for the disengagement of literariness
from aesthetic response, it follows that literature cannot be thought
of in terms of other forms of art of which the phenomenal status
seems to be more secure. What we are returned to is the necessity
of reading, but to a reading that is not reducible to the pleasurable
activity of allowing oneself to be seduced by the aesthetic dimensions of the text. De Man has no interest in denying that such
pleasures exist, but there is nevertheless an ethical tone to his
description of the divergence of an aesthetic reading from a rhetorical one at many points in his work that makes it evident where
his sympathies lie. One consequence of this rethinking of reading
is that we must learn to *read* sculpture, painting, and so on, rather
than to *look at* literature as if it were like any other phenomenal
object. The mediating role of aesthetics between art and other
phenomena is hollowed out and the role of language that was
central to the earlier notion of *theoria* reappears.

In his late essays, de Man attempts to disentangle the texts of
Hegel and Kant from the aesthetic ideology that their works supposedly generate, and one of the consequences of this scrupulous
attention to the textual detail of their texts is that materiality is
seen to be related not to the products of historicist enquiry, as

might be expected (at least by historicists), but instead to the reading practices of formalism. This is particularly the case in the essay on 'Kant's Materialism'. De Man reads a diminution of the aesthetic in the treatment of one of Kant's key terms from the third *Critique*, the sublime. As de Man points out, the sublime plays a significant role for Kant in the attempt to demonstrate the underlying unity of theoretical and practical reason, and what is crucial is that in the *Critique of Judgment* the sublime is no longer a matter of sensory experience or psychology (as it was in Kant's earlier work). Indeed, de Man proposes that: 'What makes the sublime compatible with reason is its independence from sensory experience; it is beyond the senses, *übersinnlich*. This is what makes the junction of cognition with morality possible.'[18] The sublime, then, is not fundamentally a matter of affect, and in fact one of the key features of Kant's description of the sublime is that there is *not* a phenomenal object that would allow it to be experienced. Just as the beautiful artwork is not of significance in its status as an object, so when Kant turns to the sublime it is not the sublime object but the mental encounter with the sublime that counts.

This independence from the senses does not locate the sublime in an otherworldly realm, it is instead posited as *architectonic*. The sublime is not thought of here as a form of nature (or even the 'second nature' of art), but rather as a space in which we dwell, as a kind of construction. Not nature then, but world. Yet there is no mind that forms an interior against this exterior construction, it is not the product of a psyche, not a matter of interiorisation, and thus not Idealist in character. Crucially, there is neither specular inversion nor substitution in which the mind is produced by this construction, but neither does de Man propose that this construction of space is itself simply a figure. The construction of which he speaks is not a trope, in that there is no exchange, as in metaphor, and no affect, since it is independent of sensory experience: 'The dynamics of the sublime mark the moment when the infinite is frozen into the materiality of stone, when no pathos, anxiety, or sympathy is conceivable; it is, indeed, the moment of a-pathos, or apathy, as the complete loss of the symbolic.'[19] Materiality, as here conceived by de Man, is not dependent upon a subject. What emerges from this reading of Kant is an austere formalism, and it is literature that is again stressed rather than a more generalised realm of the aesthetic. Rather than reducing the aesthetic to either idealism or abstraction, for de Man, 'the radical formalism that animates aesthetic judgment in the dynamics of the sublime is what is called materialism'. Linking this materialism precisely to the formalism that he finds in Kant, and thus opposing his reading of Kant to that more conventional one which would – often in the name of a politicised criticism – identify materialism and historicism, he continues: 'Theoreticians of literature who fear they may have deserted or betrayed the world by being too formalistic are worrying about the wrong thing: in the spirit of Kant's third *Critique*, they were not nearly formalistic enough.'[20]

In the remaining pages of this chapter, and indeed in the rest of this book, I will be following de Man's insistence on the necessity of a formalist reading practice. In the next sections, I want to go back to the relation of literature to philosophy and history, but precisely through a focus on the question of defending poetry, and in particular on the form that such defence might take. This entails a rereading of Sidney's *A Defence of Poetry* in terms of its generic status, and thus through its animation of the rhetorical forces of phenomenalisation.

V

'Again,' Aristotle says in his matter of fact way in the *Rhetoric*, 'if you cannot find enough to say of a man himself, you may pit him against others, which is what Isocrates used to do owing to his familiarity with forensic pleading.'[21] What begins as a simple enough proposition takes an odd twist as it moves to its conclusion. Attack, he seems to be saying, is the best form of defence, in rhetoric as in much else. Familiarity with the techniques of modern politics has entirely prepared us for this kind of negative strategy, but Aristotle's authority for this manoeuvre, which is itself based on a notion of familiarity, takes us on to much less familiar territory. Rather than the forensic mode of oratory offering a resource for those unable to find much of positive value to say in favour of their case, it seems that acquaintance with forensic rhetoric somehow produces this negative approach – Isocrates used this tactic 'owing to' this familiarity. Or so the Roberts translation leads us to believe.

If we turn instead to the more recent Lawson-Tancred translation, we find: 'And if you do not find these [amplificatory factors allowing for strong praise] in the subject himself, you must compare him with others, as Isocrates did through his unfamiliarity with forensic oratory.'[22] The tone is less antagonistic – 'pit against' becomes 'compare' – but, more interestingly, the familiarity of Isocrates with forensic pleading has become an 'unfamiliarity'. The Greek text might seem to offer a way out of this quandary, but in fact it does not necessarily give us a simple solution. The translator of the Loeb edition concurs with Lawson-Tancred on the basic sense: 'If he does not furnish you with enough material in himself, you must compare him with others, as Isocrates used to do, because of his inexperience of forensic speaking.'[23] The key word here, for our purposes, is rendered as 'inexperience' rather than familiarity or unfamiliarity. This slightly more practical term is explained by an editorial footnote: 'Reading ἀσυνήθειαν. He [Isocrates] had no legal practice, which would have shown the irrelevancy of comparisons in a law court, whereas in epideictic speeches they are useful. συνήθειαν gives exactly the opposite sense, and must refer to his having written speeches for others to deliver in the courts.'[24] Thus the Loeb translator justifies a decision to change the Greek from *synetheian* to *asynetheian* in order to fit what he wishes Aristotle's text had said. This seems a little shaky at best, not necessarily as a principle of translation but instead because of the reason furnished. It is not obvious, for example, what the evidence is for the stated 'irrelevancy of comparisons in a law court'.

What this editorial decision does imply is the ease of making a distinction between forensic and epideictic rhetoric. Further, it proposes that a certain form of argumentation – in which comparison takes the place of encomium – may be seen as appropriate to and even characteristic of a genre of rhetorical performance. Following this opening will tell us something about how to read certain formal aspects of Sidney's *A Defence of Poetry*.[25]

VI

Early in her book on early modern defences of poetry, Margaret Ferguson notes that 'the defense as a form calls attention to the existence of rhetorical motives'.[26] Following Kenneth Burke, however, Ferguson also notes that it is very easy to misread such motives unless one pays attention to the particular rhetorical form employed by a writer, whatever the title of a text may lead the reader to believe. Thus, she argues, 'a work like Sidney's *Defence of Poetry* may have a closer kinship to Erasmus's *Praise of Folly* or to the host of witty defenses of "indefensibles" (baldness, debt, fleas, etc.) . . . than it has to a sober treatise like Scaliger's *Poetics*'.[27] Poetry is thus aligned with these 'indefensibles', and Sidney's text becomes a defence of the indefensible. But why might poetry be indefensible? In this chapter I will offer more than one answer to this question. Taking up Ferguson's suggestive point, I will propose that the possibility of differentiating a mock-encomium from a genuine defence must face two separate problems: how to judge the form of the argument (is it persuasively presented?) and how to judge its content (is the argument logically persuasive?).[28] Thus a text such as the *Praise of Folly* offers a very powerful expression of a case that just happens to be indefensible. If we are not ulti- mately persuaded of the merits of folly (or Folly), then this is not due to a failure of Erasmus's rhetorical skill. Here, in short, is a restatement of the traditional distinction between *verba* (most simply 'style') and *res* (content).

My reason for turning now to Ferguson's reading of Sidney is that *Trials of Desire* itself offers a defence of Sidney's text that is fully alive to the ambiguities of the rhetorical tradition of which it is a part. Defending Sidney as a 'counterfeiter' (and drawing upon the use of this term made by George Puttenham in his 'trans- lation' of the names of rhetorical figures into English), Ferguson seeks to give adequate weight to the connections between form and content in the *Defence*. As such, her reading is distinct from the kind of account given, for example, by Blair Worden, who writes that:

> Sidney's *Defence of Poetry* is a rhetorical work. It pleads a case which its author half believes. Proclaiming the superiority of poetry to other forms of instruction, particularly philosophy and history, it mocks them in terms which are at odds with what he writes in other places. But what it says about the purpose of poetry has never been said better.[29]

What Worden says here is largely true, but it pleads a case that we should only half believe. What it misses entirely is the form of the text, since the description 'rhetorical work' is too broad to be helpful. While it could be objected that, in the context of his own discussion, Worden is primarily concerned with what the *Defence* can usefully tell us about the *Arcadia*, which is the real focus of his study, what should remain clear is that Sidney's text is being read solely for content. Consequently, this account begs far more questions than it answers. What kind of rhetorical work is the *Defence*? How exactly does it plead its case? Might there be something about the genre that could explain why the argument here seems to contradict Sidney's opinion in other texts? The final suggestion that 'what it says' has never been 'said better' maintains the distinction between form and content while trying to collapse it. There is little sense here that the way in which the argument is expressed may be part of the argument, little sense that this may be an aspect of the 'instruction' that Worden rightly sees behind it.

In Ferguson's reading, however, such connections between the form and the content of the argument are central to understanding Sidney's project.[30] Imitating the forensic rhetoric that we might expect in a defence, Sidney's text is also a form of *epideixis*, displaying his skill. One of the advantages of Ferguson's reading here is that it allows us to be appropriately sceptical of the apparently clear distinction between forensic and epideictic rhetoric of the type found in the Loeb editor's comments on Aristotle's *Rhetoric*. Sidney, we must not forget, is a poet writing about poetry, and poetry for him is not to be confused with or reduced to 'verse'. As Ferguson comments:

> Sidney is perfectly aware that as an effort of persuasion his treatise is in crucial respects a double of the poetry it defines and defends. He is, moreover, aware that the affinity between his own rhetoric and the 'moving' force of poetry raises questions about the use and abuse of power. When he echoes Aristotle's defense of rhetoric to formulate a definition of poetry as a morally ambiguous power, he invites us to see that, in this trial, the lawyer is as guilty or innocent as his client.[31]

Sidney's defence is thus a repetition of Aristotle's attempt to found a neutral or innocent space for art, an attempt that may also be read in Kant's positioning of the aesthetic judgement of art as disinterested.[32] But, it is also a structure that doubles or folds in upon itself, echoing the concerns of his argument to make a case for persuasion through a persuasive form of argumentation. Since this argument ultimately derives not from Aristotle's *Poetics* but from the *Rhetoric*, Sidney moves from poetry to oratory, and it is the persuasive aspect of his definition of poetry that makes the question of the relation between language and power a pertinent one. (We might still, of course, wish to ask what form this power takes.) The division that occurs in Latin between *ratio* and *oratio*, a split that is inherent in Greek in the single term *logos*, is the division that the duplex or specular nature of Sidney's text is attempting to heal. If we were to allow ourselves to translate this division into other terms, we might think of it as the agonic relation of presentation and representation, and thus as a fundamentally platonic problem. This problem returns us to the insistent role of *Darstellung* in the understanding of figures such as *hypotyposis*, but we should be wary about falling away from the necessary anti-platonic caution advocated by de Man in his elaboration of the consequences of the aestheticisation of literary study.

Rather than sketching in the whole of Ferguson's argument, I would like to focus on a particular section of it which returns us to the question of the *experience* of language as rhetoric. In her discussion of 'The Defense against Philosophy and History', Ferguson takes up the trope of *prosopopeia*. This occurs, of course, in Sidney's passage on the Psalms, in which he praises David's poetic skill, asking:

> what else is the awaking his musical instruments, the often and free changing of persons, his notable *prosopopœias*, when he maketh you, as it were, see God coming in His majesty, his telling of the beasts' joyfulness and hills leaping, but a heavenly poesy, wherein almost he showeth himself a passionate lover of that unspeakable and everlasting beauty to be seen by the eyes of the mind, only cleared by faith?[33]

In Chapter 2 I outlined some of the ramifications of this notion of 'the eyes of the mind'. *Prosopopeia* has a certain privilege for Sidney because it is referred to by Aristotle in the *Rhetoric* in a passage discussing Homer's practice of giving metaphorical life to lifeless things.[34] As Aristotle says, 'The materials of metaphor must be beautiful to the ear, to the understanding, to the eye or some other physical sense.'[35] In Sidney's account, it is this ability to move from the text to the 'eyes of the mind' that lies at the heart of the poet's craft (and that echoes Puttenham's sense of acting upon the 'mind's eye' that I discussed in Chapter 2). It is this that offers the glimpse of the golden world, beyond the brazen world that we inhabit. But there is something quite odd going on here that it would be easy to miss. As we have seen already in the earlier discussion of Ben Jonson's attitude to language, there is a kind of translation at work. The Psalmist's voice creates an image of beauty for the mind's eyes. The aural becomes the visual. Or, the written text becomes a voice, which then turns back into a picture. The visual becomes the aural becomes the visual. Just like Sidney's famous metaphor of the 'speaking picture' (itself a kind of translation), the mimetic counterfeiting that is performed in *prosopopeia* crosses the boundaries between senses, revealing the very artificiality of those boundaries and reminding us of synaesthetic possibilities. That the Psalmist's words reveal a love of a beauty that is described as 'unspeakable' only adds to the confusion of the senses.

While it is common to see Sidney's text as exemplary, somehow embodying his age, the *Defence* may be better understood if compared to other rhetorical thought. Comparison of Sidney's treatment of particular topics with that by some of his contemporaries will help to flesh out the comments so far made about the *Defence*'s formal qualities. If Sidney conjures an implicit form of translation through the trope of *prosopopeia*, for Henry Peacham this kind of translation characterises all metaphorical language. In the opening pages of *The Garden of Eloquence*, having defined tropes and figures and their sources in Greek and Latin thought, Peacham turns to what he calls the central tropes, beginning with *Metaphora*. This, he suggests, is 'when a word is translated from the proper and natural signification, to another not proper, but yet nie [near] and likely, and that eyther for necessity, or else for pleasauntnesse, thys translation is taken from many places'.[36] In this, of course, he is following the standard Latin rendering of the Greek *metaphorein* as *translatio*.

The 'many places' from which this translation begins are primarily the bodily senses. As Peacham says, 'First, we translate a word from the sences of the body, to the thinges in the mind, that is, when by any word which is proper to the sences, we signify something belonging to the mind, which translation is very usuall and common, but chiefly from the sight, which is the most princi-pall and perfect sence.'[37] Peacham's elevation of sight over the other senses is entirely conventional, but his location of the effects of language in bodily sensation and perception is instructive. The translation of bodily sensation into mental property is indeed common, as we have seen in the passages from Hobbes that were quoted in Chapter 2, but just as in Hobbes the 'chiefly' doesn't succeed in masking the impact of the other senses on this process of translation. Just as in the earlier forms of animating figure that have been discussed, such as *enargeia* and *hypotyposis*, *prosopo-peia* blurs any rigid distinctions between the senses, and draws attention to the relation of language to cognition.

The place of *prosopopeia* is a complex one. Equivalent to the Latin *fictio personae*, this figure is most commonly used to describe the attribution of human qualities either to inanimate or absent objects, which may or may not be themselves human. The term takes on the sense in the Greek root word *prosopon* of 'face' or 'character'.[38] When Peacham comes to describe *prosopopeia* (which is printed in the 1577 edition as *Prosopeia*) he immediately makes the same crossing from poetry to oratory, or poetics to rhetoric, that we see in Sidney's text:

> Prosopeia, the fayning of a person, that is, when to a thing sencelesse or dumme, wee fayne a fit person, this figure Orators use as well as Poets, an Oratoure by this figure maketh the common welth to speake: lyfe and death: vertue and pleasure: honesty and profite: welth and poverty: envy and charity: to pleade and contend one agaynst another, and sometime they rayse as it were the deade agayne, and cause them to complayne or to witnesse that they knew.[39]

In thinking about Worden's proposal that Sidney's *Defence* 'pleads a case', we need to be thinking precisely in terms of rhetorical figures such as this. Here we find a clear echo of Aristotle's notion of pitting personae against one another in forensic oration. Peacham goes on to note that inanimate objects such as stones or weapons, or even cities, are frequently made to speak, offering examples from Ovid and others. As Peacham concludes: 'The use of this figure is very profytable in perswading, chyding, complayning,

praysing, and pittying.'[40] The appeal of such a figure for a forensic
oration is obvious, but there is also an obvious element of display
in this ability to raise the dead (even if we concede the force of
Peacham's 'as it were'). Forensic rhetoric thus crosses over into
epideixis.

Similarly, Puttenham talks of *prosopopeia* as a 'Counterfait in
personation', suggesting that this occurs 'if ye wil attribute any
humane quality, as reason or speech, to dombe creatures or other
insensible things, & do study (as one may say) to give them a
humane person'.[41] As a figure designed to increase the vividness of
an oration's persuasive aspect, *prosopopeia* has affinities with
hypotyposis, which Puttenham describes two paragraphs earlier
as 'counterfait representation', as we saw in Chapter 2. In fact,
since *prosopopeia* shades into *ethopeia* (in which the position of
another is adopted in order to make a speech on their behalf more
vivid, as in a law case), and this is in turn related to *enargeia*,
prosopopeia does to some extent overlap with *hypotyposis*. All of
these figures are, as we have seen, primarily concerned with phenomenalisation, that is, with making something apparent to the
senses. When John Hoskyns offers a gloss on Sidney's *Arcadia*, he
proposes that 'to animate and give life is PROSOPOPEIA, as, to make
dead men speak'.[42] In this sense, *prosopopeia* is the specular double
of *apostrophe*, in which the inanimate or absent object is addressed
as if it were able to hear and even to respond (*apostrophe* will be
discussed further in Chapter 6). While critics working on the early
modern period may fantasise conversations with either the dead
or the living, the power of phenomenalising figures such as these
should give pause to both historicist and presentist projects.[43]
Conceived of as a form of speech act, such figures open up possible
futures that cannot be located in and limited to a 'present'
moment.

Phenomenalising figures such as these allow for the fiction of
self-presentation, allow that is for the illusion that an image could
'speak for itself' (and thus assure us of its materiality as image).
So, just as Folly in Erasmus's *Encomium* is personified as both the
subject and the central protagonist of the discussion – a paradox
presented by the title *Moriae encomium*, which can be translated
as both 'praise of folly' and 'praise by folly' – in Sidney's text
poetry and its opponents are given the opportunity to 'represent'
themselves (with the full legal sense). As Ferguson notes, this

' "counterfeit in personation" is a clever device, since it allows each competitor to act not only as a weapon against the other but also as an unwitting self-destroyer'.[44] The ingenuity of the device comes precisely through Sidney's attention to the stylistic qualities of the rivals to poetry, most obviously history and philosophy. Style becomes, in fact, the issue. Having set up the purpose of trying to decide between these rival disciplines (to which we will return in a moment), Sidney argues:

> The philosopher . . . and the historian are they which would win the goal, the one by precept, the other by example. But both, not having both, do both halt. For the philosopher, setting down with thorny arguments the bare rule, is so hard of utterance and so misty to be conceived, that one that hath no other guide but him shall wade in him till he be old before he shall find sufficient cause to be honest. For his knowledge standeth so upon the abstract and the general, that happy is that man who may understand him, and more happy that can apply what he doth understand. On the other side, the historian, wanting the precept, is so tied, not to what should be but to what is, to the particular truth of things and not to the general reason of things, that his example draweth no necessary consequence, and therefore a less fruitful doctrine.[45]

In both cases, it is the style of argumentation that renders the discourse ineffective. Either too general or too particular, philosophy and history stand in need of each other, demand in fact a third discipline that would be the product of a dialectical operation. In this, Sidney is perhaps again echoing Aristotle, since the *Rhetoric* begins with the proposition that 'Rhetoric is the counterpart of dialectic.'[46] When he goes on to explain how poetry exceeds its rivals, Sidney certainly follows Aristotle's prescription that the 'modes of persuasion are the only true constituents of the art [of rhetoric]' (1354a). By being able to produce the 'perfect picture', Sidney's poet 'yieldeth to the powers of the mind an image of that whereof the philosopher bestoweth but a wordish description, which doth neither strike, pierce, nor possess the sight of the soul so much as that other doth' (p. 32). Again, there is a movement from the image produced verbally to the image that appears in the mind, and this as we have seen is a matter of translation, which may or may not pass through a medium of 'voice'. Yet there is a distinction between the merely 'wordish' description of the philosopher, and the more persuasive language of the poet. The philosopher's style is seen to be rhetorically inert, incapable of the vividness with which the poet may render an image. Ultimately, 'the philosopher with his learned definitions – be it of virtue, vices, matters of public policy or private government – replenisheth the memory with many infallible grounds of wisdom, which, notwithstanding, lie dark before the imaginative and judging power, if they be not illuminated or figured forth by the speaking picture of poesy' (pp. 32–3). The obscurity of the mode of teaching makes philosophy less capable than poetry of prompting good action. It is the exploitation of vivid tropes such as *enargeia*, *hypotyposis* and *prosopopeia* that gifts to the poet his power. By insistently invoking darkness and illumination, Sidney reminds us of the sensory dimension of this rhetorical power.

If philosophers are criticised for their lifeless words, then historians are faced with a similar problem of stylistic inadequacy. Where philosophers remain at a level of uninspiring generality, writers of history are too in thrall to particulars that are seemingly equally incapable of delighting as they teach. As we saw in the last chapter, Sidney argues that feigned examples, that is, fictions, are as powerfully moving as true examples, that is, things that 'actually happened'. Consequently, the poet is able to accentuate the virtuous example without being constrained by the events and their circumstances to offer a balanced sense of a person's good and bad qualities or actions. As Sidney puts it, 'whatsoever action, or faction, whatsoever counsel, policy, or war stratagem the historian is bound to recite, that may the poet (if he list) with his imitation make his own, beautifying it both for further teaching, and more delighting, as it please him' (p. 37). The historian is 'bound', the poet does what he likes. As ever, the purpose of poetry is to teach and delight, and poetry is able to go 'further', it is capable of 'more'. Unlike history, then, poetry is not 'captived to the truth of a foolish world' (pp. 37–8). This foolish or brazen world, characterised by 'counsel, policy and war stratagem', may only be transcended – towards the golden world – through poetry.

In Sidney's account, 'the truth of a foolish world' is not the only form of truth available since it has no necessary relation to reason, and the establishment of the priority of poetry over philosophy must be bought by conceding the strength of history over philosophy, and vice versa. In other words, the dialectical elevation of poetry must concede strength to one rival as it points to the weakness of the other, using both as weapons against each other. The risk is that the particular quality of poetry is ceded to what is shared with either history or philosophy. The claim that poetry can *also* do something that is already done by one of its rivals is weaker than a positive claim to special status. It is precisely this form of weakness that Aristotle alludes to in the passage on forensic rhetoric; from the negative strategy employed by the speaker it may be inferred that there is little positive to say about the person who he wishes to praise. Sidney's comparison of poetry with history and philosophy raises similar doubts and questions. Where does this leave art? Why is poetry necessary, if most of what it is capable of doing may already be done in another manner? In order to offer some provisional answers to these questions, I will have to look at the relation that Sidney establishes between his three rival forms of instruction.

Central to Sidney's project is the notion of the architectonic which, M. J. Doherty claims, is elided from Ferguson's account of the *Defence*.[47] Yet Ferguson certainly does propose that the real importance of poetry comes from its 'role in the system of "dependent relations" which constitutes the body of culture'.[48] As Sidney puts it, the 'highest end of the mistress-knowledge' is denoted by the Greek word *architektonike*, 'which stands (as I think) in the knowledge of a man's self, in the ethic and politic consideration, with the end of well-doing and not of well-knowing' (p. 29). If poetry is raised up, it remains in a relation with the other aspects of the system, and it is only by virtue of this relation that it achieves such elevation. Virtuous conduct as 'the good' is the ultimate aim, and this is rendered as a version of the platonic admonition to 'Know Thyself'.[49] This end of 'well-doing' subordinates all others to it. In this, as in much else, Sidney follows Aristotle, who says: 'Every art and every inquiry, and similarly every action and choice, is thought to aim at some good; and for this reason the good has rightly been declared to be that at which all things aim.'[50] Where Sidney in his passage uses the example of the saddler, Aristotle employs the bridle-maker, both claiming that this activity is subordinate to the higher purpose of riding, and thus to its military uses. It is only for the sake of these 'master arts' that the subordinate ones are pursued at all.

The architectonic, then, allows Sidney to elaborate poetry (or at least poesie) as self-knowledge, that is, as a form of cognition.

But this cognition is precisely self-knowledge, that is, it accords with de Man's insistence that literature can tell us primarily about its own status and that of its language. It is not possible to move without mediation to knowledge of a world or of that world's history. In this, Sidney brings his conception of poetry close to the concerns of Kant's critical project, while offering a sense of the reasons why Kant's project was not ultimately able to complete itself in demonstrating the underlying unity of reason.[51] Again, it is a question of the systemic dimension of Kant's project. In defending philosophy (which *is* the architectonic of human reason in Kant) from the claims of law, theology or medicine, Kant focuses on the division between nature and freedom. In doing so, he also instances the division between a philosophy of nature (which deals with *that which is*) and a moral philosophy (which deals with *that which ought to be*).[52] As such, he maps out a territory to some extent anticipated by Sidney's opposition of history (bound irreparably to the events as they happened) and philosophy (limited in the inert abstraction of its moral prescriptions). There is much to differentiate the two projects, of course, but there is also something instructive in their similarities.[53] Both are ultimately concerned to establish a foundation that allows for the demonstration of the unity of reason with morality, and it is this that de Man and others have as their target in destabilising the cognitive assumptions that underpin such a project. But where does this leave poetry and literature?

VII

Both the modern sense of literature's hollowing out of aesthetic categories, and Sidney's concession of the ground of poetry's truth to its competing disciplines of philosophy and history, lead to the same conclusion. Poetry is indefensible. On the one hand this statement could be taken as an affirmation of an Erasmian playfulness at work in Sidney's *Defence*, in which poetry is no more elevated a topic than baldness, fleas or folly. But what we have seen in this chapter is the suggestion of something rather different. From one perspective, poetry is indefensible because there is nothing to be defended. It has neither essence nor objective status, nor does it have a privileged relation to truth. Equally, from a contrary perspective that depends on precisely the same lack of privilege, there is nothing that falls entirely outside poetry against which it could meaningfully be defended. Unless we accept the argument for the autonomy of art, and thus for an access to truth that only art can give us, we cannot accept the notion of a struggle for or meaningful defence of art. Without this autonomy, poetry is not defensible in terms of any notion of disinterested beauty or sublimity, but neither can it be taken as a source of reliable information or data about the world. This stems from the role that literature plays in revealing the susceptibility of language to a figural dimension that does not ground cognition in a secure conceptual determination. This is language's resistance to itself. As I have suggested, literature's resistance to aesthetics may best be thought of in terms of 'the resistance to theory', as de Man uses that phrase. The resistance to poetry, that which renders it in need of defence, is a resistance that poetry itself produces and that disables that which would defend it (aesthetics).[54] The first moment of this resistance is its refusal to be thought of as *just* poetry.[55] As Jean-Luc Nancy proposes in *Résistance de la poésie*, poetry is only what it is on the basis that it be able to deny [*se nier*], disown [*se renier*] and abolish itself [*se dénier et se supprimer*].[56] Poetry is thus indefensible because it harbours and exemplifies its own resistance.

Aesthetics cannot defend literature because it cannot be defended from literature. It is rhetoric, both as that which occupies the space of the aesthetic in the early modern period and as that which opens the space for resistance within the modern signification of the aesthetic, that must be embraced, but only to the extent that it reveals poetry's defencelessness.

Notes

1 P. Lacoue-Labarthe and J.-L. Nancy, *The Literary Absolute: The Theory of Literature in German Romanticism*, trans. P. Barnard and C. Lester (Albany: SUNY, 1988), p. 5.

2 Lacoue-Labarthe and Nancy, *The Literary Absolute*, pp. 5–6.

3 See, for example, the discussions in T. Pepper, *Singularities: Extremes of Theory in the Twentieth Century* (Cambridge: Cambridge University Press, 1997); P. Widdowson, *Literature* (London: Routledge, 1999); J. H. Miller, *On Literature* (London: Routledge, 2002); and the essays in E. Beaumont Bissell (ed.), *The Question of Literature: The Place of the Literary in Contemporary Theory* (Manchester: Manchester University Press, 2002). Among the more compelling

attempts to account for literature, see D. Attridge, *Peculiar Language: Literature as Difference from the Renaissance to James Joyce* (London: Methuen, 1988) and *The Singularity of Literature* (London: Routledge, 2004). Unfortunately the latter book appeared too late for me to give it the attention it deserves here.

4 See J. Derrida, 'The Time of a Thesis: Punctuations', in *Philosophy in France Today*, ed. A. Montefiore (Cambridge: Cambridge University Press, 1983), pp. 34–50.

5 This point might be illuminated by a reading of 'LECTIO: de Man's Imperative', trans. P. Fenves, in W. Hamacher, *Premises: Essays on Philosophy and Literature from Kant to Celan* (Cambridge, MA: Harvard University Press, 1996), pp. 181–221.

6 On the privileged relationship of poetry to other arts see, among many examples, Kant, *Critique of Judgment*, trans. W. S. Pluhar (Indianapolis: Hackett, 1987), §53, p. 196, and the comments of Heidegger in 'The Origin of the Work of Art': 'If all art is in essence poetry, then the arts of architecture, painting, sculpture, and music must be traced back to poesy. That is pure arbitrariness . . . Nevertheless, the linguistic work, the poem in the narrower sense, has a privileged position in the domain of the arts.' Heidegger, *Poetry, Language, Thought*, ed. and trans. A. Hofstadter (New York: Harper & Row, 1971), pp. 17–87, 73.

7 J. Derrida, 'Resistances', trans. P. Kamuf, in *Resistances of Psychoanalysis* (Stanford: Stanford University Press, 1998), p. 13. Of course, part of the positive valence of *résistance* as a term comes precisely from the French *Résistance* of the Second World War and its surrounding mythography, as Derrida himself notes.

8 See the illuminating discussions in D. Attridge, 'Derrida and the Questioning of Literature', in J. Derrida, *Acts of Literature*, ed. D. Attridge (London: Routledge, 1992), pp. 1–29; T. Clark, *Derrida, Heidegger, Blanchot: Sources of Derrida's Notion and Practice of Literature* (Cambridge: Cambridge University Press, 1992), pp. 1–19.

9 One implication of de Man's essay 'The Return to Philology' is that this is also true of those who teach literature. The key to this is the notion of *return* alluded to in the title, in which a philological or rhetorical approach to reading (what is called, with maximum de Manian irony, 'mere' reading) reveals a systematic, if not fully intentional, forgetting of the place of literature (as art) and literary criticism in a history of post-Kantian aesthetics. In *The Resistance to Theory* (Minneapolis: University of Minnesota Press, 1986), pp. 21–6, especially 24–5.

10 de Man, *The Resistance to Theory*, p. 15. For a reading which makes explicit the connections of de Man's essay to a psychoanalytic

thinking of resistance, see P. Kamuf, 'Pieces of Resistance', in *Reading de Man Reading*, ed. L. Waters and W. Godzich (Minneapolis: University of Minnesota Press, 1989), pp. 136–54.

11 de Man, *The Resistance to Theory*, p. 12.

12 de Man, *The Resistance to Theory*, p. 19.

13 de Man, *The Resistance to Theory*, p. 20. On the figure of the fall in de Man's work, see C. Caruth, 'The Falling Body and the Impact of Reference (de Man, Kant, Kleist)', in *Unclaimed Experience: Trauma, Narrative, and History* (Baltimore: Johns Hopkins University Press, 1996), pp. 73–90.

14 W. Godzich, 'Foreword' to de Man, *The Resistance to Theory*, pp. xiii–xiv.

15 Reprinted in de Man, *Aesthetic Ideology*, ed. and intro. A. Warminski (Minneapolis: University of Minnesota Press, 1996), pp. 70–90, 91–104 and 119–28. This is not the place to offer more than a cursory reading of these essays. I have benefited from the discussion in C. Norris, *Paul de Man: Deconstruction and the Critique of Aesthetic Ideology* (London: Routledge, 1988), Ch. 2.

16 C. Chase, 'Literary Theory as the Criticism of Aesthetics: De Man, Blanchot, and Romantic "Allegories of Cognition"', in *Critical Encounters: Reference and Responsibility in Deconstructive Writing*, ed. C. Caruth and D. Esch (New York: Rutgers University Press, 1995), pp. 42–91, 43. The citation is from de Man, *The Resistance to Theory*, p. 25.

17 de Man, *The Resistance to Theory*, p. 10.

18 de Man, *Aesthetic Ideology*, p. 125.

19 de Man, *Aesthetic Ideology*, p. 127.

20 de Man, *Aesthetic Ideology*, p. 128. The 'new materialism' has become a popular term in early modern studies in recent years, exemplified by critics such as David Kastan, Peter Stallybrass and Margreta de Grazia. A critique of the presuppositions of this movement might usefully begin precisely from this moment in de Man.

21 Aristotle, *Rhetoric*, trans. W. Rhys Roberts, in *Complete Works of Aristotle*, ed. J. Barnes, 2 vols (Princeton: Princeton University Press, 1984), 2: 1368a. Unless otherwise stated, all references are to this text.

22 Aristotle, *The Art of Rhetoric*, trans. H. Lawson-Tancred (Harmondsworth: Penguin, 1991), 1368a.

23 Aristotle, *The 'Art' of Rhetoric*, trans. J. H. Freese (Cambridge, MA: Harvard University Press, 1926), p. 103.

24 Aristotle, *The 'Art' of Rhetoric*, trans. J. H. Freese, p. 102.

25 For a socio-historical reading, see R. Matz, *Defending Literature in Early Modern England: Renaissance Literary Theory in Social*

Context (Cambridge: Cambridge University Press, 2000), particularly Ch. 3.

26 M. W. Ferguson, *Trials of Desire: Renaissance Defenses of Poetry* (New Haven: Yale University Press, 1983), p. 9.

27 Ferguson, *Trials of Desire*, p. 11.

28 It is worth remarking that this raises the vexed question of the relation of rhetoric to logic. The early modern period's teaching of rhetoric has been seen as remaking the crucial link between the *elocutio* emphasised in medieval teaching and the *inventio* and *dispositio* that furnished an oration's subject matter (frequently transferred in the medieval period to the domain of logic rather than rhetoric). This separation is partly what allowed rhetoric to be seen either as a mechanical set of figures of speech or as mere ornamentation. This argument is made in the editor's introduction to Richard Rainolde, *The Foundacion of Rhetorike*, ed. F. R. Johnson (New York: Scholars' Facsimiles and Reprints, 1945), pp. ix–x.

29 Worden, *The Sound of Virtue: Philip Sidney's* Arcadia *and Elizabethan Politics* (New Haven: Yale University Press, 1996), p. 10.

30 Ferguson's work is not referenced anywhere in Worden's book.

31 Ferguson, *Trials of Desire*, p. 139.

32 This notion of disinterestedness is not, however, original to Kant. See Gasché, *The Idea of Form: Rethinking Kant's Aesthetics* (Stanford: Stanford University Press, 2003), Ch. 6.

33 Sidney, *A Defence of Poetry*, ed. J. A. van Dorsten (Oxford: Oxford University Press, 1991), p. 22.

34 Aristotle, *Rhetoric*, 1411b–1412a.

35 Aristotle, *Rhetoric*, 1405b.

36 Peacham, *The Garden of Eloquence. Conteyning the Figures of Grammer and Rhetorick, etc.* (London: 1577), sig. B2r–v.

37 Peacham, *The Garden of Eloquence*, sig. B2v.

38 Thus Puttenham translates *prosopographia* as 'Counterfait countenance'. See Puttenham, *The Arte of English Poesie*, ed. G. D. Willcock and A. Walker (Cambridge: Cambridge University Press, 1970), p. 238.

39 Peacham, *The Garden of Eloquence*, sig. D3r.

40 Peacham, *The Garden of Eloquence*, sig. D3v.

41 Puttenham, *Arte*, p. 239. Puttenham is following Quintilian, *Institutio oratoria*, trans. H. E. Butler, 4 vols (London: William Heinemann, 1953), 9.2.29–37.

42 J. Hoskyns, 'Sidney's *Arcadia* and the rhetoric of English prose (*c.* 1599)', in B. Vickers (ed.), *English Renaissance Literary Criticism* (Oxford: Clarendon Press, 1999), pp. 398–427, 426.

43 This is, I realise, a very abrupt way of dealing with the complexities
   of the issue. See the famous first sentence of Greenblatt's *Shakespearean Negotiations: The Circulation of Social Energy in Renaissance
   England* (Oxford: Clarendon Press, 1988) and the barbed retort in
   T. Hawkes, *Shakespeare in the Present* (London and New York:
   Routledge, 2002), p. 4.
44 Ferguson, *Trials of Desire*, p. 142.
45 Sidney, *A Defence of Poetry*, pp. 31–2.
46 Aristotle, *Rhetoric*, 1354a. See P. Mack, 'Humanist rhetoric and
   dialectic', in *The Cambridge Companion to Renaissance Humanism*,
   ed. J. Kraye (Cambridge: Cambridge University Press, 1996), pp.
   82–99. As Mack comments: 'The humanist tradition of bringing
   together rhetoric, dialectic and grammar helped create the conditions
   in which the linguistic inventiveness of sixteenth-century writers
   could flourish', p. 96.
47 M. J. Doherty, *The Mistress-Knowledge: Sir Philip Sidney's* Defence
   of Poesie *and Literary Architectonics in the English Renaissance*
   (Nashville: Vanderbilt University Press, 1991), p. xix. Doherty believes
   the 'mistress-knowledge' to be 'the organizing metaphor par excel-
   lence of the *Defence*', p. xv.
48 Ferguson, *Trials of Desire*, p. 145.
49 Sidney was certainly aware of platonic ideas, and the commentaries
   upon them, having received a gift of Jean de Serres's *Platonis Opera
   Quae Extant Omnia* of 1578. See Doherty, *The Mistress-Knowledge*,
   pp. xiii–xiv and Ch. 4, and S. K. Heninger, Jr, 'Sidney and Serranus'
   Plato', *English Literary Renaissance* 13 (1983), 146–61.
50 Aristotle, *Nichomachean Ethics*, in *Complete Works*, 2: 1094a.
51 It is the architectonic that similarly holds a crucial place within Kant's
   three *Critiques*, most obviously in 'The Architectonic of Pure Reason'
   and in §85 of the *Critique of Judgment*. Kant, *Critique of Pure
   Reason*, trans. W. S. Pluhar (Indianapolis: Hackett, 1996), A832/
   B860; *Critique of Judgment*, particularly Ak. 438.
52 Kant, *Critique of Pure Reason*, A840/B868.
53 At this point I must signal my disagreement with Doherty's reading.
   Fascinating though much in her book is, she overstates her case for
   the centrality of the architectonic to early modern thought, and mis-
   reads Kant's work and the supposed universalising formalisms that
   she believes to follow from it. Her historicising impulse leads her to
   a reduction of both Kant and Sidney, whose own formalist tendencies
   cannot be contained as easily as her historicisation seems to
   suggest.
54 If we wished to return this insight to a historical register, we might
   follow Philippe Lacoue-Labarthe who suggests that as modernity has

unfolded, 'either art has been in complicity, or else it has been an obscure, dampened form of resistance.' He continues: 'In these works and discourses, it is aesthetics, the aesthetic project itself, strictly defined, which is called into question ... in what I'm calling resistance, at the place where art and thinking about art find it hard to accept the question of the sublime, there takes place a ruin of the presuppositions of aesthetics itself.' Lacoue-Labarthe, 'On the sublime', trans. G. Bennington, in *Postmodernism: ICA Documents*, ed. L. Appignanesi (London: Free Association, 1989), pp. 11–18, 12.

55 See the discussion in E. Scarry, *On Beauty and Being Just* (London: Duckworth, 2000).

56 J.-L. Nancy, *Résistance de la poésie* (Bordeaux: William Blake & Co., 1997), p. 10.

Part II
Reading's senses

5

To sign: *Sir Thomas More*

I

In their 1980 article 'Wit, Wisdom, and Theatricality in *The Book of Sir Thomas More*', Charles Forker and Joseph Candido lament the relative neglect of the play by literary critics, and the consequent paucity of readings of the play 'from an aesthetic point of view'.[1] Unwittingly, they use exactly the phrase that is so central to the philosophical account of aesthetics within the modern European tradition that I drew upon in the first part of this book. What I am proposing here is precisely to read this play 'from an aesthetic point of view', but I suspect that this reading does not stem from an understanding of this phrase in the sense that Forker and Candido seem to have intended. As the preceding chapters and the commentary on hands with which I will continue this chapter demonstrate, I am using the term 'aesthetic' in a broader sense. What this play offers is an opportunity to investigate what it is that writing gives to sense. As such I will be pursuing precisely the formalist agenda to which I made reference in Chapter 4. In reading *Sir Thomas More*, I am also reading the critical reception (or lack of reception) of this play and, in focusing on the role that 'hands' play in the play, I will draw together arguments concerning authorship, censorship and the thematising of signatures and subscription that the play itself stages.

In part, I am following the guiding hand of Marjorie Garber, who suggests of Shakespeare's texts that:

> again and again, the plays themselves can be seen to dramatize questions raised in the authorship controversy: who wrote this? did someone else have a hand in it? is the apparent author the real

author? is the official version to be trusted? or are there suppressed stories, hidden messages, other signatures?[2]

What I propose to focus on here is the concept of the signature as a specific mode of this relation between writing and the writer. Signing as subscription formalises relationships between the self as subject and structures of authority and law, but this formalisation is more than just a formal expression, more than just one form among others. In part (self-) denomination, the act of signing which the mark of subscription demands involves consent (and, as dictionary definitions suggest, its cognates: assent, adhesion, attestation, support, favour, sanction, concurrence, approval, agreement, acquiescence, allegiance), witnessing (acknowledgement, testimony), and submission (to sign away, yield (up), give in, submit or subject oneself to law or rule). Writing (one's name) inscribes a subject within these implied relationships, but this act of inscription does not guarantee this signing as a secure expression of intention or presence.

To sign is to attempt to recover an immediacy that writing loses, and should not be thought of simply as writing a proper name. The necessary potential for the proper name to be repeated after the death of the self that it is supposed to denominate reveals writing as a marker of absence as much as presence, but it is precisely presence that the signature offers. This presence is also haunted by a necessary capacity for the signature to be forged, and this is part of its structure. If the signature functions as a promise, that I-write-this-here-now, asserting myself as an origin (always already displaced into the signature which precisely cannot guarantee that promise), then this promise demands a countersignature. As a modality of the signature, the act of subscription opens itself to the countersignature of an *act of reading*, and, therefore, to an encounter (perhaps inevitably missed) with the other.[3] Reading, as Geoffrey Bennington suggests, might then be thought of as 'a relation of signature and countersignature'.[4]

II

Hands are all over early modern drama. Indeed, they touch upon every aspect of the literate and literary culture of this period.[5]

Hands are used to seal a bond, they are given in marriage, offered to express support, they commit acts of violence and murder, become obsessive fetishes, pray, they are cut off. In modern anthropological discourses, it is the hand that is often the locus of a distinction between human and non-human animal, since the hand is the organ of making.[6] It is this emphasis on making that might lead us to recall once again the Aristotelian sense of *poiesis* as making, that connection much-beloved of Sidney and Jonson that we have seen in earlier chapters. The poet as maker reveals writing as a form of handicraft, but it also links it to a politics of making.[7]

Shakespeare's works offer us, as we might expect, a striking range of possible treatments of the hand as figure. And these treatments are, we might say, even-handed in depicting positive and negative connotations. In *Titus Andronicus*, the hand is both the agent and target of violence. Following her mutilation, Titus pleads: 'Speak, Lavinia, what accursed hand / Hath made thee handless in thy father's sight?' (3.1.66–7).[8] The scene goes on to include an argument about which member of the Andronicus family has the most worthy hand, and proceeds to Titus's loss of his own hand.[9] In *The Winter's Tale*, Hermione's hand is said to be both hard to 'open' when Leontes woos her (1.2.103), and all too easily given to Polixenes (1.2.108, 115, 125).[10] On the one hand then, hands are seen as positive extensions of the self. On the other hand, this makes them potentially threatening, either through excess of strength or of weakness. Such characterisations of the hand come to form part of the mythography of Shakespeare as author that is inaugurated with the First Folio. As Heminge and Condell suggest in their address 'To the Great Variety of Readers', Shakespeare's 'mind and hand went together, and what he thought he uttered with that easiness that we have scarce received from him a blot in his papers'.[11] That the hand might figure the mind just as an utterance figures a thought makes sense here because the utterance is seen to be a form of writing, and it is to Shakespeare's papers that we are asked to look for evidence of this congruity. The mind is known through the actions of the hand. This easiness is, however, precisely what makes of Shakespeare's hand for some an object of suspicion. The writing is *too* easy, and thus he becomes little more than a dictation machine, copying that which comes from elsewhere (from nature, inspiration, another person who wished to use Shakespeare as a ghost-writer, and so on). To recall my earlier discussions again, it might also be seen to be copying the fancies of the thinking mind.

While they may at times be seen as an extension of the self, in that they may be willingly used or given, there is also the suggestion in *Macbeth* that hands may be beyond the control of the conscious self. Lady Macbeth's obsessive washing of her hands in sleep is well known, but another aspect of this scene is less often noted. Act Five begins with a discussion about another unconscious action. As the Gentlewoman reports:

> Since his majesty went into the field, I have seen her rise from her bed, throw her nightgown upon her, unlock her closet, take forth paper, fold it, write upon't, read it, afterwards seal it, and again return to bed; yet all this while in a most fast sleep.
>
> (5.1.4–8)

This sleep-writing is tantalisingly vague. What is being written? When we hear of this act, the paper has already been sealed but it has also already been read. The scene invites us to repeat her reading, but a reading of what? Nicholas Brooke, editor of the Oxford edition, speculates that Lady Macbeth might be writing 'a note to Macbeth, a confession, a will?'[12] The first option hardly lessens the uncertainty about the paper's contents, but the other two clearly point in the direction of a relationship between writing and death. The unconsciously moving hand reveals an act of violence, or attempts to legislate for or beyond its own disappearance. One act of the hand (murder) produces another (writing). This is succeeded by another (rubbing as 'washing'), and is ended by a final sense, in which Lady Macbeth concludes with a series of repetitive statements that interrupts repetitive action: 'To bed, to bed – there's knocking at the gate – come, come, come, come, give me your hand – what's done, cannot be undone. To bed, to bed, to bed' (5.1.63–6). Hands stabbing, writing, sealing, washing, knocking, reaching and holding are touched on throughout the play.

But in the context of early modern drama, of course, hands are not only to be found *in* plays, in any simple sense. As Jeffrey Masten has commented with regard to the prologues and epilogues to early modern plays: 'Human hands – hands that applaud, but also the hands that pay to see the play, the hand-shaking that seals the bargain, the collaborating hands of exchange and commerce – make repeated appearance in this framing material.'[13] To this we need to add, as Masten does, the hands that write (and perhaps the hands that see and read, as Derrida proposes in *Memoirs of the Blind*).[14] It is important, then, that we pay attention to the 'framing' material and to the discussions about and recourse to figures of hands that occur within the texts. Reading one against the other seems essential. The question of the frame opens the relationship of inside to outside, work to world, precisely as a question.[15] But the frame should not be treated as if it were more elaborate (or more simple) than that which it frames. Just as in the editorial speculation on the contents of Lady Macbeth's paper – whether a note, a confession or a will – what is really at stake is both the doubling of a reading and the countersignature to that reading.

What we can see from this brief exploration of hands – and I have only touched upon some of the most obvious examples here – is a series of relations between the hand and expressions of consciousness, will, desire and making sense. Hands are meaningful, but these meanings seem to tremble between subjectivity and secrecy, between the expression of an interiority (conscious or unconscious, willed or unwilled) and the phenomenalisation of that interiority in a form which cannot securely be rendered meaningful. Writing offers a form of making and of making sense (we might say, of handicraft) that cannot necessarily lead us to a sense of the priority of sense over making, or vice versa.

III

When Forker and Candido lament the paucity of readings of the play, this is due to a recognition that the question of the hand takes on a particular significance in the context of *Sir Thomas More*. The most frequent appearance of 'hands' in respect to this text is in discussion of the supposedly authorial hands that appear in the manuscript of the play, and it is in this sense that hands draw attention away from the text's supposed content.[16] Forker and Candido's recognition that a concern with *Sir Thomas More*'s authorship and date has tended to dominate critical discussion, and that there has been an unhappy failure to see 'a coherence of design uncommon among such plays', still seems largely to hold true, although there is some critical discussion to be found.[17] A further constraint upon this critical discussion, however, has been an emphasis upon censorship, which has again deflected attention from *readings* of the play. Here it is the hand of the censor which attracts attention. This chapter examines more closely some of the theoretical presuppositions of critical opinion about the play, and offers a reading which suggests that the play itself raises questions about such presuppositions that have been given too little serious attention to date. One way of thinking about this critical terrain is to see it as an example of the privileging of one mode of materiality over another. The materiality of the text in the sense of its physical manifestation as an object outweighs its materiality as text. In favouring the latter in my own reading, I have in mind the connection between materialism and formalism that I noted in Chapter 4.

The emphasis on the authorial hand dominates twentieth-century criticism of the play. Edward Maunde Thompson's attempt to identify Hand D in the manuscript of *Sir Thomas More*, for example, centres upon a comparison with Shakespeare's signatures on other, non-literary documents.[18] Despite the age of this piece, Thompson's efforts are representative of an ongoing debate about this play. But rather than simply add to this largely over-worked area, I would like here to raise some questions about the principles which guide so much of this debate. For example, that it should largely be the signatures on Shakespeare's will that ground this attribution seems particularly telling, since the signature on a will is precisely that which marks the absence as much as the presence of the one who signs. While the signature marks a will to control this absence, it cannot guarantee presence. The signature on the will performs only after death; until this point the will has no legal force which could be acted upon, and there is always the possibility of substituting another will.[19] In this respect the performative dimension of the signature might be compared to that of the promise, in that there is always the possibility of a future failure to deliver that which seems to be offered in the act of signing.

There are additionally some empirical difficulties particular to this case. W. W. Greg came down in favour of Thompson's attribution of Hand D to Shakespeare, but not before making a troubling suggestion: 'On purely palaeographical grounds there is less reason to suppose that all six signatures [attributed to Shakespeare on other documents such as wills] were written by the same hand than there is, granting this identity, to suppose that the hand of the signatures also wrote the addition to *More*.'[20] Hand-writing does not offer security and certainty. Rather than positing the author as a unified horizon of possible authority against which the text might be judged, Greg here suggests a division at the origin, in a series of signatures which cannot be used to give a positive identi-fication as singular identity. Further, as David Scott Kastan has pointed out, if Hand D is indeed that of Shakespeare, then it gives us a glimpse not of Shakespeare as unique author, but of Shakespeare as collaborator. That modern commentators have tended to sideline this impression only reinforces a process which is perhaps already at work in the decision of the compilers of the 1623 folio not to include *Sir Thomas More* in the volume. Indeed, it is likely that it is precisely this collaborative dimension that makes it impossible for this play, as for *The Two Noble Kinsmen* and *Pericles*, to be included.[21] This principle of exclusion is coun-tered, however, by those editors who desire to have as much Shakespeare as possible in a collected volume, and leads to such strange occurrences as the presence of only the excerpted Hand D section of the play appearing in Shakespeare's *Complete Works*.[22]

We might say, then, that the excerpted speech to be found in modern editions acts as a kind of dismembered limb, as a hand cut off from a body, and there are parallels to be drawn between this practice of dividing up the text and the condition of early editions of Shakespeare's plays. Heminge and Condell complain about earlier printings of Shakespeare's plays, employing this bodily metaphor: 'you [the readers] were abused with divers stolen and surreptitious copies, maimed and deformed by the frauds and stealths of injurious impostors that exposed them, even those are now offered to your view cured and perfect of their limbs, and all the rest absolute in their numbers, as he conceived them; who, as he was a happy imitator of nature, was most gentle expresser of it.'[23] Maimed and deformed, Shakespeare's texts can be cured and perfected though an appeal to the author's own 'conception' of them. They are reborn in and as the body (or corpus) of the Folio.

How then might *Sir Thomas More*, a play which calls for the reading of signatures and acts of signing, be countersigned, remembering Bennington's comments on reading as a form of countersignature? Readings of the text as a phenomenal literary *object* have led to encounters with institutionalised structures of interpretation which curiously seem to have resulted in a steady accretion of failures to read the text in any strong sense at all. The treatment of the text as a cultural artefact appears to stem from a form of 'materialism' which falls into idealism at the point where the text is taken to be a privileged mode of access to some recovery of 'material' social or cultural conditions. The manuscript of the play is undoubtedly of interest to those concerned with cultural history, especially in the areas of authorship and censorship. What is rarely taken into account in these readings, however, is the thematisation of the act of signing within the play, and this has led to a dissolution of the literariness of the literary object in favour of a concentration on its status as an object. This remains true even if we adopt a functionalist categorisation of litera-ture and literariness. My reading of *Sir Thomas More* is not, then, simply another 'thematic' reading, since the concentration upon interpretation as an act, as itself a performance, disturbs the possibility of securing such thematic concerns. The purpose of this reading is to unveil the questioning of presuppositions of pres-ence enacted within the text, and thus to reflect critically upon this dependence upon presence in modern commentaries on the play.

What I have been arguing about the authorship debate, with its inevitable emphasis on Shakespeare, should lead us to think about the contribution made by Hand D, about the 'Shakespearean' scene. The main speech provided for More in the Hand D section uses the figure of the hand explicitly, and it is used to link together notions of authority, copying and violence. Prompted by Betts's suggestion that the removal of the strangers 'cannot choose but much advantage the poor handicrafts of the city', More replies:

> Grant them removed, and grant that this your noise
> Hath chid down all the majesty of England.
> Imagine that you see the wretched strangers,
> Their babies at their backs, with their poor luggage
> Plodding to th' ports and coasts for transportation,
> And that you sit as kings in your desires,
> Authority quite silenced by your brawl,
> And you in ruff of your opinions clothed:

> What had you got? I'll tell you: you had taught
> How insolence and strong hand should prevail,
> How order should be quelled, and by this pattern
> Not one of you should live an aged man,
> For other ruffians, as their fancies wrought,
> With selfsame hand, self reasons and self right
> Would shark on you, and men like ravenous fishes
> Would feed on one another.
>
>   (2.3.78–93)

The strong hand, in its rejection of the authority of kings and majesty, provides a model that others might copy, producing a model of predation. The problem seems to be that the kind of power that the rioters envisage will bring authority itself into disrepute. They will not be kings but tyrants. The ruff leads to their identification with and thus as ruffians. But the problem seems to lie with the idea of taking something into one's hands. More attempts to divert the usage of those hands, asking that 'those same hands / That you like rebels lift against the peace / Lift up for peace' (2.3.116–18).

References to hands are not confined to the section in Hand D, however, and the play opens with Doll Williamson complaining about the way in which she is being handled by Francis de Bard, demanding 'Hand off when I bid thee' and commenting, outraged, that he 'thinkst thou hast the goldsmith's wife in hand' (1.1.7, 9–10). She later makes the same demand again (1.1.55). Preparing for death, Doll and Williamson join hands and she also takes the hands of her fellow condemned, Betts, Ralph and Sherwin. Frequently, hands are seen in precisely such a legal setting. Elsewhere, More claims that 'there are such matters in my hands / As if I pleased to give them to the jury, / I should not need this way to circumvent thee' (1.2.73–5). Similarly, when More meets up with a woman for whom he has been acting (legally speaking) in Act 5, again hands appear in proximity to writing. The woman asks: 'Now good Sir Thomas More, for Christ's dear sake, / Deliver me my writings back again / That do concern my title.' More replies:

> What, my old client, art thou got hither too?
> Poor silly wretch, I must confess indeed
> I had such writings as concern thee near,
> But the king has ta'en the matter into his own hand:

He has all I had; then, woman, sue to him,
I cannot help thee, thou must bear with me.

                                    (5.1.33–41)

This dialogue in the language of patronage, with its emphasis on
suits and clientage revolves around some ill-defined documents,
but this matter is all taken in hand by the king. This language of
suits returns when More is on the scaffold, and he says to the
Hangman: 'the law, my honest friend, lies in thy hands now'
(5.4.89–90). Taking something into one's hands – in the cases of
the rioters, de Bard, the King and the executioner – implies might
but not right, power but not justice. How, then, does this affect
the writing hand?

The rioters are described in the Hand D section as 'not men of
wisdom'. Wisdom in *Sir Thomas More* stands in for a series of
conceptual terms, in particular for law, and the pivotal scene in
More's tragedy (4.1) involves a demand for his signature to this
legal structure. In this scene, the demand for More's subscription
to a series of unspecified articles figures the demand for socialisa-
tion and conformity to law, but this figure is constituted by a dialectic which is put into motion by the divagation of a series of
oppositions in the play, such as inside/outside, law/conscience,
law/justice, wisdom/wit, wisdom/folly, wisdom/poetry.[24] If law (as
wisdom) demands writing as its ground, then the fact that revolt
in the play also demands writing presents, as we shall see, a complication of the relationship between writing and authority. As I
have already suggested in the earlier chapters in this book, this
marginalisation of the poetic that is represented by the opposition
of wisdom to poetry is paralleled in a critical inheritance which
similarly favours determinate reference over 'poetic' meaning, and
which insists on an identification between 'outside' and 'inside'
that is itself only possible through the recognition of a potential
difference (or non-identity) between the two terms. Consequently,
Sir Thomas More has been read primarily as a document rather
than as a drama, and it is necessary to reconstruct some of the
general characteristics of this commentary.

IV

As David Kastan proposes, *Sir Thomas More* offers one of the
most intriguing examples of collaboration that has survived from

the early modern period. Not printed in the sixteenth or seventeenth centuries, modern editions of the play rely upon a manuscript for a source-text, comprising a fair copy in a single hand
together with fragmentary additions or revisions in several other
hands.[25] Every year from 1586 to 1605 has been suggested for the
composition of the play's fragments, and it was long held that the
original composition and the revisions took place in quick succes-
sion.[26] More recent scholarship has suggested that the original
composition took place in the early 1590s, and that the revisions
occurred around 1600.[27]

The text thus presents a unique opportunity to examine the
methods of composition, and more particularly collaborative composition, of Elizabethan playwrights. This is not an opportunity
which has been wasted, and the intensity of the scholarly interest
which has surrounded this document has been heightened to an
unprecedented degree by the possibility that one of the hands,
Hand D, may be that of Shakespeare.[28] It was Greg who first
attempted to produce some order from the chaos of speculation
about *Sir Thomas More* that appeared in the first decades of this
century.[29] Apart from Shakespeare, contributing dramatists suggested include Anthony Munday, Henry Chettle, John Webster,
Thomas Heywood, Thomas Kyd, Thomas Dekker and George
Peele.[30] It has also been proposed that the whole thing was plotted
by Christopher Marlowe, who was unable to complete the piece
as a result of his untimely death – it is seemingly impossible to say
anything of Marlowe without mentioning plots.[31] Varying degrees
of certainty may be attached to each of these names, and Greg was
led to suggest in 1923 that: 'though certainty may be unattainable,
speculation is not therefore idle'.[32]

While we may not be entirely convinced by Greg's assertion
regarding the idleness of this speculation, it is clear that what lies
behind this critical activity is an investment in the significance of
the author. Why, though, should such investments have dominated
discussion of the play? The attempt to attach a proper name to the
hands that appear in the manuscript is an example of the chiastic
intersection of work in life and life in work: the logic appears to
be that if it were possible to establish by whom the text of *Sir
Thomas More* was written, whether singly or in collaboration,
whether for part or the whole of the manuscript, then it could be
taken into (or excluded from) an oeuvre. Thus the continuing

attempts to identify the hands of *Sir Thomas More* must always
take the form of a comparison between these hands and that of
someone whose work is already known. This search for the
same, for the already known, is haunted by the figure of the supplement. According to a curious but by now familiar logic, this
chiastic understanding of the interpenetration of life and work
renders the part in some way greater than the whole into which it
is inserted: if we believe that the play was written by Marlowe,
say, then this alters not only the status of the play but also our
knowledge of his life and work. The 'known' Marlowe from which
we begin our process of attribution is altered by the attribution
itself.

The authority of authorship is not the sole area to have pro-
voked extensive commentary in relation to *Sir Thomas More*. The
presence of another hand in the manuscript, that of Edmund
Tilney, Master of the Revels from 1579 to 1610, places the text in
an additional relationship to discourses of authority. Tilney's signature appears at the end of the following much-discussed
comment, inserted in the left margin of the first few lines of the
manuscript:

> Leaue out . . . / ye insurrection / wholy w^t / ye Cause ther off & / begin
> w^t S^r Th: / Moore att ye mayors sessions / w^t a reportt afterwards /
> off his good servic' / don being' Shriue off Londō / vppō a mutiny
> Agaynst ye Lùbards only by A shortt / reportt & nott otherwise / att
> your own perilles / E Tyllney.[33]

This statement by the censor has been the subject of much argument, including uncertainty as to whether it amounts to censorship
at all, or was in fact an attempt to make sure that the play was
performed.[34] The authority of the statement lies in the signature,[35]
and it is no doubt in large part due to its presence in the manuscript
that *Sir Thomas More* has been described by Janet Clare as the
'*cause célèbre* of Elizabethan censorship'.[36] Again we see an
emphasis on the relationship between writing and authority that
is focused upon the signature, but again this is not read in terms
of the signature's performative aspect. Tilney's signature is used
to give access to certain apparently material conditions, which are
accepted as a given. The relationship between Tilney's apparent
act of interpretation and the play's own questioning of such acts
is not addressed.

In modern criticism, *Sir Thomas More* is seen to be less (as Roland Barthes might have put it) a tissue of quotations than a series of echoes, always defined in terms of something (handwriting, stylometry, staging, vocabulary, cultural conditions) other than its textuality. The textual dimension is killed off through an overvaluation of its significance as an index of something other than itself. There is a congruity between the 'old' and the 'new' historicisms in most of the work on *Sir Thomas More*, and the text is easily lost in the speculation about authorship and censorship. Treated as a 'document', the questions that the play raises are obscured, despite the fact that these questions relate directly to the foundations upon which such documentary readings depend. These discourses of authorship and censorship insist upon secure referentiality, intertextual connection between the components identified as a given oeuvre, and the location of meaning outside the text. Concern with extrinsic significance has led to a certain blindness to the play's own thematisation of subscription, and to a diminution of its performative historicity. Yet this performativity itself troubles such thematic readings.

V

What, then, is the status of the signature in *Sir Thomas More*? When Sir Thomas Palmer enters in Act Four with a set of 'articles . . . to be viewed / And then to be subscribed to' (4.1.70–1), it seems that the intended signatories are not expected to refuse. What is proposed is not reading but viewing, since the readers are expected to sign irrespective of what they find there. Yet both Thomas More and John Fisher, Bishop of Rochester, respond in significantly different ways; More's response is cautious – 'Our conscience first shall parley with our laws' – but Fisher quickly assesses the importance of the articles:

> Subscribe to these? Now good Sir Thomas Palmer,
> Beseech the king that he will pardon me.
> My heart will check my hand whilst I do write:
> Subscribing so, I were an hypocrite.
>
> (4.1.76–9)

Fisher recognises the conflict between the authorities of heart and hand, and between inner conscience and outward affiliation, making both a matter of personal responsibility. More's words, by contrast, show his consciousness of the need to reconcile obedience to the law with his own conscience, marking the possible divergence of public and private duty. Where More sees the need for a 'parley' between public and private obedience, Fisher sees the problem as a matter of reconciling aspects of the self. The use of 'hypocrite' serves to accentuate Fisher's relation of subscription to subjectivity; the Greek etymological origin of 'hypocrisy' links religious faith to dissimulation and to acting on a stage. What Fisher's response indicates is a fundamental difference between a hypocritical attitude and a critical one.

Fisher's failure to dissimulate imperils his head, although he offers his heart to the king in place of his hand (signature) (4.1.84). His refusal to subscribe to the articles is later interpreted as a capital offence, and leads to his execution, since the heart is precisely *not* what is demanded by the articles. Performance need not entail sincerity (or even conscious will), but it may be demanded without such will. Fisher's connection of heart (conviction) and hand (subscription) echoes speeches in Act One by the rebels George Betts and Doll Williamson, which suggest the need for the open expression of resistance. Such resistance is to take the form of signature to a 'bill of wrongs' formulated by Lincoln, the leader of the citizens' revolt. Having read the bill, which is intended to be given to preachers to 'openly publish in the pulpit' (1.1.91–2), Lincoln and Betts are asked what the 'further meaning' of their action might be, that is, what effects they expect the reading of the bill to have. Betts explains that they wish to keep a written record of those who express support: 'No doubt but this will store us with friends enow, whose names we will closely keep in writing.' Subscription is presented by Betts as a challenge: 'Do ye subscribe, or are ye faint-hearted revolters?' (1.1.127–32). If the male rebels are to avoid the charges of cowardice made earlier in the scene by Doll, who expresses her disdain through a complaint about 'men's milky hearts' (1.1.56), then they must testify to their strength of purpose through writing. This written support is to be kept and used as authority for the May Day riots which will follow.[37] Doll, however, is the first to sign, and she does so in terms which also prefigure Fisher's response to the 'articles': 'Hold thee, George Betts, there's my hand and my heart' (1.1.133). The potential for rebellion is retrospectively clear in Fisher's stance, in that the alignment of heart and hand that he views as a reconciliation of aspects of the self can be employed to express dissent as much as acquiescence. Refusal to sign the articles is equated with sub-scription to the bill of wrongs through the repeated tropes of heart and hand.

More's solution to the problem of whether or not to subscribe to the articles is delay, asking for time to consider the request, but immediately resigning his chancellorship into the king's hands. Surrey and Shrewsbury, who are also present in this scene, sign 'instantly', and are seemingly unable to comprehend More's appar-ently disobedient prevarication. Surrey voices this disbelief by invoking the divine sanction of royal authority: 'Tis strange that my lord chancellor should refuse / The duty that the law of God bequeaths / Unto the king' (4.1.106–8). For Surrey, unlike More and Fisher, there is no divergence between public duty and private conscience, and his subscription is as much a submission to law and the will of the king (which are in effect the same thing) as an acquiescence or agreement. There is no need for any 'parley' between conscience and law. That Surrey represents this as a sub-mission to the law of God, rather than to temporal power, occludes the basis of the distinction that More recognises between an indi-vidual religious faith (as duty to conscience) and social responsibil-ity (as duty to law). We should not then be surprised that it is Surrey and Shrewsbury who come to take More into custody in Act Five.

Thus we are given two poles between which More's position may be situated. For Fisher, social duty must always accord with faith; temporal law must be obeyed only if it is congruent with spiritual law. Surrey is not capable of seeing faith as anything other than an aspect of a primary obedience to law; thus temporal law and spiritual law are not distinguished. More must attempt a rap-prochement between the two extremes (later this is recast as an attempt to marry wit and wisdom), and it is his inability to do so within the given political situation depicted in the play which results in his 'tragedy'. More's speech at the end of the play marks the change of position that this failure entails: 'my offence to his highness makes me of a state pleader a stage player (though I am old, and have a bad voice) to act this last scene of my tragedy' (5.4.72–5). Clearly this is meant to be seen as a critical rather than a hypocritical performance. More suggests that he is no longer a representative of state law, but is instead reduced to acting out his own death, stressing the change in his sense of agency. From identifying himself as the 'voice' of law, as a 'pleader' for the state, More now sees himself as reduced to playing a part over which he has little control.

In assessing the spiritual dimension of More's character, we must note the lack of specificity in the play about More's status as a Catholic, and about the religious dimension of the somewhat vague 'articles'. But it seems to me that it would be unwise to think, as Forker and Candido suggest, that: 'It goes without saying that the playwrights had entirely to suppress the religious beliefs for which More died (the play never mentions his Catholicism or the King's "great matter") and explicitly to vindicate the authority of the state.'[38] This gives too little attention to Fisher's role, and it would be hard not to notice that More eventually comes to the same conclusion about subscription as the Bishop of Rochester. If Fisher's decision not to subscribe to the articles is read in terms of an attempt to assert an autonomous selfhood with regard to structures of temporal authority, then More's position can also be read in this way. More's conclusions about the relationship of identity to writing and authority are not simply a matter of personal ethical choice.

More's situation between law as a sanctioned social norm (wisdom) and an individual ethical position identified by a term such as conscience (or wit) is established in his first appearance in the play in Act One. It is an attention to naming that should lead our reading here of a trial scene in which a man called Lifter stands accused of theft.[39] The Mayor asks of the accused, 'what is this fellow?' and is forced to re-pose his question: 'What is his name?' The eventual reply makes clear the connection of name and character: 'As his profession is, Lifter, my lord, / One that can lift a purse right cunningly' (1.2.10–11).[40] Lifter's crime is, then, sleight of hand. Lifter and Justice Suresby then engage in a discussion of the nature of truth and error, and they begin a paronomasia upon *more* with Lifter's explanation of his situation in court: 'Sir, I am charged, as God shall be my comfort, / With more than's true' (1.2.103–4). What is more than true, in Lifter's terms, is false. Suresby pushes this further:

> Sir sir, ye are indeed, 'with more than's true',
> For you are flatly charged with felony.

> You're charged with more than truth, and that is theft,
> More than a true man should be charged withal.
> Thou art a varlet, that's no more than true.
>
>   (1.2.105–9)

To be more than true is to be false and by extension to be a criminal, beyond the law. The Clown later echoes this notion when he
asserts that if More fails to save the rioters from the gallows as he
promises, he deals 'double honestly' with them (2.3.187–8). The
names of several other characters in *Sir Thomas More* are similarly
related to their identities: the Frenchman, Caveler (caviller); More's
servants, Robin Brewer, Ned Butler, Giles Porter and Ralph Horse-
keeper; and Smart, a plaintiff. Through the link of character to
nomination, and the play upon his name in the scene in which he
first appears, we may expect that Thomas More will go (or *be*)
beyond the law.[41]

More's behaviour in Act One confirms his ambiguous status
with regard to the law. Suresby's interpretation of the law in this
scene disadvantages both accused and plaintiff, since he seems to
be unable to distinguish between responsibility and culpability,
and holds the victim of the theft to be as guilty as the thief. In
order to prove a point, More procures a further act of robbery, at
the same time having some fun at Suresby's expense and revealing
his love of folly: to demonstrate that Suresby's attitude is unreason-
able, More asks Lifter to steal Suresby's purse.

This episode is a much-embellished version of an anecdote
taken from More's treatise on death, *The Four Last Things*, where,
in his discussion 'Of Covetousness', More tells of the failure of
proximity to death to affect those who are unable to appreciate its
significance:

> I remember me of a thief once cast at Newgate, that cut a purse at
> the bar when he should be hanged on the morrow; and when he was
> asked why he did so, knowing that he should die so shortly, the des-
> perate wretch said that it did his heart good to be lord of that purse
> one night yet. And in good faith, methinketh as much as we wonder
> at him, yet see we many that do much like, of whom we nothing
> wonder at all.[42]

The intention in this treatise is to show the vanity of worldliness,
and the worthlessness of possessions. The certainty of death
renders the thief's attachment to the purse meaningless, and More's

wider point is that we are all in the same position as the thief, and
that many of our actions are as senseless. But in the rewritten scene
in *Sir Thomas More*, More himself procures the theft and it is his
character upon which we focus rather than that of the thief. The
spiritual message is muted in favour of a meditation on law, justice
and personal responsibility, in which it is shown that a criminal
act (such as More's incitement of a theft) may have a just cause.
This spiritual dimension does, however, seem to resurface in
More's comments after his resignation that 'They that have many
names are not still best' (4.2.73), which amounts to a devaluation
of worldly ambition. In *Sir Thomas More*, we see the paradox of
a theft that is enacted in order to reinforce the prohibition against
theft.

The deception of Suresby partakes of a popular characterisation
of More as the wise fool, which is to be found, for example, in
Hall's *Chronicles* and Ellis Heywood's dialogue *Il Moro*.[43] More's
love of folly in *Sir Thomas More* is disturbing, and is indicative
of that excess which is suggested by his name. More goes beyond
the letter of the law in order to stay 'true' to its spirit. Thus law
itself is divided by More, and this might be seen as an excess in
relation to the actions of *Justice* Suresby. More resists the materiality of the letter of the law; for him justice is not simply a word or
title, and this prefigures his divergence from Surrey's position on
law with regard to subscription to the king's articles. More's crime
(in the sense that he could be said to be responsible for the theft
of Suresby's purse) is a repetition of the logic of justice in that it
depends upon reciprocity and exchange.[44]

In *Sir Thomas More*, then, More's name is related to a series
of significant acts of naming which recur throughout the play,
and the connectedness of name and authority is made explicit.
When plain Thomas More is rewarded for his part in calming the
rioters, Surrey tells him: 'Your name is yet too short . . . Rise up
Sir Thomas More' (2.3.214, 216). Following his resignation, More
announces:

> Am I not leaner than I was before?
> The fat is gone: my title's only More.
> Contented with one style, I'll live at rest:
> They that have many names are not still best.
> I have resigned mine office: countst me not wise?
>
> (4.2.70–4)

The shortening of his title registers his reversed fortunes, but it also marks his excess in relation to law – he is 'only More' – and makes the connection between 'wisdom' and worldly advance. Although in worldly terms More is reduced, as the scene with Lifter has shown to be 'more' carries its own significance. This might also impact upon his attitude to Suresby; *Justice* as a title is not necessarily the same as justice as a concept. The point is not that this process of giving identity through names is unusual *per se* in early modern texts; what is interesting here is that Thomas More, a 'historical' figure which we might be led to think of as a secure referent, can be treated in this way. In *Sir Thomas More*, the materiality of More's name creates his characterisation in a way which is not determinately referential but is instead anti-mimetic; More is thus 'more': additional, excessive, supplementary. This is thematised in the plot, since More's fall is brought about by his eventual refusal to sign his name to the unspecified articles that stand in for the Oath of Supremacy. More seems to recognise that his name is his identity, and that subscription equals submission. More thus becomes a figure of self-knowledge; it is here that some form of cognitive control seems to be being asserted as an intentional brake on the supplementary effects of More's name.

Elsewhere in the play, it appears that it is not the manifest content of written discourse but the act of writing itself that is subject to interpretation by authority. When More attends to the rioters he uses a figure of writing to show that even those unaware of the penalty for rebellion must be held responsible for their actions, and that there are performative effects of language which lie outside knowledge or intention:

> For silly men
> Plod on they know not how, like a fool's pen
> That ending shows not any sentence writ,
> Linked but to common sense or slightest wit,
> These follow for no harm, but yet incur
> Self penalty with those that raised this stir.
> (2.2.36–41)

The fool's pen writes without reason, just as the Clown's speeches earlier in the play give the impression of being a flow of significa-tion that follows signifiers rather than signifieds or referents. These

speeches rely upon homophonic substitutions and puns, progress-
ing through surface textuality rather than establishing semantic
links. Just as words flow into words seemingly independent of their
speaker (in, for example, the slippage from 'rule' to 'roost' to
'roast' in 2.1.1–3), liquid issues from the pens of fools in a senseless flow. Although they may not write a linguistic sentence
linked to wit, their folly allows the imposition of a legal sentence
of death for their offence. The fool's pen inscribes its place within
a legal discourse, since in More's figure it is the act of writing
itself, irrespective of intended signification, which leads to a
self-condemnation.

This textual model of semantic effects outside knowledge
threatens to undo the stability of the self-knowledge that More
figures. In More's speech the law of authorship places the responsibility for inscription in the *hand*(s) of the fool. Interpretation is
one-sided: it is enough that the enforcers of law know the penalties
to be imposed; the lawbreakers may remain unaware of the 'law's
debt' (2.2.35), but they are still rendered culpable, and this culpability stems from a belief that hearts follow hands. Inscription and
subscription have material effects, and the fool may not claim
diminished responsibility. This notion of the law's debt is that
referred to by Surrey when he speaks of the duty that the law of
God bequeaths (4.1.106–8). As the play progresses, however, it
becomes clear that a space opens up between the expression of law
and More's own position. Cognitive determination comes from
outside the self, and this can be read in the supplementary
effects of the name which cannot be dominated by a closed, reflex-
ive self-knowledge. More believes that this debt to God can be
repaid through his death; in other words, as Prince Hal reminds
Falstaff, 'thou owest God a death'.[45] That payment of this debt
must take place through something more permanent than mere
speech reinforces Doll's claim that 'Words are but words and pays
not what men owe' (2.4.106). The circulation of the name after
death, as I have already suggested, marks absence as much as presence, and cannot, therefore, be used to underwrite one's debts.
This seems in part to be a recognition of the failure of law, including censorship, to control the effects of language, but it also marks
the binary opposition of word and act. This binary is, of course,
undone by the potentially performative aspects of semantic
indeterminacy.

The focal point of the play is the staging of the interlude, 'The Marriage of Wit and Wisdom', and it is here that the issues addressed in my reading can also be most clearly seen. This scene brings into focus the key binaries noted above, and shows the striking problems that the 'theme' of subscription presents for thematic readings. As Forker and Candido and others have noted, the interlude performed is a version of an extant piece entitled *Lusty Juventus*.[46] More's insistence in the play that the performance must be of 'The Marriage of Wit and Wisdom' demands that we remark the significance of the central terms in this title. More's initial attraction to this piece lies in his appreciation of the difficulty that the title presupposes:

> To marry wit to wisdom asks some cunning:
> Many have wit that may come short of wisdom.
> We'll see how master poet plays his part,
> And whether wit or wisdom grace his art.
>
> (3.2.67–70)

The significance of the idea that the poet may 'play a part' becomes apparent when More himself takes on a role in the interlude. Indeed, since he is forced to improvise, More seems to take on the poet's part in producing his own lines. This is only one of numerous references to More's 'poetic' character, and already in the play this has been glossed in unfavourable terms. Surrey complains (echoing Plato) that 'Poets were ever thought unfit for state' (3.1.195), and More admits that 'This is no age for poets' (3.1.203). More's response is notable, however, for rejecting the universalising platonic sentiment in favour of a statement more obviously located in a specific cultural moment. Certainly More is concerned about the content of the interlude, and he is unhappy at the thought that there may be no folly in the play, arguing that if there is no folly, 'Then there's no wit in't, I'll be sworn: folly waits on wit as the shadow on the body, and where wit is ripest, there folly still is readiest' (3.2.159–61). Without folly there is no wit, thus both wit and folly are opposed to wisdom.

More steps in to take the part of Good Counsel and intervenes in 'improvised' rhyming couplets. The advice that More as Good Counsel offers to the young Wit reiterates the scene in which More tests Erasmus (3.1), stressing the importance of a sceptical attitude towards outward appearances:

> Wit, judge not things by the outward show:
> The eye oft mistakes, right well you do know.
> Good Counsel assures thee upon his honesty
> That this is not Wisdom, but lady Vanity.
>   (3.2.274–7)

These are More's last words within the interlude, since it is halted
here by the return of Luggins, who was to play the part taken by
More. This attempt to reconcile wit and wisdom is unsuccessful,
since there is no opportunity for Wit to take advantage of the
advice of Good Counsel. More is unhappy with his performance,
complaining that 'fools oft times do help to mar the play' (3.2.289),
and this expression of his dissatisfaction echoes his 'own' text *The
History of King Richard III*: 'For they that sometime step up and
play with them, when they cannot play their parts, they disorder
the play and do themself no good.'[47] This 'self'-citation brings us
out of the world of the play-within-the-play into the world of *Sir
Thomas More*, and suggests that playing may be more than a
matter of entertainment, keeping in play Fisher's critical/hypocriti-
cal division. Just as the writing of the fool's pen may become
subject to legal penalty, so More's improvisation is similarly subject
to disruption by external forces, metatheatrically reinforcing the
political dimension of performance.

The players voice the significance of this recognition. Inclination is astonished at More's proficiency as an actor, remarking
particularly upon the proximity of More's improvisation to the
written script of the interlude:

> Do ye hear, fellows? Would not my lord make a / rare player? O, he
> would uphold a company beyond all ho, / better than Mason among
> the King's players. Did ye mark / how extemprically he fell to the
> matter, and spake / Luggins's part almost as it is in the very book
> set down? (3.2.295–9)

Almost as it is in the very book: text provides validation for a
performance that is better than that of a professional actor, and
it is notable that the player in question is one of the King's men;
More is thus 'more' than one of the King's servants. But the idea
of More as an actor is troubling for Wit, and he silences
Inclination:

> Peace, do ye know what ye say? My lord a player? Let us / not meddle
> with any such matters. (3.2.300–1)

It is not obvious what 'such matters' might be, and they are not specified, but the emphasis on performance for the King reinforces the allusion to *The History of King Richard III*: 'these matters be kings' games, as it were, stage plays, and for the more part played upon scaffolds'.[48] These are the stages upon which More plays, and these performances may end not in applause but in death. In recognising the danger implied in the theatrical metaphor, Wit comes closest to wisdom. Thus, although Forker and Candido are right to note the 'biographical' significance of More's choice of interlude, the political implications are not to be overlooked.[49] That More insists upon the title of the interlude should again alert us to the place of nomination in the structure of *Sir Thomas More*.

VI

Naming in *Sir Thomas More* opposes a number of terms: law/conscience, wisdom/wit, wisdom/folly, wisdom/poetry and law/justice. In part, this opposition is enacted through a distinction between temporal and spiritual authority, and the divagation of outward expression and inward belief. Wisdom and law are worldly, externalised and institutional; Wit marks the points at which the individual is potentially forced to come into conflict with these structures of authority, and vice versa. Thus Surrey complains of the rioting citizens that they are 'not men of wisdom' (2.3.40), and we should not be surprised that he is the speaker of this line when we remember his later view on obedience to law (in 4.1 cited above). It is the signature, or subscription, that formalises the dualism these oppositions mark, but it is already apparent in the different attitudes to law expressed by More and Suresby. The inscription of the name marks both submission to the authorised institutional meanings (the articles, and the implications of duty that they embody), and the potential diremption of such submission from the belief that subscription should externalise. More's advice to Wit in the guise of Good Counsel reveals his consciousness of the possibility of separating belief and expression. He ends as a player in his own tragedy upon a scaffold provided by the king, and the performance ends in death.

What seems to appear in the consideration of subscription that takes place in *Sir Thomas More* is a model of critical debate. The metonymics of heart and hand mobilise a questioning of presence and absence which impacts upon the various appeals to institutions of authority within much of the modern commentary on the play. The focus upon the signature in terms of authorship and censorship reveals a desire for presence which announces itself in a paradoxical illumination of an ineluctable absence, marking the co-implication of presence and absence within the same system. Such critical readings strive for wisdom, they have faith in a logic of mimesis that can secure a referential connection of hand and heart. In other words, they subscribe to law.

And yet there is always the question of wit in *Sir Thomas More*, the knowing laughter of folly. This deferred, poetic response, a response to poetics that leads to death, can only trouble the security of such a faith. Recognitions of the failure of interpretative strategies which rely too credulously on appearance, subscription and writing are expressed at various times in the play by the characters of More, Doll and Good Counsel, and they should make us alert to the difficulties inherent in reading *Sir Thomas More*. In countersigning such acts of subscription through our acts of reading, our desire to witness all too easily falls into consent and submission to the institutionalised structures of law. Our readings attest only to our failures to read.

Notes

1 C. R. Forker and J. Candido, 'Wit, Wisdom, and Theatricality in *The Book of Sir Thomas More*', *Shakespeare Studies* 13 (1980), 85–104.

2 M. Garber, *Shakespeare's Ghost Writers: Literature as Uncanny Causality* (London: Methuen, 1987), p. 26.

3 This necessarily schematic account of the signature is, of course, based upon the work of Jacques Derrida. Derrida recognises that the 'concept' of the signature cannot be understood simply as an act of writing one's name, although it is in part precisely this. See, most obviously in Derrida's work, 'Signature Event Context', in *Margins of Philosophy*, trans. A. Bass (London: Harvester Wheatsheaf, 1978), pp. 309–30. For Derrida's account of the modalities of the signature, see *Signéponge/Signsponge*, trans. R. Rand (New York: Columbia University Press, 1984).

4 Bennington and Derrida, *Jacques Derrida*, trans. Bennington (Chicago: Chicago University Press, 1993), p. 162.

5 Throughout this chapter, I touch upon areas explored in J. Goldberg, *Writing Matter: From the Hands of the English Renaissance* (Stanford: Stanford University Press, 1990).

6 See, for example, E. Scarry, *The Body in Pain: The Making and Unmaking of the World* (Oxford: Oxford University Press, 1985), p. 252. Heidegger returns to the figure of the hand on many occasions. See Derrida, 'Geschlecht II: Heidegger's Hand', in *Deconstruction and Philosophy*, ed. J. Sallis (Chicago: University of Chicago Press, 1987), pp. 161–96; and Goldberg, *Writing Matter*, particularly pp. 291–302.

7 See the discussion of this in terms of the work of Jacques Rancière below, pp. 123–4.

8 Shakespeare, *Titus Andronicus*, ed. E. M. Waith (Oxford: Oxford University Press, 1984).

9 It is hard to avoid the suspicion that this scene may be motivated by a play upon the 'and' syllable in both h*and* and *And*ronicus.

10 Shakespeare, *The Winter's Tale*, ed. J. H. P. Pafford (London: Methuen, 1963).

11 Cited from Shakespeare, *The Complete Works*, ed. S. Wells and G. Taylor (Oxford: Oxford University Press, 1988), p. xlv.

12 Shakespeare, *Macbeth*, ed. N. Brooke (Oxford: Oxford University Press, 1990).

13 J. Masten, *Textual Intercourse: Collaboration, Authorship and Sexualities in Renaissance Drama* (Cambridge: Cambridge University Press, 1997), p. 15.

14 Derrida, *Memoirs of the Blind: The Self-Portrait and Other Ruins*, trans. P.-A. Brault and M. Naas (Chicago: University of Chicago Press, 1993).

15 On framing, see Derrida, *The Truth in Painting*, trans. G. Bennington and I. McLeod (Chicago: University of Chicago Press, 1987).

16 A recent example of this phenomenon is to be found in B. Vickers, *Shakespeare, Co-Author: A Historical Study of Five Collaborative Plays* (Oxford: Oxford University Press, 2002). In several discussions of *Sir Thomas More*, he offers nothing that could be called an interpretation of the play. See especially pp. 34–43, 67–72, 87–90, 127–33.

17 Forker and Candido, 'Wit, Wisdom, and Theatricality', p. 85.

18 See E. M. Thompson, 'The Handwriting of the Three Pages Attributed to Shakespeare Compared with his Signatures', in *Shakespeare's Hand in the Play of Sir Thomas More*, ed. A. W. Pollard (Cambridge: Cambridge University Press, 1923), pp. 57–112.

19 The debates on Shakespeare's authorship parallel the numerous 'anti-Stratfordian' claims. Nicholas Royle reads aspects of this question,

centring on Freud's interest in the matter, in relation to deconstructive notions of naming and signature that intersect with my own reading of this play. See *After Derrida* (Manchester: Manchester University Press, 1995), pp. 85–123.

20 W. W. Greg, 'Shakespeare's Hand Once More', *Times Literary Supplement*, 24 November and 1 December 1927, p. 871, p. 908.

21 D. S. Kastan, *Shakespeare and the Book* (Cambridge: Cambridge University Press, 2001), p. 66.

22 This is, for example, what Wells and Taylor chose to do in compiling the single volume Oxford edition of Shakespeare's plays (cited above), and the excerpt thus also appears in the *The Norton Shakespeare*, ed. S. Greenblatt and others (New York: W. W. Norton, 1997).

23 'To the Great Variety of Readers', p. xlv. Reproduced in the Norton Shakespeare.

24 All quotations are from A. Munday and others, *Sir Thomas More*, ed. V. Gabrieli and G. Melchiori (Manchester: Manchester University Press, 1990).

25 British Library, Harleian MS. 7368.

26 See G. H. Metz's survey in ' "Voice and credyt": The Scholars and *Sir Thomas More*' in *Shakespeare and 'Sir Thomas More': Essays on the Play and its Shakespearian Interest*, ed. T. H. Howard-Hill (Cambridge: Cambridge University Press, 1989), pp. 11–44.

27 S. McMillin asserts that *Sir Thomas More* must be read as a theatrical rather than a literary text. McMillin's dating of the play rests upon the issue of casting: the role of More in the play is exceptionally large (over eight hundred lines), and the *dramatis personae* is also exceptional, with over twenty speaking parts within the first five hundred lines. See McMillin, *'The Book of Sir Thomas More*: Dates and Acting Companies', in *Shakespeare and 'Sir Thomas More'*, pp. 57–76. This essay is based upon his earlier work on the subject, *The Elizabethan Theatre and 'The Book of Sir Thomas More'* (Ithaca: Cornell University Press, 1987) and *'The Booke of Sir Thomas More*: A Theatrical View', *Modern Philology* 68 (1970), 10–24.

28 The presence of Shakespeare's hand in the manuscript was first suggested in R. Simpson, 'Are there any Extant MSS. in Shakespeare's Handwriting?', *Notes and Queries* 183 (1871), 1–3.

29 Greg identifies one main scribal hand, Hand S, which was responsible for (at least) the copying of the original text, and five others, Hands A, B, C, D and E, who wrote out the additions and revisions. Although the matter has by no means been resolved to everyone's satisfaction (assuming this were possible), the following attributions are the most likely combination of scribes: S = Anthony Munday;

A = Henry Chettle; B = Thomas Heywood; C = Playhouse book-keeper; D = William Shakespeare; E = Thomas Dekker. See Greg (ed.), *The Booke of Sir Thomas More* (Oxford: Malone Society, 1911); 'The handwritings of the manuscript', in *Shakespeare's Hand in the Play of Sir Thomas More*, 41–56; 'T. Goodal in *Sir Thomas More*', *PMLA* 46 (1931), 268–71; 'Autograph Plays by Anthony Munday', *Modern Language Review* 8 (1913), 89–90; 'Shakespeare's Hand Once More'; 'Was *Sir Thomas More* Ever Acted?' *Times Literary Supplement*, 8 July 1920, p. 440.

30 S. Tannenbaum argues that A was Chettle, C was Kyd, B was Heywood, and that D was not Shakespeare, in *The Booke of Sir Thomas More: A Bibliotic Study* (New York: 1927). Tannenbaum's attributions to Chettle and Heywood have been largely accepted, not so his comments on Kyd and Shakespeare. Peele was suggested in A. Acheson, *Shakespeare, Chapman, and Sir Thomas More* (London: 1931), pp. 265–73. Webster is proposed in C. Chillington, 'Playwrights at Work: Henslowe's, Not Shakespeare's, *Book of Sir Thomas More*', *English Literary Renaissance* 10 (1980), 439–79.

31 Marlowe is the obvious (if unstated) candidate put forward in E. A. J. Honigmann, 'The Play of "Sir Thomas More" and Some Contemporary Events', *Shakespeare Survey* 42 (1990), 77–84.

32 W. W. Greg, 'The handwritings of the manuscript', p. 50.

33 This is the transcription given by Gabrieli and Melchiori in their edition of *Sir Thomas More*, p. 17.

34 See W. B. Long, 'The occasion of *The Book of Sir Thomas More*', in *Shakespeare and 'Sir Thomas More'*, pp. 45–56, who wishes to challenge the commonly-held idea of Tilney, and by extension the Revels Office, as the 'implacable foe of much that playwrights wished to write and even of dramatic representation in general' (p. 45). Comments on the operation of the Revels Office in relation to *Sir Thomas More* are also made by Chillington, Honigmann, and in G. H. Metz, 'The Master of the Revels and *The Booke of Sir Thomas More*', *Shakespeare Quarterly* 33 (1982), 493–5.

35 In an indenture of licence of 1583 granted to the Earl of Worcester's Men, a note on travelling companies makes clear the power of the censor's signature: 'No play is to bee played, but suche as is allowed by the sayd Edmund, and his hand at the latter end of the said book they doe play.' Quoted in E. K. Chambers, *The Elizabethan Stage*, 4 vols (Oxford: Oxford University Press, 1923), 2: 222; see J. Clare, *'Art made Tongue-tied by Authority': Elizabethan and Jacobean Dramatic Censorship* (Manchester: Manchester University Press, 1990), p. 13.

36 See Clare, p. 30. See also R. Dutton, *Mastering the Revels: The Regulation and Censorship of English Renaissance Drama* (Basingstoke: Macmillan, 1991) and *Licensing, Censorship and Authorship in Early Modern England: Buggeswords* (Basingstoke: Palgrave, 2000). See also the readings in T. Hill, ' "Marked Down for Omission": Censorship and *The Booke of Sir Thomas More*', *Parergon* 17 (1999), 63–87, and S. Longstaffe, 'Puritan Tribulation and the Protestant History Play', in *Literature and Censorship in Renaissance England*, ed. A. Hadfield (Basingstoke: Macmillan, 2001), pp. 31–49.

37 This connection between language and authority is also made by Shrewsbury when More is arrested. Shrewsbury suggests to More: 'My Lord, 'twere good you'd publish to the world / Your great offence unto his majesty' (5.4.68–9).

38 Forker and Candido, 'Wit, Wisdom, and Theatricality', p. 103.

39 For a discussion which in part uses this play to note the way in which naming functions in Shakespeare's texts, see P. Stallybrass, 'Naming, renaming and unnaming in the Shakespearean quartos and folio', in *The Renaissance Text*, ed. A. Murphy (Manchester: Manchester University Press, 2000), pp. 108–34.

40 This is analogous with the relationship between appearance and identity on the early modern stage. See Stephen Orgel's telling comment that the 'wrong' costume is as expressive of a character's essence as the 'right' one, citing the scarcity of instances of anyone seeing through the numerous examples of disguise on the Elizabethan stage. *Impersonations: The Performance of Gender in Shakespeare's England* (Cambridge: Cambridge University Press, 1996), pp. 2, 104.

41 Other examples of this production of 'character' through names might be seen in Thomas Stapleton's link of More to St Thomas and Thomas Becket, establishing More's sanctity through his saintly namesakes, and Richard Hall's connection of John Fisher to John the Baptist. Having made the connection, Hall pushes this further, representing Henry VIII as Herod and Anne Boleyn as Salome. See Stapleton, *The Life and Illustrious Martyrdom of Sir Thomas More*, ed. E. E. Reynolds and trans. P. E. Hallett (London: Burns & Oates, 1966), p. xvi; and R. Hall (attrib.), *The Life of Fisher*, ed. Ronald Bayne, EETS Extra Series: 117 (London: Oxford University Press, 1921), p. 136.

42 *The Four Last Things* in *The English Works of Sir Thomas More*, ed. W. E. Campbell, 2 vols (London: Eyre & Spottiswoode, 1931), 1: 491.

43 Hall, *The union of the two noble and illustrate famelies of Lancastre & Yorke* (London: 1548), f.ccxxvi^v; *Il Moro: Ellis Heywood's*

Dialogue in Memory of Thomas More, ed. and trans. R. L. Deakins (Cambridge, MA: Harvard University Press, 1972). See also my 'Translatio mori: Ellis Heywood's "Thomas More"', in *Travels and Translations in the Sixteenth Century*, ed. M. Pincombe (Aldershot: Ashgate, 2004), pp. 73–87.

44 It is for reciprocity and justice that the Londoners revolt in the opening scenes. Disadvantaged in law compared to an immigrant population which is shown in the first scene to be exploiting its privilege, the English citizens see their only course of action as a rejection of law itself.

45 Shakespeare, *Henry IV, Part 1*, ed. D. Bevington (Oxford: Oxford University Press, 1987), 5.1.126.

46 Forker and Candido, 'Wit, Wisdom, and Theatricality', p. 89.

47 *The History of King Richard III and Selections from the English and Latin Poems*, ed. R. S. Sylvester (New Haven: Yale University Press, 1976), p. 83.

48 More, *History of King Richard III*, p. 83.

49 Forker and Candido, 'Wit, Wisdom, and Theatricality', p. 89.

6

Swansongs

I

'Which voice would speak of voice?'[1] The implications of Jean-Luc Nancy's question will resonate throughout this chapter, since the focus will be on what will be for most readers an unknown voice, that of the seventeenth-century royalist woman poet Hester Pulter.[2] The female voice has become a common concept in early modern and feminist studies, and is central to many discussions of the relationships between writing and subjectivity.[3] Voice, it has been suggested, also has a privileged relationship to manuscript text which print cannot match.[4] Yet to speak of Pulter's 'voice' is perhaps already too hasty, for there are many different tonalities in the manuscript which contains her work. Equally, it would not be wise to move forwards in reading this poetry without reflection on the extent to which the voice or voices that we hear in this work may be described, unequivocally, as 'hers'. While I cannot offer a conspectus of the voices in Pulter's work here, I hope to demonstrate through a reading of two of the poems why an emphasis on voice as the expression of subjectivity might not be the best line of enquiry to take.

A passage from Peggy Kamuf offers one of the clearest expressions of the doubts that should, I think, occur when tackling the problem of voice in women's writing. Noting the unease that she felt when encountering the critical treatment of the relation between signature, authorship, and the gender of the writer or of writing, Kamuf explains:

> I was pursued by a persistent dissatisfaction with the way in which these terms tended to get confused or even collapsed into one another

by most discourse concerned with the relation between writer and
writing, and especially between the woman writer and her writing.
That relation continued to be thought largely according to notions
of representation, expression, the fully present intentionality of a
subject, and so forth. I had been convinced for some time by dem-
onstrations, most notably in the writings of Jacques Derrida, that
such notions contributed essential elements to the metaphysical construction of women's exclusion, to the 'phallocentrism' at the base
of virtually all Western habits of thought. I was also convinced,
therefore, that deconstructing this exclusion could not be a matter
only of enlarging the field of expression to include 'feminine' subjects, or writers, or writings. Unless this expansion is accompanied
by a rethinking of some fundamental categories that have classified
us *as* subjects, however discerning or changed the aspects of that
subjectivity may appear, then the chances for the displacement of the
fundamental structures of exclusion are no doubt considerably
lessened.[5]

What Kamuf gives voice to (and we'll see in a moment why that
phrase needs some thought) is a profound concern over the hasty
eradication of necessary structural distinctions. Such distinctions
demand preservation since it is precisely the fact of relation *as*
relation that threatens to be lost in the move from linguistic utterance to a subjectivity posited as the source of that utterance.
Rather than presenting a textual idealism, or some notion of language all the way down (or of 'text as far as the eye can see'),
Kamuf (following Derrida) points up *that there is a relation*
between writer and writing. Such a relation cannot be thought of
too quickly as an identity, or as any of its hypostases such as
'expression', 'unique voice', 'individuality', or so on. Since writer
and writing are in relation, that relation must itself be part of a
system of other relations that will break down the terms of the
opposition. That gender as a category exceeds anything that may
be adequately labelled as an opposition between male/female (most
obviously in terms of race, class and sexuality) seems self-evident,
and we must also be wary of what Jonathan Goldberg has called
the tendency towards a 'legend of good women' (following Natalie
Zemon Davis, who generated the idea of an emergent tradition of
'Women Worthies').[6] Such a 'positive' approach to gender, however
well-intentioned, offers little genuinely critical purchase on the
texts that we now have available. What I am trying to argue,
however, is not simply for a more complex sense of subjective

relations but instead, as Kamuf does, to question the bases of the movements from writing to subjectivity at all.

Analogously, Jean-François Lyotard makes a proposal about the structure of that to which writing is (too) often opposed, namely *voice*:

> Every *voice*, *vox*, in as much as, since the Bible, this has been the name borne by the pure actuality of the event, comes to us recorded, phenomenalized, formed and informed, if only in the tissue of spatio-temporal agencies, in the 'forms of sensibility', here and over there, not yet and already no longer, etc. Not to mention the meanings pre-inscribed in the 'language' spoken by the voice.[7]

Even if we let the dazzling 'not to mention' slide past us here, what Lyotard calls 'forms of sensibility' takes us back to the notion of *aisthesis*, offering a recognition of the cultural basis of the frequently naturalised sense of voice with which we have become familiar. It is a recognition of this notion that would begin to trouble the idea of someone's 'own' voice.

Voice has become a major theme within literary and critical thought in part because of its central place within the history of political philosophy.[8] The 'foundation' of such thought is to be found in a famous passage from Aristotle's *Politics*. It follows only a few lines after the description of man as a 'political animal':

> Nature, as we often say, makes nothing in vain, and man is the only animal who has the gift of speech. And whereas mere voice is but an indication of pleasure or pain, and is therefore found in other animals (for their nature attains to the perception of pleasure and pain and the intimation of them to one another, and no further), the power of speech is intended to set forth the expedient and inexpedient, and therefore likewise the just and the unjust. And it is a characteristic of man that he alone has any sense of good and evil, of just and unjust, and the like, and the association of living beings who have this sense makes a family and a state.[9]

The central distinctions here are clear. Man possesses speech, whereas animals only possess voice, and man possesses knowledge of the difference between good and evil (and its cognates such as just and unjust, and so on) whereas animals can only communicate pleasure and pain. It is not obvious whether we are supposed to think here of the perception of good and evil as the consequence of the faculty of voice, or whether speech emerges in order to give expression to moral distinctions. This would be a matter of deciding whether concepts depend upon language or vice versa, and that is not a matter to be reopened here.[10] Instead, we might wish to translate this Aristotelian notion as follows: Human animals are endowed with a faculty that goes beyond that which is shared with non-human animals. This emerges in the discourses of democracy as an idea of the expression of opinion as a form of political representation – or of 'having a say' – and is marked most obviously in a play such as Shakespeare's *Coriolanus*, with its emphasis on the voices of the people and on the rhetorical power of even Menenius' belly fable. But this source in Aristotle should already create some disquiet. Perhaps we should have been talking about speech rather than voice all along. Speech, of course, remarks the remove from the body of the subject in a way that voice, apparently at least, does not.

As Jacques Rancière notes, the Aristotelian distinction between human and animal can only be the result of a rather unlikely forgetting of Plato. In particular, it involves suppressing the passages in the *Republic* that are all too clear on the animalistic nature of crowds who, at the instigation of an orator, will express pleasure and displeasure.[11] Rancière argues that far from being the beginning of politics, this Aristotelian passage is a long way from giving us such an origin:

> the simple opposition between logical animals and phonic animals is in no way the given on which politics is then based. It is, on the contrary, one of the stakes of the very dispute that institutes politics. At the heart of politics lies a double wrong, a fundamental conflict, never conducted as such, over the relationship between the capacity of the speaking being who is without qualification and political capacity. . . . For before the debts that place people who are of no account in a relationship of dependence on the oligarchs, there is the symbolic distribution of bodies that divides them into two categories: those that one sees and those that one does not see, those who have a logos – memorial speech, an account to be kept up – and those who have no logos, those who really speak and those whose voice merely mimics the articulate voice to express pleasure and pain. Politics exists because the logos is never simply speech, because it is always indissolubly the *account* that is made of this speech: the account by which a sonorous emission is understood as speech, capable of enunciating what is just, whereas some other emission is merely perceived as a noise signaling pleasure or pain, consent or revolt.[12]

As the italicisation indicates, the key word here for Rancière is *account*, since it is this notion of 'what counts' (and thus of what is thought worthy of taking into account) that opens up the question of what may be perceived in a given social organisation. In a book such as *The Names of History*, Rancière explicitly refuses this distinction between those who speak and those who only make noise. While it is always dangerous in the case of this thinker to excerpt sentences without a reconstruction of the context, it is hard to avoid the positive impact of a statement such as the following: 'Everything speaks, everything has meaning, to the degree that every speech production is assignable to the legitimate expression of a place: the earth that shapes men, the sea on which their exchanges take place, the everyday objects in which their relations can be read, the stone that retains their imprint.'[13]

It would be a relatively easy matter to see how Rancière's rethinking of the Aristotelian source could be translated into thinking about women's history in the early modern period. The distribution of bodies, not just in the sense of class distinctions but rather in terms of an *aisthesis* of visibility and invisibility, of those who are held to be of account and those who are not, is precisely a matter of a qualification to speak and of the political capacity that consequently stems from this process of division. Much of the work of feminist and other scholars has been concerned with changing this visibility, of recognising the speech of those formerly held to be of no account as speech. Such voices thus become capable of drawing attention to the fact of distribution and division, they take on this capacity to enunciate what is just, and not merely to be the mimicry of an articulate voice. But, of course, this is not primarily conceived in terms of the expressly political content – what we might otherwise term the 'commitment' – of such speech.[14]

I rehearse this sense of the relation between voice and *aisthesis* because an emphasis on voice in criticism of lyric poetry is commonplace. Of course, despite the familiarity of the link between the written form of the lyric and the spoken word, there are reasons to be cautious about collapsing too quickly the distinction between speech and writing. As in earlier chapters, what I am primarily interested in here is the role of reading, and how that reading is affected and effected through an attention to all the senses of sense. What Hester Pulter's writings seem to demonstrate is that recourse in any reading to the referential security of a discourse which seeks to phenomenalise rhetorical figures (including the figure of the author) might lead us into problems that cannot simply be side-stepped. If this is in part a matter of *ethos* (in an Aristotelian sense), it is also a question of the relationships between rhetoric and politics.[15] For if the lyric is the poetic form most readily associated with subjectivity, then lyric poetry is the poetry of the subject, it is a 'subjective' genre. As such, its history partakes of the history of the subject, which is perhaps another way of saying that it is intimately linked to the project of modernity.[16] This question will remain a concern which guides these readings of voice in Pulter's poetry.

It will rapidly become apparent that the reading I offer here is not based upon an appeal to 'female experience' in any simple sense. I appreciate that there are debates around the question of reading women's writing, and that the approach taken here does not sit comfortably with aspects of these discussions.[17] But what I wish to emphasise here is that this is precisely a matter for critical debate. While I have no desire to diminish nor deny the specificity of the experience of a woman writer in the seventeenth century, I also wish to avoid a retreat from a *reading* of the poetry into areas of biography, cultural history or 'historicism', however conceived. Where such areas of historicist concern are indicated, as in my sketching in of a 'context' for the readings of the poems that follow, this is done to throw into relief the distance between the procedures that would tend to characterise such readings and my own.

II

The 'political' connection that tends to be made between the spoken voice and will or intention is mirrored in a sense of the status accorded to the tongue and to speech, especially women's speech, in the early modern period. It is also important to remember that rhetoric was often itself criticised for an apparent 'effeminacy'.[18] Emphasis on the tongue points up the strangeness of voice in relation to the other senses and their organs (as we will see in the next chapter). Obviously the tongue has two distinct functions, one as the organ that allows for the articulation of voice, and the other as that which enables the faculty of taste. The tongue is thus divided between an intimate, proximate sense of tasting as touching, of contact and tactility, and the intercession of distance that allows one to project sounds into the air. (This is also reversed in the idea of being 'touched' by a speech, especially in an early modern usage of that word.) Divided in this way, the tongue is drawn into the path of two contradictory movements, from the world into the body, and from the body into the world.

Two texts will serve as illustration here of the terrain, though there is not the space here to do justice to their complexity. Both appear under the title *Lingua*.[19] The first of these texts is by Erasmus, and is thought to have been completed in 1525.[20] Erasmus has a decidedly ambivalent attitude towards the tongue, seeing it both as poison and as medicine (p. 262). He is also far from seeing an unbridled tongue as a specifically female attribute: 'I would address myself especially to women, who commonly are reproached on this score, if I did not see all around me so many foul-tongued men that women appear subdued and restrained in comparison' (p. 264).[21] But he is quite clear on the negative connotations of uncontrolled speech: 'Eloquence is never found without sense, and equally loquacity is always combined with stupidity' (p. 272). Knowledge of rhetoric, if it is not aligned with moral reasoning, leads to error (p. 276). Praising sense without eloquence over a fluent senselessness, and offering the usual warnings against gossip, drunkenness, inopportune humour and flattery, most interesting perhaps is the privilege that Erasmus gives to the tongue compared to the other sensory organs. Humans possess two eyes, two nostrils and two ears, but only one tongue, and its position in the body accentuates its importance. The tongue, claims Erasmus, is the 'spokesman of the heart and mind', set between the two and acting as the mind's 'interpreter' (pp. 265–6). The tongue should be employed last, after the other senses have been consulted, especially the faculties of sight and hearing which have 'primacy among the perceptions'. Even these are not the summit, however: 'Yet it is much more important to consult the inner perceptions of the soul, intelligence (or reason) as well as memory; both of these have their place and workshop in the brain' (p. 266). Such a notion of work might lead us to think about the relation to *poiesis*.

The idea of the tongue as the mind's interpreter, however, is an odd one, and it recalls the sense of language as a translation of the mind's *phantasma* that we have encountered in earlier chapters. Rather than asserting the identity of tongue and mind (whether we locate reason in the brain or in the heart), the notion of interpretation precisely marks that which comes between the two. As might have been predicted from my earlier comments on the tongue as an organ of tactile experience, here it approaches the hand. Erasmus also makes a connection between taste and touch, between the tongue and other organs that rely on contact (pp. 265–6). It is tempting to remark the connection between Erasmus's sense of the tongue as interpreter and Heminge and Condell's comments on the relationship of Shakespeare's mind and hand, and of the easiness with which the utterance of his thought passed to paper (see p. 93). The movement of Shakespeare's hand is a form of utterance just as the movement of the tongue is a form of interpretation; both are mimetic tools (to follow the workshop metaphor) which enact the becoming sensible of thought.

The second text is attributed to Thomas Tomkis, and was printed in 1607.[22] Here the water is less muddied by scruples about fairness to the sexes, and the functions of the tongue are divided so that the character of Lingua personifies voice but not taste (which is personified by Gustus). Tomkis's play is structured around a battle between the senses, in which Lingua bids for her rightful place (as she would see it) as a sixth sense alongside the conventional five. What she stresses are precisely the affective benefits of rhetorical elaboration:

> Delightfull speeches, sweet perswasions
> I have this long time usd to get my right,
> My right that is to make the Senses sixe;
> And have both name and power with the rest.
> Oft have I seasoned savorie periods,
> With sugred words, to delude *Gustus* taste,
> And oft embellisht my entreative phrase
> With smelling flowres of vernant Rhetorique,
> Limming and flashing it with various Dyes,
> To draw proud *Visus* to me by the eyes:
> And oft perfum'd my petitory stile,
> With Civet-speech, t'entrap *Olfactus* Nose,
> And clad my selfe in Silken Eloquence,
> To allure the nicer touch of *Tactus* hand,
> But all's become lost labour, and my cause
> Is still procrastinated.
>
> (A4v)

Tomkis thus works with a version of rhetoric that stresses its
capacity to activate the senses, that is, to open up the question of
aisthesis. As we might expect, however, the female Lingua battles
against the five male senses in vain and her case is ultimately dismissed. Her 'vernant Rhetorique' fails to persuade. The division
of rhetoric into one part that is thought of as linguistic elaboration
or embellishment and another seen as persuasive argument allows
for the distinction necessary to judge against Lingua. What is also
apparent is the negative sense of rhetoric. Even Lingua speaks of
using 'sweet perswasions' to delude, to draw, to entrap and to
allure. Much of the play shows Lingua employing deceit and flattery to create dissension. The obstacles to her success were always
going to be great, however, and this is made clear very early on
by Auditus:

> Good *Iove* what Sense hast thou to be a Sense;
> Since from the first foundation of the world,
> We never were accounted more then five;
> Yet you forsoth, an idle prating Dame,
> Would faine increase the number, and up-start
> To our high seates, decking your babling selfe
> With usurpt titles of our dignitie.
>
> (A3r–v)

Lingua's pretension to the status of a sense may flow from ambition, yet this babbling has a distinct advantage. In one of the
stronger arguments presented, Lingua claims priority over the
other senses because of her ability to testify to more than just what
may be immediately sensed. Lingua can refer to the past and
future; the other senses are only able to know the things of the
present. As such, there is a memorial capacity in tongue-as-speech
which seems to surpass the other senses, revealing them as quasi-
animalistic expressions of little more than pleasure and displeasure. The 'dignity' of the senses is undercut by this emphasis on a
form of sensation that is disjoined from memory, reversing the
prejudice against oratory that comes from the platonic objection
to its power to sway the passionate but unthinking crowd.

The charges levelled against Lingua prove harder to escape. Ten
charges are presented. She is accused of high treason and sacrilege
against the Commonwealth of Letters, 'for under pretence of prof-
iting the people with translations, shee hath most vilye prostituted

the hard misteries of unknowne Languages to the prophane eares of the vulgar' (F3r–v). Equally, she is said to have wrongfully imprisoned truth, to be a witch, to be a prostitute (since she lets everyone 'lie with her'), to taunt authority and create strife between friends, to give wives weapons against their husbands, to be responsible for all the misuses and deceptions of language, to have made rhetoric 'wanton', to be a tell-tale and, finally, '(which is the last and worst) that shee's a Woman in every respect, and for these causes not to bee admitted to the dignitie of a Sense' (F3v). Lingua is found guilty of most of these charges and, after a little more plotting, is finally confined to imprisonment in Gustus's house (that is, the mouth). The realm of the senses is thus asserted to be a masculine domain, opposed to a feminised speaking tongue. What, then, might this tell us about the relation between writing and the female poet?

III

The manuscript that constitutes the only extant version of Hester Pulter's work (Leeds MS Lt q 32) contains almost one hundred and twenty poems, and seems from the evidence of the dates given in the manuscript itself to have been written between 1646 and 1665. The first folio bears the title *Poems Breathed Forth by the Noble Hadassa*. The poetry is attributed in the manuscript to Hester Pulter, and this attribution is reinforced by the use of the name 'Hadassas', a biblical synonym for Esther, in its title. Also on the first folio is a description of the poems as 'Hadassas chast fances Beeinge the fruett of solitary and many of them sad howers', and a couplet instructs the reader: 'Marvail not my names conceald / In beeinge hid itt is reve'ld.'

It is possible to distinguish three types of poetry in Pulter's writings. Much consists of responses to events of the civil war period, and subjects include the execution of Charles I; the deaths of Sir George Lisle and Sir Charles Lucas, shot at Colchester in August 1648 for their parts in the Kentish insurrection; Charles's imprisonment at Holmby in 1647, figured as a lament by the River Thames; the death of Arthur, Lord Capel of Hadham; Sir William Davenant's loss of his nose through syphilis; the suicide of a young woman at Oxford whose royalist lover was killed during the war; and the destruction of the effigy of Robert Devereux, third Earl of Essex, in Westminster Abbey. This political poetry is explicitly royalist, and is pervaded by a sense of anger and loss. Pulter is often polemical, condemning what she describes as the 'hydra' of the Parliamentarian 'mob' and the perceived chaos that the wars brought.

The other two categories of poetry in the manuscript are devotional and, for want of a better term, 'domestic' poetry, and much of the latter is about or addressed to Pulter's children. She explains in the titles of some of these poems that she tended to write them during her 'confinement' periods. That she had fifteen children might explain her relatively prolific poetic output. While Pulter's work does not seem to have been printed, this should not be taken as an indication that this is 'private' poetry, nor is it indicative of the texts' quality. As Margaret Ezell and others have argued, the circulation of texts in manuscript should not be read only in terms of a relationship to print. Arthur Marotti, for example, notes that a critical tendency to judge the literature of the civil war predominantly in terms of printed texts has produced an inaccurate picture of cultural production in the period.[23] Similarly, Ezell remarks on the unfortunate consequences of this emphasis for the writing of women's literary history, in which writers prior to the eighteenth century are rendered far less visible because the importance of manuscript texts is not sufficiently appreciated.[24] It was not uncommon for writers' work to be transmitted in this manner, often among members of a 'coterie' audience, and this can be seen in certain cases as a conscious choice. We should not forget here the 'stigma' of print, particularly for aristocratic writers, although even this idea has come under some pressure.[25] Equally, the attempts to control print made by Parliament in these years may also be a determining factor.[26] Nor does this 'failure' to publish apply only to the work of women, and Donne and Sidney would be the obvious examples of male writers whose work only reached print in posthumous editions. The compilation of a manuscript such as Pulter's thus implies a potential readership, even if that readership cannot be identified with any certainty.

I have chosen here two elegies, one satirical and political, the other more personal.[27] As I noted above, it has been suggested that manuscript texts have a privileged relationship to the idea of a 'voice' in (or behind) writing.[28] The subject of the first of these poems is perhaps adequately described by its title, 'On the Fall of that Grand Rebel the Earl of Essex his Effigies in Harry the 7th's Chappel in Westminster Abby'.[29] Robert Devereux, third Earl of Essex, after Cromwell the most prominent Parliamentarian general, died after a stroke on 14 September 1646. As part of the grandest state funeral since the death of James I, an effigy of the Earl was constructed which was included in the procession. Following the funeral, this effigy of Devereux remained in Westminster Abbey, where it became the centrepiece of a Puritan shrine which attracted many visitors. The sermon which formed part of the funeral itself was given by Richard Vines and, by order of 'the House of Peeres', this sermon was published in October 1646, under the title *The Hearse of the Renowned, the Right Honourable Robert, Earle of Essex*.[30] In the sermon, Essex is compared to the biblical precedents Jonathan and Abner, linking their attempts to defend Israel to Essex's military role in the parliamentarian cause, particularly at Edge Hill. Essex is described as a defender of the liberty and property of England, and his death is said to bring about a 'universall lamentation' (p. 3). Vines's somewhat trite chiasmatic conclusion is that: 'Hee lived *a good Generall*, Hee died *a Generall good*' (p. 36). Although the emphasis that Vines gives to his sermon centres on a theological rather than a more straightforwardly political message, stressing the vanity of mortal fame and the inevitability of death ('Death is a fall from every thing but grace', p. 12), there are some phrases in the sermon which produce curious effects when viewed with the benefit of hindsight. While towards the end of the text Vines claims of Essex's memory that 'it will be such a Monument that every stone of it will speak a History' (p. 36), there is also the suggestion in 'The Epistle Dedicatory' (A3v) that, even in the cases of the great and good, 'their very Monuments are mortall'. In a retrospectively extraordinary passage towards the end of his text, Vines comments:

> the losse wee have susteined is great tho he never had wore Buff but onely Parliament Robes, & they say that when a limb or part of a man is cut off, *anima retrahitur*, the soule is retracted, I wish the Phylosophy may be verified in the retraction of his reality and faithfulnesse unto you; that so he may remayne among you in quintessence and vertue, being as it were divided among you, as they say of *Romulus*, that he was discerpt by the Senate, when he died, and every Senatour got a piece of him. (p. 37)

This desire for a *metempsychosis*, in which the soul of Essex would be transported from his living body to the other parliamentarians, is prompted by a perceived mutilation or dismemberment of Essex's dead body. The interest of this passage becomes more apparent when we realise what happened to the effigy of Essex. His monument did indeed seem to be 'mortal', and the figural dismemberment that Vines wishes for becomes literalised by the actions of one who did not share in the universal lamentation for the general's death.

For on the night of 26 November 1646, the effigy of Essex was mutilated by the cavalier John White. White concealed himself in the Abbey, attacked the Inigo Jones-designed catafalque with an axe, slashed the effigy's clothing, which included a coat worn by Essex at Edge Hill, and chopped off the effigy's head. Finally, he stole a gilt sword. He was captured two weeks later, imprisoned in the Gatehouse, and questioned in the House of Lords, where he also admitted to accidentally breaking off the nose of a statue of William Camden, the antiquarian. Despite his pleas for clemency, White was allowed to starve in the Gatehouse. The effigy was restored and placed in a glass case to prevent further attacks, and it was only removed from the Abbey in 1661, by Charles II's order.[31] Although Essex's image was not submitted to further damage, he was the subject of numerous satires and polemics. One such is the poem to be found in Pulter's manuscript.

> When that Fierce Monster had usurp'd the Place
> W^{ch} once (ah mee) our Royall King did grace
> One of her Heads, on topp of Fortune's Wheel
> W^{ch} ever turns, grown giddy 'gan to reel
> 5   Just like Bellerophon mounting to the skie
> And looking down – like him did brainsick die
> Or like that Boy who thro' his fond desire
> had almost sett Heav'ns axle-tree on fire
> Or like the Cretian youth who flew soe high
> 10   His borrow'd plumes began to sindge & Fry
> So this Bold Earl blown up with Pop'lar breath
> Unenvy'd and unpitty'd fell to Earth
> This was the man or rather the half Beast
> Not like Alcides's Tutor who exprest
> 15   Both Natures & from both the best did Cull

This like Lybian Hammon had a horned skull
This was the first who had the bold Commision
from Cannon's mouth to thunder out partitions
The Copy came from Hell, thence such thoughts spring
20   With sulph'rous breath to parly with their King
Yett hee that ne're gain'd Honour here on Earth
By Order they made triumph after Death
And in derision of our Antient Kings
his horned Image they to th'Temple bring
25   because he was a member of the Dragon
they sett him up just like the Idol Dagon
by Israel's sacred Ark O bold Assumption
& certainly unparallel'd presumption
Butt down he fell loosing his hands & head
30   his Father serv'd so, living, hee so dead.
such End such honour lett all Trayters have
but our Augustus Heav'n protect & save.

This poem looks like a straightforward royalist polemic, celebrating the desecration of Essex's monument. Essex is described as an overreacher, with references to Bellerophon, Icarus and others, and the well-worn topos of fortune's wheel. This is shown to be a familial trait, as the reference to the execution of the second Earl at the end of the poem suggests. Pulter's recurrent image of the parliamentary supporters as a hydra appears here in the suggestion that Essex is one of the fierce monster's heads, and this prepares the way for the decapitation of the effigy. There is a recurrent movement between a use of third-person description and the use of collective terms (such as hydra, our, they, and so on) which suggests that Essex, or at least his effigy, has a synecdochal significance. The destruction of the effigy thus becomes a symbolic victory against the parliamentarians, and the link to the second Earl also produces the figure of a posthumous execution; the effigy, a figure of the body, is subject to the same punishment as a physical body. This might be connected to the practice of destroying effigies in cases where a criminal is seen to have escaped justice, but what also takes place is an inversion of the symbolism of the parliamentarian funeral. John White's actions are figured in the poem as a literal reading of the effigy as a representation of Essex's body.

The hydra might also be read, however, as an image of the inhuman, or more precisely the not fully human, and it is not the only figure of this type to intervene in this poem. The connection made between Essex and the Lybian Hammon (l. 16), like the reference to the Idol Dagon (l. 26), is more than just an assertion of relationship between the effigy and idolatry. Hammon, or Ammon, is usually represented as half-man, half-beast, frequently with the head of a ram or a horned skull. Similarly, Dagon is commonly half-human, half-fish.[32] Such characterisations in Pulter's poem might be read as the adoption of a royalist poetic convention, which shows the parliamentarians as less than human. The horns of Ammon might also be read as the cuckold's horns, however, thus becoming an allusion either to Essex's first marriage to Frances Howard, annulled amidst allegations of Essex's impotence and his wife's alleged adultery with Robert Carr, or else to his second, about which there were also suspicions that he had been cuckolded.[33] James Loxley notes the irony in the discrepancy between Essex's martial and marital reputations: 'That the military leader of the revolt should be the Earl of Essex, a man famously divorced for impotence, allowed royalist satire to locate emasculation in a figure who was the iconic centre of the parliamentarian cause for most of the first civil war.'[34] The implication may be then not so much that Essex is less than fully human but that he is less than a man, with the emphasis on his masculinity.

Phenomenalisation of the voice and subject is always necessarily implied in the lyric, but here it would seem that some strategy must be found for avoiding the full phenomenalisation of Essex's body. The body of Pulter's text should not stand in for Essex's body, since this would make the text itself an effigy. Unlike the figure used in the funeral procession, the poem is not intended to be a memorial of Essex, indeed it might best be read as the commemoration of a dismembered body, through its repetition of the dis-*figuring* of the effigy. This avoidance of the animation of Essex as textual monument is in part attempted through the creation of a less than fully human figure. The broken effigy thus remains as the accurate figuration of a human body which is itself incomplete.

The question of gender raised by this attention to masculinity takes us into an area that has not yet been taken into account in this reading of the poem. What of the fact that this is written by a woman? Pulter's adoption of an avowedly royalist poetic position seems to negate any sense of female passivity, particularly if we accept the connection made in so much royalist poetry between writing and fighting. The idea of writing as commitment, and more particularly as committed political action, stands in opposition to the notion of a cavalier withdrawal into drinking, friendship and *otium*. This might be read as a means of engagement for the non-combatant female writer. Yet the rhetoric of masculinity which underpins so much royalist writing, especially if conceived through an attack upon the masculine virtues of its opponents, must be disturbed by its presentation through an apparently female voice. As Loxley has suggested: 'The corporeal agency such poetry demands is marked as biologically male, defined against a particularly physical lack.'[35] As Loxley also notes, however, acceptance of this demand without interrogation of its bases threatens to grant voice a privileged access to presence and corporeality. The gender difference that this royalist concentration on masculinity is attempting to assert and define is precisely rhetorical. A non-linguistic, corporeal origin must ground the claim for an actively masculine poetic, and yet the claims for poetry as activity and the definition of masculinity upon which this claim is grounded can only take place in the poetry itself. That which is posited as ontologically prior to its linguistic expression turns out to be itself a product of that expression, and the corporeal origin is dispersed into reiterated linguistic acts of positing. Any identification of Pulter's writing as an attempt to enter this discourse as a royalist female combatant necessarily threatens the royalist principle of poetry as action, since such action is predicated on a masculinity that precedes writing. It might then be possible to read Pulter's focus on the question of Essex's masculinity as a matter of deferral. The place of the woman writer within this masculine poetic convention is displaced through the projection of a perceived physical lack onto the subject of the poem rather than the speaking persona.

IV

And yet, to read Pulter's poetry in this way may also allow too much to the ontological claims of voice. In a very different poem to be found in the Pulter manuscript, it is possible to read a far less secure operation of voice. While the Essex poem can be read

as an attempt to avoid monumentalising its subject, 'On the same'
is an elegiac lament for the death of one of Pulter's daughters, Jane.
The title refers to a poem which precedes this one in the manuscript, entitled 'Upon the death of my deare and lovely daughter
J.P.', to which a note has been added: 'Jane Pulter, baptized May
1. 1625. Buried Oct. 8 1646 at 20'.[36]

Tell mee noe more her haire was lovly brown
Nor that it did in Curious curles hang down
Or that it did her snowey shoulders shrowed
Like shineing Cinthia in A sable Clowd
5   Tell mee noe more of her black Diamond eyes
Whose cheerfull looke made all my sorrowes fly
Like Glittring Phebus Influence and light
After a northern winters halfe years night
Tell mee noe more her cheeks exceld the Rose
10   Though Lilly leaves did sweetly interpose
Like Ruddy Aurora riseing from her bed
Her snowey hand shadeing her Orient he'd
Tell mee noe more of her white even nose
Nor that her Ruby Lipps when they disclose
15   Did soe revive this drooping heart of mine
Like Golden Aples on A silver shrine
Tell mee noe more her bre'sts were heaps of snow
White as the swans where Cristall Thams doth flow
Chast as Diana was her virgin Bre'st
20   Her noble Mind can never bee exprest
This but the Casket was of her rich soule
Which now doth shine above the highest pole
Tell mee noe more of her perfection
Because it doth increase my hearts dejection
25   Nor tell mee that shee past here happy dayes
In singing Heavenly and the Museses layes
Nor like the swans on Cristall Poe
Shee sung her Dirges ere shee hence did goe
Noe never more tell my sad soule of Mirth
30   With her I lost most of my Joyes on earth
Nor can I ever raise my drooping spirit
Untill with her those Joyes I shall inherit
Those Glories which our finite thoughts transcend
Where wee shall praises sing World without end
35   To him that made both her and mee of Earth
And gave us spirits of Celestiall Birth

> Tell me noe more of her Unblemished fame
> Which doth I mortalize her virgin name
> Like fragrant odours Aromatick fumes
> 40 Which all succeeding Ages still perfumes
> Nor why I mourn for her aske mee noe more
> For all my life I shall her loss deplore
> Till infinite power her dust and mine shall raise
> To sing in Heaven his everlasting praise.[37]

'On the same' begins as an apostrophe to an unidentified interlocutor, to one who seems to serve as an uncomfortable reminder of a
daughter's death. Who is this addressee? Several possibilities
present themselves, and attempts to make any identification natu-
rally rest in part upon our definition of lyric poetry and the figure
of apostrophe.[38] Lyric poems always imply a voice, speaking or
singing, and necessarily imply someone or something to whom this
voice speaks. It need not be a person, fictional or otherwise,
and cannot easily be identified by the catch-all term of 'reader'
(whether intended, implied, universal, ideal, embodied, specifically
named, or otherwise). This unidentified interlocutor is precisely
not present, but neither in any strong sense is the author. We
must preserve the distinction between author and speaking
persona, even or perhaps especially in a poem which appears to
be so evidently autobiographical. The reader, however conceived,
is thus a hearer, or perhaps, in John Stuart Mill's phrase, someone
who (or, we may wish to add to Mill, something that) overhears.[39]
This distinction is important here, since on one level it is impossible not to think of a reader as an addressee. Yet it is also possible
to think of a reader inhabiting the position of the persona who
speaks in the poem, most obviously when the poem is read
aloud.

   This might be better understood if we think more carefully
about the figure of apostrophe, that is, if we read the poem in
relation to rhetorical notions of performativity. Apostrophe seeks
to animate that which is inanimate, and in this it is related to
figures such as *enargeia*, *hypotyposis* and *prosopopeia* that I discussed in earlier chapters. As Barbara Johnson suggests: 'Apostrophe is a form of ventriloquism through which the speaker throws
voice, life, and human form into the addressee, turning its silence
into mute responsiveness.'[40] The refrain of this poem – 'Tell mee
noe more' – seemingly enacts not so much a desire to hear or to

appropriate the voice of the other as a wish for silence. Response in this case is to take the form of muteness. There are contrary impulses here; an apostrophic address which calls the other to animation also marks a conversation which is already in progress and that the discourse of the poem seeks to end. That this is the second poem on this subject – and that, therefore, its title announces it as being in some sense a repetition – reinforces the sense of a traumatic working through. Of course, it is almost too obvious to say that this is a poem about absence, about loss and mourning.[41] Yet we should not be too quick to establish or locate a strict opposition between animate and inanimate. If apostrophe is a figure of animation, and in particular the animation of the inanimate, then such oppositions become hard to ground, and this poem clearly marks the painful presence of that absence, marks the failure of the poem to recover 'life'.

For Godsake hold your tongue, and let me mourn, might be an accurate summation of the tone of the beginning of this poem. The implied dialogue that the poem enacts offers an apparent divergence between *two* speakers which a reader may only hear as a single voice, and this is accentuated by the call for the silence of the interlocutor. The repetition of the interlocutor's words, placing the blazon-like description of the daughter's qualities in invisible quotation marks, blurs any clear distinction between the supposedly antithetical positions. We also hear that these words are themselves repetitions; Tell mee *noe more*, not again, not now. (I will return to the question of the temporality of this 'now'.) The repetition of the descriptions makes the poem's apparent literal meaning untenable: the act of asking not to be reminded of the daughter's qualities is itself a form of reminder. Of course, for a reader, this is a repetition which comes 'for the first time', it is an origin already marked by its secondarity, even without recourse to a mimetic notion of the representation of the actual body of the deceased. Thus the desired muteness of the interlocutor is substituted for in the speaker's own locutions.

We might expect this act of mourning to be predicated on the loss of the human, yet the comparisons that are made are conventionally hyperbolic: Jane is 'Like shineing Cinthia', 'Like Glittring Phebus Influence and light', 'Like Ruddy Aurora', 'Chast as Diana', 'her cheeks exceld the Rose', 'her bre'sts were heaps of snow', and her body is merely the 'Casket' for her soul. Although such descriptions sound familiar as poetic conceits, we should be aware that most of these are rejected, they are the words that should not be repeated. Perhaps it is the movement into conceit that is the problem, the movement, marked by the repetition of 'like', away from the body itself (if we can use that word here). More particularly, the poetic conventions in question belong to the tradition of the male love lyric, and the poem thus presents the possibility of reading against this tradition. It would have to be said, however, that this tradition includes a strong sense of writing against itself, and thus the apparent opposition runs the risk of presenting itself as a thoroughly conventional turn against convention. There is an element here of echoing Shakespeare's 'false compare' of Sonnet 130. Evidently, the refrain echoes Carew's 'A Song', with its repeated response – 'Ask me no more' – given to a series of impossible demands.[42] This alone aligns Pulter's poem with a rhetoric of love lyrics, and this gives us another tonal twist. Indeed, if it were not for the title of the previous poem, it would not be obvious from the opening lines of 'On the same' that this is in fact an elegy. Unlike Lady Mary Wroth, Pulter does not make an explicit effort to distance herself from a line of male love lyrics.[43]

The question of temporality becomes significant here. The emphasis on human corporeal finitude, on the need to transcend finite thoughts in favour of a recognition of infinite power and everlasting praise, opens the text to a reading as a memorial. Jane Pulter's body becomes monumentalised through the very act of repressing the memory of its component qualities. We might, then, think of this poem as an effigy. The substitution of a poetic text for an absent human body is not of course uncommon. The most famous examples are perhaps Ben Jonson's claim for 'his best piece of poetry' in the elegy for his son, or Shakespeare's claim for the memorial quality of his sonnets.[44] Similarly, then, when Pulter remarks on her daughter's reputation the immortalisation is enacted in the utterance which requests its own cancellation in lines 37–40. The temporal location of the speaker's claim here should be remarked; there is an implication that the speaker already knows what the deceased's reputation will have been. There is an impossibly transcendent position suggested here, but it is also apparent that this attempt to move beyond finite perfection is rejected. More pointedly, perhaps, 'fame' immortalises 'name', but it is not the name that is the object of mourning. What, we might ask, is in a name?[45]

The sense of temporal dislocation that appears here is not restricted to this moment in the text. The notion of the daughter singing a swan's dirge (ll. 27–8) revives the classical conceit that swans are supposed to sing but once, and that before their deaths. This familiar image, used by Donne and by Shakespeare in both *Othello* and *Lucrece*, might be read as the voice of the future anterior; it can only be interpreted, after the fact, as that which will have announced death.[46] Is this poem, then, an apostrophe to death? Here might be another candidate for the unidentified interlocutor, for there is another *telos* here, that of Pulter's own death, and life in death.

The question of what it might mean to write an apostrophe to death, what it might mean to attempt to animate death, or to see death as a force capable of animation, is not one which should be answered too quickly here. Donne's resort to paradox in the movement from 'Death be not proud' to 'Death, thou shalt die' might exemplify the difficulties inherent in such a project.[47] Jonathan Culler suggests that 'apostrophe takes the crucial step of constituting the object as another subject with whom the poetic subject might hope to strike up a harmonious relationship'.[48] But in this context it seems pertinent to ask: is it possible to have a harmonious relationship with death? Given time, perhaps. And given the rhetorical resources. Apostrophe is the trope which, through an obliteration of temporality, attempts the instantiation of the poem as an event in the ever-present 'now' of a reading. Culler suggests that it is here that lyric is to be opposed to narrative. This is perhaps where Pulter's poem itself, as memorial and as an instance of voice, attempts to enact the transcendence of finitude.

This is then a memento mori, but it does not rest upon a strict division between presence and absence.[49] Pulter might be seen to attempt to dwell, to borrow a line from another of her poems, 'amongst the caverns of the dead'.[50] Memory and memorial are always intended towards the future, even if this must be figured in a future anterior. Just as identification with a royalist poetic cannot guarantee the production of a stable female voice of political engagement, neither can the border between the living voice and the dead voice be located, once and for all. The Muses' lays cannot bring back the dead, but neither can that song be simply silenced within memory. Jane Pulter's voice can also be heard, by the speaking persona at least, in this poem. It is her voice, as much as that of the interlocutor, which acts as a painful reminder. When Hamlet suggests in his dying words that 'the rest is silence', he can give no guarantees; the rest of the play should already have told him (and us) that.

Notes

1 The implications of this question are played out in J.-L. Nancy, 'Vox Clamans in Deserto', trans. N. King, in *The Birth to Presence*, ed. B. Holmes (Stanford: Stanford University Press, 1993), pp. 234–47, 236.

2 The poetry in question is contained in MS Lt q 32, held by the Brotherton Collection at the University of Leeds. I am grateful to Leeds University Library for permission to use these texts. Further biographical and bibliographical descriptions may be found in Pulter, *Poems*, ed. M. Robson (Leeds: Leeds Studies in English, 2007).

3 See, for example, E. D. Harvey, *Ventriloquized Voices: Feminist Theory and English Renaissance Texts* (London: Routledge, 1992); J. Goldberg, *Voice Terminal Echo: Postmodernism and English Renaissance Texts* (London: Methuen, 1986); L. Dunn and N. Jones (eds), *Embodied Voices: Representing Female Vocality in Western Culture* (Cambridge: Cambridge University Press, 1994); K. Chedgzoy, M. Hansen and S. Trill (eds), *Voicing Women* (Keele: Keele University Press, 1997).

4 The suggestion is made in W. J. Ong, *Orality and Literacy: The Technologizing of the Word* (London: Routledge, 1982), for example, p. 132. This is discussed in chapter 4 of H. Love, *Scribal Publication in Seventeenth-Century England* (Oxford: Clarendon Press, 1993), especially pp. 141–4.

5 P. Kamuf, *Signature Pieces: On the Institution of Authorship* (Ithaca: Cornell University Press, 1988), p. vii.

6 See the introduction to Goldberg, *Desiring Women Writing: English Renaissance Examples* (Stanford: Stanford University Press, 1997), pp. 3–15, 5.

7 Lyotard, *The Inhuman: Reflections on Time*, trans. G. Bennington and R. Bowlby (Stanford: Stanford University Press, 1991), pp. 147–8.

8 Such a concentration is, of course, also prevalent in the wider sphere of critical thought. Among only the most obvious references would

be Barthes's investigation of authorship, Blanchot's work on the neutral voice and literature, Levinas on the Saying and the Said, Kristeva on polyphony, Lyotard on discourse and the differend, Lacan on speech and psychoanalysis and all the works on gendered or 'ethnic' voices.

9 See *Politics*, Book I, in *The Complete Works of Aristotle*, ed. J. Barnes, 2 vols (Princeton: Princeton University Press, 1995), 2: 1253a1. Some of the material in the following paragraphs is taken from my 'Introduction: Hearing Voices', *Paragraph* 29: 1 (2005), 1–12. Special issue: *Jacques Rancière: Aesthetics, Politics, Philosophy*. See also my 'Reading Hester Pulter Reading', *Literature Compass* 2 (2005), 17C 162, 1–12.

10 Although it is necessary to note Jacques Rancière's comments: 'my idea is that politics is not based on a linguistic destination to community, that it is not based on any anthropological disposition to the common. I start from the "speaking animal" to show that this animal is split up from the beginning: "understanding language", Aristotle says, is not the same as "possessing" it. Speaking is not the same as speaking.' From §2 of 'The Thinking of Dissensus: Politics and Aesthetics'. Paper presented at the conference 'Fidelity to the Disagreement: Jacques Rancière and the Political', Goldsmiths College, London, 16–17 September 2003.

11 See *Republic*, Book VI, particularly 493, in *The Collected Dialogues of Plato, including the Letters*, ed. E. Hamilton and H. Cairns (Princeton: Princeton University Press, 1963).

12 Rancière, *Disagreement: Politics and Philosophy*, trans. J. Rose (Minneapolis: University of Minnesota Press, 1999), pp. 22–3.

13 Rancière, *The Names of History: On the Poetics of Knowledge*, trans. H. Melehy (Minneapolis: University of Minnesota Press, 1994), p. 65.

14 See, for example, Rancière's criticism of a Sartrean notion of literary commitment in 'The Politics of Literature', *SubStance* 33: 1 (2004), 10–24.

15 See Aristotle's *Rhetoric*, in *The Complete Works of Aristotle*, 1365a. *Ethos* in this sense is related to persona and questions of authorial identity. The longevity of this concept may be indicated by T. S. Eliot's 'The Three Voices of Poetry', in *On Poetry and Poets* (London: Faber & Faber, 1957), pp. 89–102, in which the Aristotelian notion of an original, organising voice linked to authorial intention is maintained.

16 On the political consequences of this shared 'experience', testified to by the work of Paul Celan, see P. Lacoue-Labarthe, *Poetry as Experience*, trans. A. Tarnowski (Stanford: Stanford University Press, 1999).

For the definition of 'experience' as Lacoue-Labarthe uses it in this text, drawing upon its strict sense as 'a crossing through danger' rather than as something that is 'lived', see p. 18.

17 See, for example, the very different readings in P. S. Hammons, *Poetic Resistance: English Women Writers and the Early Modern Lyric* (Aldershot: Ashgate, 2002) and L. McGrath, *Subjectivity and Women's Poetry in Early Modern England: 'Why on the Ridge Should She Desire to Go?'* (Aldershot: Ashgate, 2002).

18 See W. A. Rebhorn, *The Emperor of Men's Minds: Literature and the Renaissance Discourse of Rhetoric* (Ithaca: Cornell University Press, 1995), Ch. 3.

19 I am not the first to bring them together. See P. Parker, 'On the Tongue: Cross-Gendering, Effeminacy, and the Art of Words', *Style* 23 (1989), 445–65.

20 Erasmus, *Lingua: The Tongue*, in *The Complete Works of Erasmus* (Toronto: University of Toronto Press, 1976–), 29: 257–412.

21 But see also the comment: 'Consider children, old people, and women: their tongue is less controlled because their mental powers are weaker' (p. 283) and the repetition of the proverbial wisdom that women can't be trusted even after their deaths, although he extends this to friends (p. 298).

22 Tomkis, *Lingua: Or, The Combat of the Tongue, And the Five Senses For Superiority. A Pleasant Comœdie* (London: 1607).

23 A. F. Marotti, *Manuscript, Print, and the English Renaissance Lyric* (Ithaca: Cornell University Press, 1995), p. 73. Marotti's discussion of women's manuscripts occupies pp. 48–61.

24 M. J. M. Ezell, *Writing Women's Literary History* (Baltimore: Johns Hopkins University Press, 1993), pp. 37–8.

25 This was most notably argued in J. W. Saunders, 'The Stigma of Print: A Note on the Social Bases of Tudor Poetry', *Essays in Criticism* 1 (1951), 139–64; but see also S. W. May, 'Tudor Aristocrats and the Mythical "Stigma of Print"', *Renaissance Papers 1980* (1981), 11–18.

26 These attempts, and the resistance to them, are discussed in the first chapter of L. Potter, *Secret Rites and Secret Writing: Royalist Literature, 1641–1660* (Cambridge: Cambridge University Press, 1989), pp. 1–37.

27 Marotti notes the popularity of death as a subject in manuscript collections, *Manuscript, Print, and the English Renaissance Lyric*, pp. 129–30.

28 See note 4 above. My readings are guided by a similar concern for voices, but in the debate between Ong and Derrida that Harold Love interestingly sets up, the readings presented here would be much

closer to the Derridean line than to that of Ong. The texts of most relevance in Derrida's corpus would be *Of Grammatology*, trans. G. C. Spivak (Baltimore: Johns Hopkins University Press, 1976); *Speech and Phenomena, and Other Essays on Husserl's Theory of Signs*, trans. D. B. Allison (Evanston: Northwestern University Press, 1973), although many other passages might be cited here.

29 MS Lt q 32, f. 85r–v.

30 R. Vines, *The Hearse of the Renowned, the Right Honourable Robert, Earle of Essex* (London: 1646). The connection with the House of Lords is given on the title page.

31 Much of the following information is to be found in *Whole Proceedings of the Barbarous and Inhuman Demolishing of the Earl of Essex Tomb on Thursday Night Last, November 26, 1646* (London: 1646); and V. F. Snow, *Essex the Rebel: The Life of Robert Devereux, the Third Earl of Essex, 1591–1646* (Lincoln: University of Nebraska Press, 1970), especially p. 494.

32 The complaint about the proximity of the monument of Essex to Israel (l. 27) might also be a reference to the analogy drawn between Essex and the biblical defenders of Israel made in a text such as Vines's sermon.

33 On Essex and Frances Howard, see D. Lindley, *The Trials of Frances Howard: Fact and Fiction at the Court of King James* (London: Routledge, 1993). Ammon is also associated with Alexander the Great, and this may reinforce the critical attitude towards Essex's martial prowess.

34 J. Loxley, 'Unfettered Organs: The Polemical Voices of Katherine Philips', in *'This Double Voice': Gendered Writing in Early Modern England*, ed. D. Clarke and E. Clarke (Basingstoke: Macmillan, 2000), pp. 230–48, 240. See also Loxley's *Royalism and Poetry in the English Civil Wars: The Drawn Sword* (Basingstoke: Macmillan, 1997).

35 Loxley, 'Unfettered Organs', p. 239–40.

36 Pulter, MS Lt q 32, f. 16v.

37 Pulter, MS Lt q 32, ff. 17v–18v.

38 For a discussion of lyric poetry which has influenced my approach here, see T. Bahti, *Ends of the Lyric: Direction and Consequence in Western Poetry* (Baltimore: Johns Hopkins University Press, 1996).

39 Mill, quoted in Bahti, *Ends of the Lyric*, p. 3.

40 B. Johnson, 'Apostrophe, Animation, and Abortion', in *A World of Difference* (Baltimore: Johns Hopkins University Press, 1987), pp. 184–99, 185.

41 For a useful discussion, see M. Greenfield, 'The Cultural Functions of Renaissance Elegy', *English Literary Renaissance*, 28:1 (1998),

75–94. For the status of particular genres in the civil war period, including elegy, see N. Smith, *Literature and Revolution in England, 1640–1660* (New Haven: Yale University Press, 1994).

42 It is to be noted that Henry King's 'Sonnet' begins with the phrase 'Tell me no more', but it does not maintain this in the manner of a refrain. Scott Nixon addresses the manuscript circulation of Carew's poem in ' "Aske me no more" and the Manuscript Verse Miscellany', *English Literary Renaissance* 29: 1 (1999), 97–130.

43 I am grateful to Michael Brennan for this suggestion.

44 Jonson, Epigram 45 'On My First Son', in *The Oxford Authors: Ben Jonson*, ed. I. Donaldson (Oxford: Oxford University Press, 1985), pp. 236–7.

45 For an indication of just how lacking in innocence this question is in the context of a discussion of mourning, see Derrida's 'Aphorism Countertime', trans. N. Royle, in *Acts of Literature*, ed. D. Attridge (London: Routledge, 1992), pp. 414–33.

46 Donne, 'An Anatomy of the World: The First Anniversary', in *The Complete English Poems*, ed. A. J. Smith (Harmondsworth: Penguin, 1983), p. 281, l. 407; Shakespeare, *Othello*, ed. N. Sanders (Cambridge: Cambridge University Press, 1984), 5.2.245–6; *Lucrece*, in *The Poems*, ed. F. T. Prince (London: Methuen, 1969 [1990]), ll. 1611–12.

47 Donne, *Divine Meditations*, 'Holy Sonnet X', in *The Complete English Poems*, p. 313.

48 J. Culler, 'Apostrophe', in *The Pursuit of Signs: Semiotics, Literature, Deconstruction* (London: Routledge, 1981), pp. 135–54, 143.

49 Among many discussions of the function of the memento mori in England in this period, notable is N. Llewellyn, *The Art of Death: Visual Culture in the English Death Ritual c.1500–c.1800* (London: Reaktion, 1991), especially Ch. 4.

50 Pulter, 'The complaints of Thames 1647 when the best of kings was imprisoned by the worst of Rebels at Holmbie', l. 108, MS Lt q 32, f. 10r. This poem also contains the image of the swan's dirge, l. 104.

7

To hear with eyes

I

Where is an ear? Is an ear part of the inside or the outside of a body, and how can we distinguish its own inside and outside surfaces? Where is the ear of an era, the ear of the early modern? And what of the ear of Shakespeare? Such quibbling might seem of little consequence, serving to irritate rather than illuminate, and yet irritation is sometimes productive. It is the foreign body that puts the body to work.[1]

These questions resonate in the context of the various debates within early modern studies on the body, on orality and aurality, on speech and writing, on the voice and the gaze. In particular, these questions have a special pertinence in the context of recent calls for an attention to sense, and to the senses, and the proposal that such attention might best come through a phenomenological approach. For it seems clear that phenomenology quickly embeds itself within a visuality that supplants and supplements orality. In other words, the eye and the ear change places, but without ever being able to eliminate the residue of the one in the other, like a foreign body, continuing to work like the grit within the oyster shell. Or within the shell of an ear.

As we shall see, it is language that becomes this foreign body, entering the ear as voice or the eye as writing. And again, this is a cause for profound ambivalence, as the possibilities of persuasion offered by rhetorical work upon the senses are perceived as both opportunity and threat. In the discourse of early modern writing, the foreign body that is language is given an ethical import because it can make something happen. In Sidney, as I suggested in earlier chapters, this is the positive dimension of poetry. But there is also a negative capability. Just as the foreign body may give rise to a pearl, it may also lead to a form of poisoning or of infection.

II

In Shakespeare's works, the ear is treated with an ambivalence that cannot be simply idiomatic. One of the most famous invocations of the ear is, of course, Antony's 'Friends, Romans, countrymen, lend me your ears!' (3.2.65) in *Julius Caesar*.[2] Antony's rhetorical display is one of the clearest examples of persuasion as force, and stands against seemingly more naive alternative views in Shakespeare's works, such as that expressed in *Othello* by Brabantio: 'words are words; I never yet did hear / That the bruis'd heart was pierced through the ear' (1.3.216–19).[3] The irony of Brabantio's lack of insight is that Desdemona is indeed won over by Othello's stories, and the play, which is more frequently read through Othello's desire for 'ocular proof', is full of references to the ear. Indeed, it is Othello's failure to 'see' the threat that lies within speech that contributes to his tragedy. At 1.3.377, Iago suggests that he will 'abuse Othello's ear' and the editor of the Cambridge edition glosses 'abuse' as 'deceive'. But is it that simple? Might it not rather be that Iago is simply going to exploit the openness of Othello's ear, an image reinforced by his later claim that he will 'pour this pestilence into his ear' (2.3.323)? Antony's recognition of the power of speech is closer to Augustine's sense of the ear as the route to the heart: '*Whisper in my heart, I am here to save you.* Speak so that I may hear your words. My heart has ears ready to listen to you, Lord. Open them and *whisper in my heart, I am here to save you.*'[4] Yet the ear, unlike the eye, is always open, always ready to receive, and can only be 'closed' with difficulty, just as the sailors in Book 12 of Homer's *Odyssey* must stop their ears with wax if they are to avoid the trap of the Sirens' song. Thus there is always the possibility of the call, but this call cannot be 'screened'; to decide whether or not to 'listen' to a speech, one must already have heard it. One can only reserve the right not to answer the call; any pestilential content will already have been incorporated. The difficulty arising is analogous to the problems of interpretation posed by an injunction such as 'Do not read this sentence.' One can only obey its prescription after having broken the law that it attempts to institute.

In this respect, the ear is analogous to the tongue. As we saw in the previous chapter, the tongue is positioned within two movements, from the body into the world (as speaking organ) and from the world into the body (in tasting).[5] Both ear and tongue are able to sense threats only when it may be too late; it is only possible to recognise the 'poison' after it has entered the body. As we will see in a moment, the figure of speech as poison may be literalised in this sense of taste. From here it is not difficult to see that any notion of art as having a positive influence upon the one who experiences it (good art leads to a good influence) has to counter the problem that art may also be capable of having a damaging effect. This is the force of the platonic objection to the Aristotelian or Sidneian emphasis on the moral nature of poetry, and is what lies behind their insistence that it must be a concern for morality that motivates poetic acts. Aesthetic 'taste', then, to take the figure seriously, can only reject that which it has already experienced. The idea of rhetoric as poison or as harmful – and Erasmus too recognises the tongue as both poison and medicine in *Lingua* – becomes the source of drama in several of Shakespeare's texts.[6]

The problem regarding the spatial definition of the ear finds its way into critical accounts of the plays. Thus Jonathan Bate, in a discussion of Olivier's film adaptation of *Hamlet*, finds himself saying: 'At the very centre of the play is Hamlet's lacerating confrontation with his mother in her bedchamber. In this iconic moment, Hamlet is forcing Gertrude back on to the bed; he seems on the verge of piercing not just her ear but her body.'[7] *Not just her ear but her body.* What notion of the ear is Bate working with here, if he is able to distinguish the ear from the body? This might appear to be a mistake on Bate's part, but I would like to suggest that it is rather a symptomatic example of the difficulties which surround (without lying 'outside') the ear.

Part of the fascination with the ear and hearing stems from a clear connection between the ear and the tongue, emphasised by the fact that one can hear oneself speak in a way that one cannot see oneself seeing, cannot taste oneself tasting, and so on. This link between a form of self-awareness and the voice makes hearing an *intimate* sense. But although this has led to a privileging of the ear and the tongue over other organs, there are indications in the literary texts of the early modern period that suggest we be cautious about endorsing this privilege. Adopting another perspective, over thirty years ago Jacques Derrida suggested that: 'Hearing oneself speak is not the inwardness of an inside that is closed in upon itself; it is the irreducible openness in the inside; it is the eye and the world within speech.'[8] At the time, Derrida was attempting to account for the familiar association of speech with a sense of intimacy and interiority, and for the privilege of this sense over others within a philosophical tradition which culminates (without ending) in phenomenology. Of particular interest here is the movement from hearing to 'the eye and the world within speech'. Rupturing any sense of the self-enclosed relay from tongue to ear, Derrida counts self-overhearing as an indication of the continuity of speech and world that refuses to be closed off as an expression of 'self'. It is not that there is not a world elsewhere, it is that it refuses to remain safely 'over there', outside the body. It is worth restating here, however, that those who read statements such as this, as well as Derrida's by now infamous *'il n'y a pas de hors-texte'* ['there is no outside-text'], as a gesture of textual idealism are clearly wrong.[9]

In part why I choose to cite Derrida here is that in three recent works of pertinence to my discussion, there has been a suggestion that phenomenology might provide a way to think through questions of the senses.[10] I think that such a movement is to be welcomed, but I also think that we should be clear about the trajectories that such phenomenological investigations might take. The dominant trend in Western philosophy, it is sometimes argued (and as I showed in my introductory chapters), is the history of a sustained movement from the sensual to the supersensual.[11] Thinking, in this tradition, is not something that can be equated with sensing, or at least not with the actions of or impressions received by the senses. This is the difference between making sense and sensuality. This movement then from the physical to the metaphysical has a long and elevated history, even if that history now appears to be under a certain amount of stress. Bruce Smith's recent work has offered an alternative to this separation of the realm of the senses from early modern textuality, emphasising the embodiedness of readers and audiences in an aural world. Smith's work raises some important questions relevant to the debates on textuality and performativity in the early modern period. Yet there are ways in which certain early modern texts, and the ones chosen here are simply emblematic of a much wider (perhaps even interminable) project, might intervene in these debates. What I would like to offer in this chapter is merely an indication of a sense of unease that arises about the movement away from a philosophy (and by extension any theory) associated with the privileging of the supersensual and back to the embodied reader or audience member.

That philosophy need not be abandoned in our return to a concern for the senses is ably demonstrated by Jonathan Rée's wonderful *I See A Voice*. While I might not fully endorse all that this book contains, there is a short passage which I think is instructive in opening up the significance of these questions. Noting the privilege afforded to voice (even by those most apparently keen to attack that privilege), Rée suggests that there are four basic 'delusions' that govern the arguments around voice: 'first, that the voice is intrinsically connected with the existence of a self-identical soul, spirit, or inward subjectivity; second, that experience must ultimately be analysed into the distinct contributions made by the various bodily senses; third, that hearing is specifically concerned with time, and vision with space; and fourth, that language has two fundamentally different forms: audible speech which occupies time but not space, and visible writing which occupies space but not time'.[12] As Rée suggests, such delusions do not evaporate simply because they can be recognised, the only way to approach them is through treating the world as phenomenon rather than object. This parallels the approach to literature on which I have insisted throughout this book, and particularly in Chapter 4. Literature is not best thought of as either individual (or collective) expression, and the senses do not contribute to the processes of making sense in isolation from each other. Equally, speech and writing cannot be simply opposed, but nor should they be collapsed into versions of the same 'thing', even if that thing falls under the numinous concept of language. In this chapter, some of the ideas on hand and voice that I discussed earlier will be rethought, deepening my earlier analysis by involving other senses.

The topics that I address here are worthy of far more extended elaboration, and there are many connections back to the discus-

sions in earlier chapters that will remain implicit, but I think that
the readings that I am proposing can act as exemplary figures for
the larger debates on to which they open. My central point will
be that much of the work on the orality of early modern English
literature (and this also includes certain of the questions about
performance with regard to dramatic texts) repeats a very familiar
opposition of speech and writing that the texts that are purportedly being read complicate. The confusion of the senses that the
title of this chapter indicates acts as a marker of a difficulty that
has to be attended to by early modern criticism, even if that criticism presents itself in a phenomenological mode. Phenomenology
must not lose sight of the linguistic processes of phenomenalisation, especially when such processes are explicitly centred on the
matter of *aisthesis*.

III

It is commonly accepted, I think, that early modern England was
a predominantly oral culture. Many critical examples of this belief
might be cited, but for now I would like to call upon only a couple
of textual witnesses. The first is from Robert Weimann's well-
known article on *Hamlet*, in which he claims that: 'Even when
deeply indebted to the humanist poetics of inscribed language,
these [Shakespeare's] plays remained close to a culture of voices,
a civilization of oral signs and practical privileges where blindness
itself (and the unliterary spectator) could be told to "look with
thine ears".'[13] In this quotation from *King Lear*, Weimann demonstrates the practical privileges that he gives to the spoken over
the written, and this forms part of his critical argument in this
essay.

The second text is Robert S. Miola's recent *Shakespeare's
Reading* in which, as part of a discussion of early modern
reading practices and the education which formed them, he states
that:

> Students acquired extraordinary sensitivity to language, especially
> to its sound. The practice of reading aloud and of reciting verse
> developed acute inner ears that could appreciate sonic effects which
> are lost on moderns. . . . Elizabethan aural sensitivity led to delight
> in wordplay of all kinds, repartee, *double entendre*, puns, and
> quibbles.[14]

Both critics suggest that the emphasis on orality and the aural is a fundamental part of audience response and thus conditions the ways in which texts are written and read. Both imply that this sensitivity to sound should also, then, inform modern critical readings. Where Weimann stresses a connection to (and distance from) traditional forms of mimesis, Miola rightly points to the role of 'wordplay of all kinds', which cannot adequately be subsumed under the heading of mimesis at all. As I have argued in earlier chapters, language has the capacity to transcend forms of referral, to allow for the perception of phenomena for which there are no objects in the world, and to follow the materiality of signification to make connections that reach beyond the semantic. It is worth pausing for a moment over these insistent references to sound, since a question poses itself here. How do Weimann and Miola know that this was an oral culture? The answer is by reading texts, both Shakespeare's works and contextual documents. The senses of the activity of ear and voice come from texts which are primarily perceived through the eye.

I have no desire to deny the strength of orality within early modern culture, but I do wish to complicate a model which seems all too easily to privilege the spoken over the written. It is by following Miola's lead here that I think we can begin to elaborate the relationship of *oratio* to *ratio*, and also to recognise that not all early modern texts support the notion of a happily oral culture. In the rush to embrace oral culture, what early modern writing has to say *about* orality must not be overlooked. What is being offered here, then, cannot be thought of as a thematic reading. Neither can a concern with the ear and the eye be taken simply as a reading of particular metaphors, however powerfully conceived.

Among Shakespeare's texts, *Hamlet* and *Venus and Adonis* thematise the problems posed by orality in clear ways, but also in ways that exceed thematisation.[15] Equally, while *Hamlet*, as a dramatic text, fits neatly into the performance context of Shakespeare's work in which a concentration on speech over writing is more familiar, *Venus and Adonis* leads us firmly into the territory indicated by Miola, since this narrative poem also displays a preoccupation with the oral and the aural. *Venus and Adonis* is, furthermore, a key text because it is, of course, the first that was published with Shakespeare's name on the title page. It seems to be a good place, therefore, to begin to think about the relationship of orality to the written or the visual in his work. By a happy coincidence which is not to be thought of as an accident, we might wish to think about this as a modality of the *tympan*, since the tympan or tympanum denotes both the membrane which separates and communicates between the inner and outer ear, and is also the name given to part of the mechanics of the printing press, and especially the hand press. That it is also the name for a drum should prompt us to think about rhythm and the beat of Shakespeare's verse, which leads to considerations of metrics (as in a recent article by George T. Wright) and repetition or repro-duction.[16] This might help us to draw together sonic rhyme and the 'eye-rhyme'.

Eye rhyme presents its own problems, however. The writer of the entry on rhyme in the *The New Princeton Encyclopedia of Poetry and Poetics* points to the fascinating etymological and conceptual genealogy which links rhythm to rhyme, especially around 1600 at which point we find the word 'rythme', which is supposed to have been pronounced in the same way as 'rime'. Eye rhyme is the very axis along which the relationship of the aural to the visual in poetry can be measured, but its identification is always a matter of privileging one sense over the other. Thus the *Princeton Encyclopedia* is forced to concede that:

> Genuine cases of eye rhyme raise the issue of the relations of sound to spelling in language and poetry – notice, for example, that spelling differences in aural rhyme are invisible, whereas spelling similarities in eye rhyme are opaque; they are the marked form. Rhyme is by definition sound-correspondence, but insofar as spelling is meant to denote sound, we must both ignore it and – when necessary – pay attention to it . . . In this, eye rhyme points up the very question of the aural and (or versus) the visual modes of poetry.[17]

Much hinges on that opening 'genuine', since it is the question of being able to determine what may or may not be a genuine case of eye rhyme that is at stake. The oral mode of rhyme involves privileging the eye over the ear, in that the ear cannot distinguish between two words which are spelt differently (flaws/floors), whereas in visual rhyme, conversely, similarities in the written forms of words emerge which the ear would not detect (though/ plough/rough/through/ought). Yet in a period in which spelling is far from conventionalised, and in which pronunciation can produce effects not detectable by the modern ear, we must be cautious in identifying eye rhyme at all (if we accept that eye rhyme *in strictu sensu* cannot be picked up aurally as rhyme). Stephen Booth, in his voluminously-annotated edition of the Sonnets, makes a revealing comment which is germane to our discussion here:

> the evidence of Elizabethan puns and rhymes is not definitive, but the words we spell 'her', 'here', 'hear', 'hair', 'hare', 'heir', and – since initial *h* was ordinarily silent in common words – 'ear' and 'air', all apparently sounded enough alike to be confusable.[18]

In another context, it would be necessary to trace all of the connections which a comment such as this one suggests, for these linkages seem to be more than just sonic coincidences.[19] And certain of these examples, including 'hear' and 'ear', are related to the perception of sound itself. Further, there is no doubt something to be made in the context of a reading of *Hamlet* of this connection between 'ear', 'air' and 'heir'. One place that we might look for some of this consonance would be to the Dedication (to the *Ear*-l of Southampton) of *Venus and Adonis*:

> But if the first *heir* of my invention prove deformed, I shall be sorry it had so noble a godfather, and never after *ear* so barren a land, for fear it yield me still so bad a harvest.

The strongest sense of 'ear' in this quotation is plough or till. Poetic invention is linked to notions of organic and sexual productivity but also to incision or penetration, marking a conventional notion of the paternal, disseminatory writer. The ear here is seen to be productive, but the play upon 'heir' and 'ear' offers another possible resonance, since it is hard to avoid thinking of *Hamlet*. The openness of the ear can be viewed as an asset to those who wish to persuade, but it can also be seen as a threat, since it may be penetrated for good or ill, as the comment from Iago cited above suggests. This perhaps leads to the rhyming of 'ear' and 'fear'. Rhetoric is persuasion but also force, and the unease that this recognition causes is part of the classical inheritance. As we have seen, the platonic warnings concerning the pliability of a crowd are precisely an admission of the power of rhetoric, and this may be seen to underpin texts such as *Coriolanus* or *Julius Caesar*. A figure for this is the relationship of *sound* to *wound*, which occurs as a rhyme in *Venus and Adonis*. This relationship expands through the poem, echoed in songs which delight and destroy (as in the nurse's song or the mermaid's or sirens' song).

Again, we need to think about exactly how this works. Sound/wound: is this a full sonic rhyme or an eye rhyme? If it is a sonic rhyme then it seems to be part of a more general connective web (it is also used in *Lucrece*), but if it is instead a visual rhyme, then this implies, since this is a rhyme on *sound*, that the potential for wounding through the ear is one that the ear itself may not be able to detect.[20] Here wounding is, perhaps against expectations, produced by a visual consonance.

Another way of linking the non-dramatic to the dramatic verse would be to turn to Sonnet 23. In elaborating the relationship of ear to eye, we find that Weimann's citation of *Lear* – in which we are invited to look with ears – might be reversed:

> O, let my books be then the eloquence
> And dumb presagers of my speaking breast,
> Who plead for love and look for recompense
> More than that tongue that more hath more expressed.
> > O, learn to read what silent love hath writ;
> > To hear with eyes belongs to love's fine wit.
> > > (ll. 9–14)

The connection of speech to writing is repeatedly made and broken. The books promise eloquence, but it is a silent love which writes. The eye must then phenomenalise the voice, reversing the common insistence on speech giving an image to the mind's eye (as discussed in Chapter 2). Jonson's 'speak, that I may see thee' becomes 'read, that you will hear me'.

Sonnet 23 begins with the persona of the 'unperfect actor on the stage' and the theatrical metaphors are continued as the poem progresses in 'books', which might allude to the dramatic script, and the 'dumb presagers', perhaps a reference to staged dumb shows.[21] Of course 'books' as a reading has been queried, with some editors preferring 'looks'. In either case the emphasis is on a distinction between the visual and the aural, but in both cases it is deflated by the suggestion that one must learn to 'hear with eyes'. As Vendler suggests, 'Silent reading carried in Shakespeare's day a powerful reminiscence of oral reading (to oneself or an audience), and the number of auditory puns in the *Sonnets* testifies to

Shakespeare's own ever-active ear, trained, of course, by his constant writing for oral delivery on the stage.'[22] Yet surely it cannot be simply that the ear is writing here, however counter-intuitive that may sound? Our evidence for the oral nature of this text is given in and as the written word, and it is in this sense that the text demands that we hear with eyes if we are to appreciate its orality. The ear called up by this poem is then the product of a knowledge which can only be attained through the eye. Vendler's invocation of Shakespeare's career as a dramatist, despite the fact that she is discussing a poem that begins with reference to a metaphorical actor, seems to miss the force of her own insight regarding silent reading.

What, then, of the plays? Acting as an idea is also linked to the senses in *Hamlet*. The metaphor of acting brings together the force of rhetoric with the force of the visual image in such a way that the boundaries between the two faculties become blurred, and this is revealed in *Hamlet* through the use of the word 'cleave', which itself exhibits a violent sense. Cleave can mean both to part or divide, to pierce or penetrate, and to adhere or cling to, but it is clearly the first cluster of meanings that concerns Hamlet here:

> He would drown the stage with tears,
> And cleave the general ear with horrid speech,
> Make mad the guilty and appal the free,
> Confound the ignorant, and amaze indeed
> The very faculties of eyes and ears.
>
> (2.2.556–60)

But what does it mean to cleave an ear, however general? Hamlet's advice to the players repeats the criticism: 'O, it offends me to the soul to hear a robustious periwig-pated fellow tear a passion to tatters, to very rags, to split the ears of the groundlings, who for the most part are capable of nothing but inexplicable dumb-shows and noise' (3.2.8–12). Cleaving as splitting is again emphasised, but we are no nearer to sensing what it means (its sense). Editors of these speeches such as Harold Jenkins, G. R. Hibbard and Philip Edwards seem to think that they are self-evident, and offer no explanation of what it might mean to cleave or split an ear.[23] Is this a puncturing, in which the ear is itself penetrated, or is it rather a splitting off from something else (reason, the body, the other senses, and so on)? Might Bate's sense of the ear as separate from the body be implied here? Intriguingly, the sense that this might be a shared ear offers the prospect of a body politic which might be dismembered through the voice of the actor. Oratory again takes on a political dimension, influencing its auditors through the force of its sensory appeal.

IV

In a characteristically provocative statement which comes in the final lines of his essay 'Shakespeare's Ear', the late Joel Fineman suggests that 'for Shakespeare it is specifically the ear that is the organ of the text, of the specifically typographic text'.[24] Fineman was regrettably unable to make good his proposal that this could be proven through a reading that would begin with Sonnet 46. But the idea that the ear could function as a privileged organ which has an intimate connection to *typography* is a fascinating one, and intimacy is one of the things that Fineman stresses most clearly, particularly in his reading of the 'salacious ear that both covers and discovers the genitals of Queen Elizabeth' in the Rainbow Portrait (p. 229). This 'exceptionally pornographic ear' (p. 228) reinforces Fineman's reading, in his earlier *Shakespeare's Perjured Eye*, of a fetishistic erotics, in which the vulva-like ear figures and disfigures an equally fetishistic principle of sovereign power, which is also to be found in Shakespeare's *Sonnets*. It is worth noting the apparently obvious fact that the pornographic, fetishistic quality of the ear can only be seen in the painting, not heard.

One further element must also be added to this before we can proceed, and that is Fineman's characterisation of the ear, drawn in large part from the section on hearing from John Davies's *Nosce Teipsum*, which Fineman sees as feeding into the iconography of the painting. In Davies's poem, the ear functions as an organ of delay and deferral, indeed Fineman makes the familiar connection between this organ and Derrida's notion of *différance*, and the ear's labyrinthine convolutions allow its identification with 'temporal distension and dilation' (p. 230). There is a historical dimension to Fineman's brief argument in which he proposes an elaboration of his central contention (made more fully in *Shakespeare's Perjured Eye* and outlined again in this essay) that there is a specific connection between Shakespearean texts, more particularly the sonnets, and the 'invention' of a governing model of subjectivity within literary history.[25] The performative dimension of the sonnets enacts a movement from the visual to the verbal, and generates a model of subjectivity which operates such that 'in our literary tradition it is necessarily writing, as such, that exists as that which constitutively intermediates between voice and vision' (p. 226). The challenge that Fineman lays down is for us to be able to think beyond this model of subjectivity, and he asserts that even the most deconstructive thought is still in relation to this 'invention'. Consequently, he argues, the Shakespearean ear, understood in terms of its relation to temporality, 'eventually determines Derrida's account of the reader's, any reader's, relation to a text, any text' (p. 230).[26] In order to make good on this proposal, it is incumbent upon him to show that the ear is the organ of the specifically typographic text. It is Sonnet 46, of course, that begins with the 'mortal war' between the eye and the heart, and while it is possible to imagine the lines that Fineman's argument may have taken, it would not be prudent to attempt to invent such a reading here.

Fineman's argument is nonetheless suggestive for several reasons. Firstly, it allows us to trace a connection between textuality, sexuality and sovereignty that raises some of the more obvious problems facing certain historicisms.[27] The notion of temporal dilation that the figure of the ear allows to be seen troubles both any sense of linear, progressive temporality and also the assumed connections between the texts of a synchronic 'period' or culture. But we should also be aware of the spatial dimension here that is so clearly a part of the invocation of *différance*. Fineman's emphasis on the typographic and, thus, visual significance of the ear again helps to reinvigorate the sense that I am trying to assert here of the necessary, indeed ineluctable, interpenetration of eye and ear. In this recognition of the interpenetration of spatial and temporal aspects, Fineman avoids the trap – identified by Rée – of mapping ear and eye on to time and space.

It is in *Hamlet* that we see perhaps the clearest thematisation of the problems of the ear in Shakespeare's works. What, in *Othello*, Iago calls a 'pestilence' is literalised in *Hamlet* in the murder plot, but in the latter play it also becomes a metaphorical refrain for other characters, and their insight into the workings of language as persuasion is recurrently undercut by their own statements or actions. Thus Laertes warns Ophelia that she must 'weigh what loss your honour may sustain / If with too credent ear you

list his [Hamlet's] songs, / Or lose your heart, or your chaste treasure open / To his unmaster'd importunity' (1.3.29–32). Hamlet's
songs are potentially as threatening as those of the Sirens. Almost
immediately, we see Laertes himself receive advice from his father,
who suggests: 'Give every man thy ear, but few thy voice' (1.3.68).
But this turns out to be (characteristically) bad advice, and in fact
prepares the way for the tragic denouement. Upon his return following Polonius's murder, Claudius recognises that this openness
to persuasive speech makes Laertes a potential threat, since he:

> Feeds on this wonder, keeps himself in clouds,
> And wants not buzzers to infect his ear
> With pestilent speeches of his father's death,
> Wherein necessity, of matter beggar'd,
> Will nothing stick our person to arraign
> In ear and ear.
>
> (4.5.89–94)

Again the emphasis is on speech as a form of infection, as a pestilence
that enters through the opening of the ear, and Claudius notes with
trepidation the power of his enemies' indictments. In the next lines,
Claudius goes on to equate this series of accusations against him with
a 'murd'ring piece' which brings him 'superfluous death' (perhaps
looking forward to the fact that he is both stabbed and poisoned in
the play's climactic scene). The focus upon the power of discourse is
maintained even once Claudius has regained control. Having persuaded Laertes to take part in his plot to kill Hamlet, and thus having
exploited the openness of his ear for his own ends, Claudius suggests
that Laertes has heard 'with a knowing ear' (4.7.3).

The idea that words may threaten and perform as weapons is
enfolded within the text in several places, as well as appearing
elsewhere in Shakespeare's work. Thus Hamlet's suggestion 'I will
speak daggers to her [Gertrude], but use none' (3.2.387) proves
effective, and Gertrude begs:

> O speak to me no more.
> These words like daggers enter in my ears.
> No more, sweet Hamlet.
>
> (3.4.94–6)[28]

What Gertrude fantasises here is, of course, a parodic repetition
of the death of her former husband, although she cannot

experience it as such, since the repetition is an unconscious one on her part and, therefore, it is precisely as experience that this event remains unavailable to her. In the Ghost's relation of the murder, there is a shuttling between literal and metaphorical ears which mimics the literal and metaphorical royal bodies. The Ghost is aware of the power of narrative, warning Hamlet that a more disturbing story yet might be told but that 'this eternal blazon must not be / To ears of flesh and blood' (1.5.21–2). The blazon again inserts this figure of dismemberment into a discourse on ears. Neither Hamlet nor the audience hear this tale. The use of the word blazon of course heralds the interplay between memory, figuration and disfiguration that runs throughout the Ghost's speeches, yet the fable of the murder is also a narration that begins with an invocation to attend to hearing:

> Now, Hamlet, hear.
> 'Tis given out that, sleeping in my orchard,
> A serpent stung me – so the whole ear of Denmark
> Is by a forged process of my death
> Rankly abus'd.
>
> (1.5.34–8)

Hamlet's ear is called for, but so is the ear of the state of Denmark. If the body of the country may be 'abus'd' through speech (as is Othello's), then the poison which kills the king cannot be limited to a literal interpretation. The metaphorical permeability of the social body is indicated through the literal penetrability of the individual body. This inability to limit the effects of treacherous words is also related to the ear's openness, since it is through 'the porches' of the former King's ears that the poison enters, to course through the 'natural gates and alleys of the body' (1.5.59–67). The public sense of the gates and alleys marks the capacity for the inwardness of the body to be entered like an ill-defended city. Hamlet, however, is aware that the call for him to listen is itself leading him into the same dilemma, and this lies behind his initial suspicion that the Ghost might be a 'goblin' sent to lead him into damnation (1.4.40).[29]

V

An indication of where all of this speculation about the senses might lead can become apparent if we return to a consideration of a non-dramatic text such as *Venus and Adonis*, since there is a less obvious implication of this text in the oral culture of theatrical performance, although the oral, rhetorical training of the writer and reader remains. The sensuality of the poem is readily acknowledged, but we must also note the sense of its senses. *Venus and Adonis* is, of course, an epyllion, that genre which is opposed to lyric, and most frequently defined as a minor epic or narrative poem. Despite this apparent movement away from lyric, the poem itself is deeply concerned with questions of voice, tongues and rhetoric. Like Marlowe's *Hero and Leander*, which shares a similar Ovidian source and tone, its central scene is an attempted seduction, and this sets up a structure of mirroring between the seduction of one character by another and the seduction of the reader by the text. There are many invocations of the power of voices to persuade and to undo, disseminating the connection of sounding and wounding throughout the text into figures such as the mermaid's voice. Two-thirds of the way through the poem, Adonis recognises the power of the tongue to seduce, and at the same time makes a claim for the strength of his defences:

> 'If love have lent you twenty thousand tongues,
> And every tongue more moving than your own,
> Bewitching like the wanton mermaid's songs,
> Yet from my heart the tempting tune is blown;
>   For know, my heart stands armed in mine ear,
>   And will not let a false sound enter there;
>
> 'Lest the deceiving harmony should run
> Into the quiet closure of my breast,
> And then my little heart were quite undone,
> In his bedchamber to be barr'd of rest.
>   No, lady, no; my heart longs not to groan,
>   But soundly sleeps, while now it sleeps alone.'
>   (ll. 775–86)

We might wish, from the material discussed thus far in this chapter, to reserve the right to doubt the security that Adonis feels. While the attempt to seduce Adonis by Venus is the most obvious aspect of persuasion in the poem, what should alert us to the fragility of Adonis's position is the sense that Venus's words have indeed lodged themselves inside him. For his reference to the mermaid's song is in fact an inversion of something that she has already claimed regarding his power to seduce. Not only does she note the force of speech, Venus also argues for the disruption of the senses caused by Adonis:

> 'What, canst thou talk?' quoth she, 'hast thou a tongue?
> O would thou hadst not, or I had no hearing!
> Thy mermaid's voice hath done me double wrong;
> I had my load before, now press'd with bearing:
>   Melodious discord, heavenly tune harsh-sounding,
>   Ears' deep sweet music, and heart's deep sore wounding!'

Each is convinced that the other's voice is the mermaid's song. The seductive element in Adonis's voice brings Venus pleasure and pain, and this is figured as a double wrong. His speech contains the positive and negative aspects marked in the 'Melodious discord', heavenly and harsh, reaching to the depths of ear and heart. Here is where sounding and wounding come together, with sounding also used to measure the depth of his tongue's effect on her. There is no defence against Adonis's voice other than deafness, but it is not hearing alone that is the problem, and Venus continues:

> 'Had I no eyes but ears, my ears would love
> That inward beauty and invisible;
> Or were I deaf, thy outward parts would move
> Each part in me that were but sensible:
>   Though neither eyes nor ears, to hear nor see,
>   Yet should I be in love by touching thee.
>
> 'Say that the sense of feeling were bereft me,
> And that I could not see, nor hear, nor touch,
> And nothing but the very smell were left me,
> Yet would my love to thee be still as much;
>   For from the stillitory of thy face excelling
>   Comes breath perfumed, that breedeth love by smelling.
>
> 'But O what banquet wert thou to the taste,
> Being nurse and feeder of the other four.
> Would they not wish the feast might ever last,
> And bid Suspicion double-lock the door,
>   Lest Jealousy, that sour unwelcome guest,
>   Should by his stealing in disturb the feast?'
>
> (ll. 421–50)

This is, of course, precisely the Ovidian banquet of sense to which Chapman objects, as we saw in Chapter 2. Venus asserts a kind of synaesthesia, in which one sense replaces and compensates for another, but each leads to the same conclusion, that she will love Adonis. Rather than different senses giving access to different experiences or forms of knowledge, all lead to the same end: love. As more than one critic has noted, the sense of 'banquet' that Venus employs echoes a common name for Plato's *Symposium*, in particular as read through the 1471 translation and commentary of Ficino. The potential tension, then, between a Neoplatonic insistence on the movement from the sensual to the supersensual and the sensualist tenor of Venus's speech is clearly marked. The problem of the location of beauty, of drawing a clear distinction between inside and outside, is side-stepped. With it goes the problem of which sense to use in the perception of beauty. While I have focused on the relationship between the aural and the visual, it would be wise to note the further step in Venus's speech; from eye to ear, from ear to touch, from touch to smell, from smell to taste. Behind this it is also possible to render this progression through the senses differently; from sight to blindness, blindness to hearing, hearing to deafness, and from deafness to touch, and so on. One sense touches on and activates another, but only at the cost of its own deprivation.

This allows for a recognition of the manner in which Shakespeare's poem transforms its source in ways that highlight the place of the senses in this sensual genre. It is worth pausing to outline briefly the early modern sense of Ovidian narratives. As Catherine Belsey puts it in a reading of the poem and its critics in terms of visuality that is indebted to Lacan: 'What the Renaissance in general and this text in particular adopt from Ovid is above all the notion of erotic metamorphosis itself: the object the lover finally possesses is not the object of desire but something else, a substitute, a stand-in. At the moment when the desiring subject takes possession of the object, something slips away, eludes the lover's grasp, and is lost.'[30] While I broadly agree with Belsey's reading of the erotic aspects of the poem (and equally of the critical heritage that it has spawned), there is something that needs to be addressed in the framing of her essay, and that is the choice of the trompe-l'oeil as a central motif. What should be apparent by now is the complexity of the relationship between knowledge, reading and visuality. This complication comes precisely from the implication of the visual in and with the other senses (and vice versa).

Belsey's essay reads *Venus and Adonis* through Lacan's reading of the Zeuxis and Parrhasius story, which is plausible enough for several reasons, not least because it is referred to in the poem.[31] The Lacanian reading of this story is still an attempt, I believe, to unveil the 'true' trompe-l'oeil in a thoroughly classical (that is, metaphysical) manner.[32] That it is a veil that is painted by Parrhasius unveils the reading of this moment as an allegory of reading, in that here truth is revealed as a moment of anamorphic 'unveiling' (*aletheia*), not in the sense that something is shown to lie behind the veil but, instead, that the veil is revealed as something other than a veil. The strength of this as a reading comes down to the plausibility of an attempt to decide between a true and false trompe-l'oeil. Belsey's Lacanian analysis offers a powerful account of the general arc of the poem, but the speeches that we have just seen from the poem, and their emphasis on the interdependence of the senses, also suggest something else. The metamorphosis of the object of desire might be said to prompt a transformation of the perception of desire, in other words, it may be necessary to change or exchange senses in order to maintain an attachment to the object. Venus's rhetorical display, in which she attempts to argue her way into Adonis's affections, parallels Shakespeare's desire to persuade and seduce the reader. But in this Venus attempts to work upon more than just the sense of sight. Like that of the character within the poem, the ear of the reader is open to penetration, to another form of productive 'earing'. Yet again, the senses cross.

In the poem, penetration of the heart comes through the ear, as in Augustine, but for the reader this is enacted through the eye. Only if the text is given a voice does the reader as listener occupy the position of Adonis. That is, a speaker capable of giving voice is phenomenalised through the text's rhetorical animation of its own materiality. Or, the seduction of the language posits a seductive speaker, just as the language that expresses that speaker's desire makes the one desired seem desirable. But, as we have seen, we should be wary of rushing to identify this as a subjective voice. From the positioning of the reader as listener that the poem seems to wish to enact, we might argue that the text phenomenalises the figure of the reader *as listener* in order to assert the figure of a speaking, lyric voice as well as evoking an object of that speech. *Poiesis* is again at the heart of this poetic form of making (as mimesis); but it asserts its status as event, as an event of fiction, and not merely as representation. So we must also be attentive to the extent to which language enacts a referral to itself. It is not, perhaps, that sound creates a wound, but that the appearance of the wound renders the voice visible. There is a wound, therefore there will have been a voice. There is a seduction, therefore there will have been a rhetoric of persuasion.

The temporal schemes involved are rendered more complex by the possibility of a tragic reading of the poem. The position of Adonis is certainly a potentially tragic one, but there is some unease generated by the tone of the poem as a whole.[33] One way of thinking about this is to reread the death of Adonis in terms of the connection between language and temporal and spatial delay. It is from a final wounding that Adonis dies, but it is only at the moment of this death that many of the prior speeches are activated in their performative, prophetic dimension. For a modern reader to recognise the source of this wound, its textual determination, it is necessary to look with ears, and to hear with eyes; to look both to a phenomenology of the acoustic world of the early modern period, and to the phenomenalisation of 'the eye and the world within speech'. But the poem also leaves us with another possibility. Rather than an ending, it offers us a vision of transformation. Adonis becomes the flower. And flowers are commonly used as a figure for rhetoric and for poetry.

Notes

1 On the critical significance of the foreign body, see N. Royle, *After Derrida* (Manchester: Manchester University Press, 1995), Ch. 7.

2 References are to Shakespeare, *Julius Caesar*, ed. M. Spevack (Cambridge: Cambridge University Press, 1988).

3 References are to Shakespeare, *Othello*, ed. N. Sanders (Cambridge: Cambridge University Press, 1984).

4 Augustine, *Confessions*, trans. R. S. Pine-Coffin (Harmondsworth: Penguin, 1961), p. 24.

5 In a typically strange and playful variation, Rabelais offers a glimpse of how we may get out of the ear and into the world in his account of the birth of Gargantua, who is born through his mother's ear. He links this apparently unbelievable event to classical parallels, including the birth of Adonis from the bark of a tree. See Book I, Ch. 6 of

   F. Rabelais, *The Histories of Gargantua and Pantagruel*, trans.
   and intro. J. M. Cohen (Harmondsworth: Penguin, 1955), pp.
   52–3.

6 Erasmus, *Lingua*, in *The Complete Works of Erasmus* (Toronto:
   Toronto University Press, 1976–), 29: 259–62.

7 J. Bate, *The Genius of Shakespeare* (London: Picador, 1997),
   p. 262.

8 J. Derrida, *Speech and Phenomena, and Other Essays on Husserl's
   Theory of Signs*, trans. D. B. Allison (Evanston: Northwestern
   University Press, 1973), p. 86.

9 'Il n'y a pas de hors-texte' is, of course, to be found in several places
   in Derrida's *Of Grammatology*, most obviously as the 'axial proposition' of the section entitled (in the translation) 'The Exorbitant.
   Question of Method'. See *De la grammatologie* (Paris: Minuit, 1967),
   p. 227; *Of Grammatology*, trans. G. C. Spivak (Baltimore:
   Johns Hopkins University Press, 1976), p. 158. As well as the discussions cited above, see also Derrida's 'Tympan', in *Margins of Philosophy*, trans. A. Bass (Hemel Hempstead: Harvester Press, 1982), pp.
   ix–xxix; *The Ear of the Other: Otobiography, Transference, Translation*, trans. P. Kamuf (New York: Schocken Books, 1985); and 'Heidegger's Ear: Philopolemology (*Geschlecht* IV)', trans. J. P. Leavey,
   Jr, *Reading Heidegger: Commemorations*, ed. J. Sallis (Bloomington
   and Indianapolis: Indiana University Press, 1993), pp. 163–218. The
   latter is a reading of Martin Heidegger's *The Principle of Reason*,
   trans. R. Lilly (Bloomington and Indianapolis: Indiana University
   Press, 1996), Lecture 6. But see also, M. Jay, *Downcast Eyes: The
   Denigration of Vision in Twentieth-Century French Thought*
   (Berkeley: University of California Press, 1993).

10 This suggestion underpins B. Smith, *The Acoustic World of
   Early Modern England: Attending to the O-Factor* (Chicago: Univer-
   sity of Chicago Press, 1999), J. Rée, *I See a Voice: A Philosophical
   History of Language, Deafness and the Senses* (London: Flamingo,
   2000), and W. Folkerth, *The Sound of Shakespeare* (London:
   Routledge, 2002). Rée's title is, of course, a quotation of Bottom from
   A Midsummer Night's Dream, and I am indebted to his work for
   several passages in this chapter. Essays which address some of these
   issues in a different manner are to be found in D. Hillman and C.
   Mazzio (eds), *The Body in Parts: Fantasies of Corporeality in Early
   Modern Europe* (London: Routledge, 1997).

11 This is discussed in K. Silverman, *World Spectators* (Stanford:
   Stanford University Press, 2000).

12 Rée, *I See a Voice*, p. 6.

13 Weimann, 'Mimesis in *Hamlet*', in *Shakespeare and the Question of Theory*, ed. P. Parker and G. Hartman (London: Methuen, 1985), pp. 275–91, 276.

14 Miola, *Shakespeare's Reading*, Oxford Shakespeare Topics (Oxford: Oxford University Press, 2000), pp. 2–3. I do not propose to follow this line of wordplay here, but an indication of the territory can be discerned in Mahood's *Shakespeare's Wordplay* (London: Methuen, 1957), and in Patricia Parker's work, including *Shakespeare from the Margins: Language, Culture, Context* (Chicago: University of Chicago Press, 1996).

15 All quotations will be from the Arden editions: *Hamlet*, ed. H. Jenkins (London: Methuen, 1982); *Venus and Adonis*, in *The Poems*, ed. F. T. Prince [1960] (London: Routledge, 1990).

16 Wright, 'Hearing Shakespeare's Dramatic Verse', *A Companion to Shakespeare*, ed. D. S. Kastan (Oxford: Blackwell, 1999), pp. 256–76.

17 *The New Princeton Encyclopedia of Poetry and Poetics*, ed. A. Preminger and T. V. F. Brogan (Princeton: Princeton University Press, 1993), p. 399.

18 Shakespeare, *Sonnets*, ed. S. Booth (New Haven: Yale University Press, 1977), p. 170.

19 Margreta de Grazia and Peter Stallybrass examine the heir/hair/air connection in *Macbeth* in their 'The Materiality of the Text', *Shakespeare Quarterly* 44 (1993), 255–83. See Parker, *Shakespeare from the Margins*, p. 297.

20 *Lucrece*, in *The Poems*, ed. F. T. Prince [1960] (London: Routledge, 1990), ll. 1464/6.

21 See Booth (ed.), *Sonnets*, p. 172.

22 Vendler, *The Art of Shakespeare's Sonnets* (Cambridge, MA: Harvard University Press, 1999), p. 137.

23 Shakespeare, *Hamlet*, ed. P. Edwards (Cambridge: Cambridge University Press, 1985); *Hamlet*, ed. G. R. Hibbard (Oxford: Oxford University Press, 1987).

24 Fineman, 'Shakespeare's Ear', *The Subjectivity Effect in Western Literary Tradition: Toward the Release of Shakespeare's Will* (Cambridge, MA: MIT, 1991), pp. 222–31, 231. Further citations are referenced in the text. With more space, it would be possible to trace Fineman's essay with much more care than I am doing here, as well as to engage with its development in Ned Lukacher's work. See *Primal Scenes: Literature, Philosophy, Psychoanalysis* (Ithaca: Cornell University Press, 1986) and *Daemonic Figures: Shakespeare and the Question of Conscience* (Ithaca: Cornell University Press, 1994).

25 J. Fineman, *Shakespeare's Perjured Eye: The Invention of Poetic Subjectivity in the Sonnets* (Berkeley: University of California Press, 1986).

26 In establishing his characterisation of Derrida's thought, Fineman quotes a passage on Nietzsche from 'Otobiographies', trans. A. Ronell, in *The Ear of the Other*, ed. C. McDonald (New York: Schocken, 1985), p. 36. Seasoned Derrida readers will be right to flinch at the notion of 'a text, any text', which is directly contrary to Derrida's own sense of reading as responsive and responsible.

27 On some of the relationships here to gender in particular, see P. Berry, *Shakespeare's Feminine Endings: Disfiguring Death in the Tragedies* (London: Routledge, 1999), Ch. 3.

28 This notion of the dagger thrust into the ear is also fantasised in a literal manner by Hamlet in Branagh's film version in which, in a neat folding of the revenge plot back upon itself, we see Claudius's ear pierced through the grille of the confessional box. K. Branagh, *Hamlet by William Shakespeare: Screenplay, Introduction and Film Diary* (London: Chatto & Windus, 1996), p. 102.

29 Hamlet also returns to the matter of the senses when he speaks to Gertrude in the closet scene, attempting to find a reason for her transferral of affections from his father to his uncle (3.4.71–81).

30 C. Belsey, 'Love as Trompe-l'oeil: Taxonomies of Desire in *Venus and Adonis*', *Shakespeare Quarterly* 46 (1995), 257–76, 261. See also J. Bate, *Shakespeare and Ovid* (Oxford: Clarendon Press, 1993).

31 The Zeuxis and Parrhasius story is well-known in the early modern period, derived from Pliny. Lacan's reading is in *The Four Fundamental Concepts of Psycho-analysis*, ed. J.-A. Miller, trans. A. Sheridan (London: Peregrine, 1986), pp. 111–12.

32 Belsey, 'Love as Trompe-l'oeil', p. 257.

33 This is, however, only one possibility. There is also a comic reading in which instead of a lament we hear (or are invited to supply) a laugh.

8

Blind faith

I

At the conclusion of the previous chapters, we were left with largely negative images: of Venus and the deprivation of the senses; of the defacement engendered by the lyric subject; of the failure to read that ensues from an overhasty subscription to structures of 'authorised' witnessing. In this chapter I would like to draw together these images into a consideration of a particular instance of textualised perception. Returning to the example of Thomas More, I would like to offer a reading of the hagiographical and historiographical tradition that emerges in the decades following his execution in 1535 in order to examine more closely the relations between the senses, and in particular sight, and notions of witnessing. Testimony to martyrdom offers a striking example of attempts to make visible an object or event through the linguistic expression of perception of that object or event. In the phenomenological sense, testimony is always intentional, it is always testimony *to* something. And yet, even at the point where *aisthesis* might seem to be most securely in evidence – in the moment at which an apparently real event and a commitment to the truth to which the event testifies come together – it remains a matter of reading the textual representation or presentation of that response, and to ask what the status of the event as object might be in such linguistic forms.

The textual and visual representations of martyrdom enact a specific relation to history and to various conceptions of presence and the present which, as Julia Lupton argues, stand at a crucial juncture in the secularisation of the Christian foundations of

modernity.[1] The presentations of More's execution provide exemplary instances of this transition from a form of 'faith-ful' representation that draws upon an authorised sense of what can be
taken to constitute truth (or Truth) to a more 'modern' sense of
fidelity to the truth of history (that is, to some verifiable notion of
'what actually happened'). By the early years of the seventeenth
century, even More's Protestant opponents begin to recognise what
we would think of as a more modern form of historiographical
truth. Christopher Lever, for example, opens his discussion of
More by making a distinction between religious truth, described
as 'that profession which I hold for truth', and the truth that he
believes to be the 'moving soule of all Historie'.[2] In both cases
there is a relationship between an objective and a subjective realm:
the 'profession' is external but must be held to; the truth of history
appears through writing. Earlier in the text, Lever suggests that it
is precisely a matter of being able to *see* the truth:

> God doth never suffer the light of his truth to be utterly extinct,
> though many times in that degree of adversity, as that the eye of this
> world cannot see it. This is evident in the sacred Stories of the *Bible*,
> and also in the condition of these times whereof I write. When Igno-
> rance and Error like a double vaile did blinde the face of Truth: yet
> God whose eye of providence is ever open, seeth the envie of evill
> men. And (in the time of his good pleasure) he taketh off this double
> Vaile, and presents Truth naked to the view of all men.[3]

Despite his differences from More's religious position, and this is
one of a series of texts in which he endorses the break with Rome,
Lever nonetheless laments the partiality of accounts of the Reformation and stresses the need to recognise the good even in his
opponents if truth is to be preserved. Partisan polemic only leads
to a blindness to the truth. In my discussion of More's representation in this chapter, then, the focus will be on the ways in which
truth may be perceived. In particular, I want to examine truth's
emergence through a deliberate testimonial blindness.

  This reading of perception takes us back to thinking about the
role of witnessing in relation to *aisthesis*. As we saw in the introductory chapters of this book, the roots of our sense of *aisthesis*
are to be found precisely in the movement from seeing and testify-
ing to sense perception, that is, in what Wlad Godzich identifies
as the opposing of *theorein* to *aisthesis* (see above pp. 65–6). Yet

in the context of discussions of martyrdom, the concern with aesthetics must also take on an ethical dimension. In the readings that follow, I want to suggest that this ethical moment devolves precisely from the question of exemplarity. Just as martyrdom raises the problem of fidelity in testimony, so the employment of examples prompts us to think about our own senses of fidelity in our treament of those examples. In *Topographies*, J. Hillis Miller suggests that 'No example is innocent. Argumentation by way of examples depends on insinuating the validity of that most problematic of figures, synecdoche. Example asserts that the part is like the whole.'[4] There is, then, always a figural implication to exemplarity, and the early modern use of More as an example (both textually and otherwise) can tell us a great deal about the caution with which we should read these 'insinuating' figures. This applies as much to my own presentation of these examples as to the work of those I read.

Indeed, the very discourse of martyrdom stems from a concern with witnessing, testimony and forms of proof. The rhetorical term *martyria* (and its Latin equivalent *testatio*) refers to attempts to prove something through an appeal to personal experience. Similarly, in the discussions of exemplarity to be found in rhetorical treatises, emphasis is placed on the persuasive aspects of the use of examples. Thus in the *Rhetorica ad Herennium* (sometimes attributed to Cicero), it is stated that examples 'serve the purpose of testimony . . . For an example is used just like testimony to prove a point.'[5] Similarly, Thomas Wilson proposes that 'He that myndeth to perswade, muste neades be well stored with examples', and he recommends the careful trawling of chronicle histories in search of resources.[6] And when Puttenham comes to discuss 'historicall Poesie', he comments:

> There is nothing in man of all the potential parts of his mind (reason and will except) more noble or more necessary to the active life then memory: because it maketh most to a sound judgement and perfect worldly wisedome, examining and comparing the times past with the present, and by them both considering the time to come, concludeth with a stedfast resolution, what is the best course to be taken in all his actions and advices in this world: it came upon this reason, experience to be so highly commended in all consultations of importance, and preferred before any learning or science, and yet experience is no more than a masse of memories assembled, that is, such

trials as man hath made in time before. Right so no kinde of argument in all the Oratorie craft, doth better perswade and more universally satisfie then example, which is but the representation of old
memories, and like successes happened in times past. For these
regards the Poesie historicall is of all the other next the divine most
honorable and worthy.[7]

In his emphasis on the mobilisation of memory, and in particular
in his insistence that such memories are directed towards future
conduct as much as towards the commemoration of past glories
and infamies, Puttenham draws together the vivid, persuasive and
performative aspects of the employment of examples. Close to
Sidney's sense of the moral possibilities of poesy, Puttenham recognises the ethical link between oratory and action, but he is equally
aware of the competition with other disciplines that offer an access
to truth. In his closing suggestion that historical poesy is second
only to divine poesy, Puttenham also shows the special place of
discourses of martyrdom, in which it is possible for the divine and
the historical to coincide in one exemplary figure.

Of course, some readers will already be wary of my own insistence on talking about martyrdom in terms of representation,
textuality and figures. Surely, in the discussion of an execution at
least, we should be very clear about the fact that there is a corporeality at stake. Terry Eagleton, for example, asserting a continuity
of bodily experience that is not so much unhistorical as given by
the continuity of the species, proposes that such bodily continuity
is troubling for a left-historicist avoidance of universals, essentials,
and so on:

> No doubt this is why the body in pain, despite a few splendidly per-
> ceptive accounts of it, has scarcely been the most popular of topics
> in a body-oriented academia, hardly able to compete with the sexual,
> disciplined or carnivalesque body. It conforms much less readily to
> a case about historical pliability. And the suffering body is largely a
> passive one, which does not suit a certain ideology of self-fashioning.
> It is of no particular consolation to the victims of torture to be told
> that their anguish is culturally constructed, as it is, perhaps, to be
> told that one's lowly place in the hierarchies of gender or ethnicity
> is a changeable historical affair.[8]

Eagleton is, as so often, half right. It is certainly true that an
individual's suffering will not be alleviated by any analysis of it.
But it is clearly not the case that the body in pain might ever be

perceived by anyone other than the victim without a degree of cultural construction, and it is far from obvious that even the one suffering the pain experiences this pain in a purely non-cultural or 'authentic' manner. One might counter, for example, with a phrase from Wittgenstein: 'The man who cries out in pain, or says that he has pain, *doesn't choose the mouth which says it.*'[9] Or, as Elaine Scarry puts it, 'Physical pain has no voice, but when it at last finds a voice, it begins to tell a story.'[10] Such stories are always culturally constructed, and it is with such narratives that I am concerning myself here.

I would also want to ask an additional question: what purpose does the representation and analysis of pain serve? There is a problem with trying to put such physical experiences to some kind of 'use'. An initial difficulty arises because those who inflict pain always do so with some end in sight. This might be (as readers of Foucault will immediately sense) to display technologies of power through a demonstration of the capacity to discipline and punish the body. Or else it can be done in order to discover a hidden knowledge, to force the revelation of a truth that will not willingly be yielded up. Or there may be some pleasure to be derived from the administration of pain. Such justifications of the use of pain inevitably impact upon the contrary motivations to resist them, to deny the power of a sovereignty, to keep knowledge hidden, to withhold the taking of pleasure. Such resistances may find themselves incorporated into an economy such that they testify to the same truth as the rituals of punishment, even in their opposition to them.

In the material at the heart of this chapter, a further problem arises with the idea of treating bodily pain. The martyrs, of course, cannot speak for themselves at all. But despite the fact that there were plenty of resources available to them, those who chose to represent More's execution tended to elide bodily sensation altogether.[11] This is, then, one of the primary problems with our notion of exemplarity. Is it permissible or even desirable to reconstruct a narrative of pain, to testify to that which is missing from their testimonies, or should we respect (or at least try to understand) why these writers and artists avoid the representation of pain? While I am not arguing for a historicist avoidance of anachronism, nor for a rejection of presentist concerns, nor for a kind of fidelity to the intentions of early modern authors, I believe that there is an ethical sense of 'doing justice' to texts. And justice is precisely what these texts are about. But as we know, justice is often said to be 'blind'.

II

First example. An illumination and a word. A kneeling figure in red: a man about to be executed. Two other men, one with a sword, the other in blue holding a sceptre: an executioner and a king. Behind them, a tree. At their feet, water. In the distance, a range of blue mountains scattered where the land begins to dissolve into the sky. The executioner and the king look beyond the frame of the picture into an unseen space, their eyes perhaps directed towards some object known to them but not to us. They look neither to the spectator nor to the kneeling figure who has brought them to this place. Or, perhaps, they simply look away. The word, underlining the illumination, is *videbam*. This Latin word in the first person calls attention to the act of looking, to an act that, imperfect or inceptive, is also unfinished: *I was seeing* or perhaps, *I began to see*. But to see what? As presented here, the solitary word has nothing to qualify it.[12] It is the act of looking that is underlined, sight itself. Attention is therefore directed back from the word to the illumination. What the viewer sees, and what the artist has seen, are seemingly the same. This is an act of double witnessing in the present tense.

The kneeling figure is as unaware of this sequence of 'looks' as he is of the executioner and king themselves. Having turned his back on his companions, the condemned man is not engaged with the objects of the world given in the illumination nor with the possible shame of its inhabitants. In fact, his eyes are closed. In this gesture, this world is emptied of significance. Just as he has been distanced by the artist from the world of the picture, so he has equally been cut off from the world of the spectator. With eyes closed, the figure whose hands are locked in prayer frustrates the gaze of the observer, refusing to return it. The observer as spectator is simply an onlooker at the scene of an execution, one of many possible spectators, and seemingly unworthy of the attention of the man about to be executed. The two worlds of the picture and of the spectator become one in their insignificance for the man who kneels and prays – even before the moment of his impending

1 Odinet Godran, 'Expositio Mortis Thomae Mori'.

death, he is already absent from them. This kneeling figure is
Thomas More, the man in blue is Henry VIII, and the occasion is
More's execution on 6 July 1535.[13]

I would like to begin with a consideration of one of the ways
in which this image has been 'read' in the past. Stanley Morison
makes the following comment: 'Vivid though it is, the miniature
has clearly no relation to any portrait of More based on reality.'[14]
Part of what seems to disturb Morison is the handling of the
subject matter, and it is odd to call this a portrait, or even to
compare it with portraits. Morison chooses not to reproduce the
image in his book, and what leads him to dismiss it with only a
brief description of the scene depicted is signalled by his use of the
word 'reality'. Since he was obviously not present at the execution
himself, Morison is depending upon a specific body of knowledge
as the source for the picture, and this leads him into a more general
statement about the status of More's execution in the latter years
of the sixteenth century:

> already at the end of his own century, More's death and the circum-
> stances of it were not remembered by a world habituated to
> savagery – where persecution was normal everywhere in every Chris-
> tian sect that had the power. It was More's literary works that were
> commemorated, not the cause for which he died. Outside Rome there
> was no interest in More's martyrdom. Not only so, but the Catholics
> themselves were forgetful of More's execution.[15]

This forgetfulness is explained by Morison as a consequence of
the persecutions in England of both Protestants and Catholics that
took place under Mary and Elizabeth. He suggests that these suf-
ferings were so fresh in the minds of the faithful that by the end
of the century it was 'too late' to assert the martyrdom of More,
John Fisher and the Carthusians.[16]

There is much in this that is questionable, both on the level of
factual accuracy, and, of more immediate concern here, in the
presuppositions upon which Morison's argument is predicated.[17]
Morison's reproduction of the image is withheld on the basis of a
perceived non-identity of reality and representation. Throughout
his book on the posthumous pictorial representations of More,
Morison has frequent recourse to concepts of authenticity. Such
authenticity seems to rely on a perceived mimetic relationship
between the details of More's execution and the representation

produced, and images are accorded value by Morison in respect of their approximation to the known details of More's life and death. For Morison the origin of the work of art, then, may be located in the known and remembered world, a world in which memory functions unproblematically as a transparent and stable faculty which records in a literal (rather than a figural) manner. Morison's reading of the image, or rather his failure to produce a reading in any strong sense, exemplifies what seems, I think, to be a somewhat simplistic form of historicism, which seeks to locate meaning in an accessible 'historical' moment unmediated by his own perception of it.

Of course, Morison is right to stress the divergence of the Godran picture from what is now known of More's death. In the first *Life of More*, written by his son-in-law William Roper in the 1550s, we are told:

> so was he [More] by m*aster* Leiuetenaunte brought out of the Tower, *and* from thence led towardes the place of execution. Where, goinge uppe the scaffold, which was so weake that it was ready to fall, he saide merilye to m*aster* Leiuetenaunte: 'I pray you, m*aster* Leiuetenaunte, see me salf uppe, *and* for my cominge downe let me shifte for my self'.[18]

Roper writes of 'all the people thereabout', and Nicholas Harpsfield's only slightly later account adds details of those who met More on his route to execution, including a woman concerned about the evidence for a case in which she is involved.[19] More despatches her with a joke, pointing out that the King will soon relieve him of concern with worldly business. The chronicler Edward Hall supplies the observation that More was 'brought to the Skaffolde on the Tower hill where on a blocke his head was striken from his shoulders'.[20] Morison thus has a reasonable amount of information about the execution upon which to base his judgement of the Godran picture. Yet in dismissing this illumination, Morison not only invokes a conception of the truth in representation that we may wish to question, but also runs the risk of an anachronistic expectation. Whoever the artist responsible for the production of the Godran picture may have been, it is likely that the account of the execution used as a basis for the illumination pre-dates those that I have just cited, since the picture is unlikely to have been produced by an eye-witness. (I will return to this idea of witnessing in the context of this image later.) Although it circulated in manuscript, Roper's text was not printed until 1626, forty years after the terminal date for the picture (since Godran died in 1581), and Harpsfield's account – while also circulating in manuscript – did not appear in print until 1932. Both texts drew upon a more accessible source, namely the so-called *Paris News Letter*, which appeared very soon after the execution and was quickly disseminated in various translations across Europe. This text gives only the slightest detail of the execution:

> he was beheaded in the open space in front of the Tower. A little before his death he asked those present to pray to God for him and he would do the same for them . . . He then besought them earnestly to pray to God to give the King good counsel, protesting that he died his faithful servant, but God's first.[21]

Let us look again at the picture. The kneeling figure in the portrait is a young, beardless man, recalling but cancelling the joke preserved initially in Hall's text about More's beard, in which he asks the executioner to be careful not to cut it, since *it* has not offended the king. In Godran's picture, the axe has been transformed into a sword, and there is no block on which the victim could lay his head. Indeed, there is no scaffold that More could ascend, with or without the help of 'master leiuetenaunte'. Further, the Godran scene accords with European styles of execution, not English ones, and this is confirmed by the number of depictions of the executions of kneeling figures by men with large swords in European artworks.[22] Similarly, the setting is quite clearly not the Tower of London as any eye-witness would recognise it.

Having suggested that addressing the possible specificity of the context of the Godran illumination's production can help to elucidate something of the image's relationship to mimesis, I would like to propose that it is precisely the image's *denial* of specificity that should prompt the next stage of our reading. If Morison's interpretation denies aspects of the specificity of the moment of production, the work itself denies that of the moment represented. For example, contrasting Godran's representation with that of Antoine Caron (dated circa 1590), we see in Caron's work an ambiguous attempt to remain 'true' to the documentary evidence. Morison is happy to reproduce the Caron picture in his book, and indeed makes a strong claim for its inclusion, despite the idiosyncrasies of guards in Roman armour and a conventional temporal conceit allowing the artist to show both More's procession to the scaffold in the foreground and the execution itself in the background.[23] Caron, like the artist of the Godran scene, shows a kneeling executionee rather than the use of a block, but what is most strikingly different about the Caron version is the presence of the crowd. Caron's picture is evidently not invested with the same relationship towards 'authenticity' as Godran's image, and it clearly communicates the social dimension of punitive practice.

Caron's markedly different version must be seen as a romanticisation of the standard accounts to be found in Roper and others, but unlike the Godran picture it does not appear to be so wilfully

2 Antoine Caron, 'The Arrest and Supplication of Sir Thomas More (1478–1535)'.

discordant with Morison's conception of 'reality'. While it may be possible to explain the Godran picture in terms of its putative source in a written text which imparted little material to the illuminator, other more revealing motivations suggest themselves. The Godran illumination is not so much a representation as an icon, allowing elements such as the tree and the water to be read as symbolic. The water may be taken for an image of cleansing, of the washing away of guilt and sins, and the tree may be seen as a symbol both of life and knowledge, of death and rebirth. The kneeling figure of More, already seemingly in the space between one world and the next, is framed in his distanciation from the specificity of his execution by the repetition of the endlessly graftable symbols of an ahistorical Christian continuum. The act of remembrance attested to by the artwork is analogous to the comment of Thomas Stapleton in his 1588 biography of More:

> let us speak of More, the great and glorious martyr. But as it is not the death but the cause that makes the martyr, we will be at pains to make the cause clear, all the more that hitherto it has not been thoroughly understood by foreign writers.[24]

The repetition of a phrase also to be found in Augustine – 'quod martyres veros non faciat poena, sed causa' – marks the existence of a tradition and aligns both Stapleton's text and More's death with the centrality of the Catholic 'cause'. [25] The necessity of contextualization in terms of a cause if the death is to carry the 'correct' significance is emphasised since 'foreign' writers have misunderstood the cause itself.

Behind Morison's denial of the Godran picture lies an identification of the artwork as dependent upon its concordance with a notion of mimesis which can be characterised as a reflection of a known and remembered reality.[26] If we are reluctant to discard this representation, as Morison does, then a movement beyond this limited form of mimesis is necessary, and leads us to posit a characteristic of artworks in essence, not simply in this specific example. In other words, this becomes recognisable as an allegorical figure. The allegorical nature of the artwork, its capacity (following the etymology of allegory) for saying something 'other', is implicit in the icon. This should come as no great surprise. As Derrida reminds us, *icon* may be translated as *allegory*.[27]

III

In one respect, the Godran image is far from unique. More's exemplary status has frequently been offered as the motivation for his execution, if we think of example here as in the phrase 'to be made an example of'. Indeed, it has been suggested that the posthumous representation of More is simply the continuation of a process that More himself set in motion. Clark Hulse relates this commodification and exchange to role-playing. With verbal echoes of Greenblatt's and of Richard Marius's readings of More, Hulse makes a distinction between More's ability to play a variety of self-chosen symbolic roles whilst alive, and his posthumous subjection to the desires of others:

> More proclaims himself a character in the Renaissance theater of individuality, and yet makes himself into a symbol first of humanist reform, then of ecclesiastical resistance, and finally of endurance in the face of annihilation. Alive he can wrestle with his own thingness – his body, his desires, his roles and obligations. Dead, he is altogether a thing for others to use, a bodily metaphor in the struggle between the Church and the king, or, in our own era, a floating sign in the struggles to define the utopian element in humanism. His portraits, whether in paint or in writing, are signs of signs that are produced, circulated, and consumed in furtherance of this transformation of the body into metaphor and the incorporation of metaphors into the body.[28]

More begins here as a series of living self-created symbols (of humanism, Catholicism and martyrdom), becoming a bodily metaphor (of the battle for spiritual sovereignty), and, more recently, a floating sign (of humanism again, this time in a utopian form). We are thus presented with a movement from an ideality of the self as symbol, through a pragmatic application of the other as metaphor, to an ideality of the other as sign. The proper name of 'Thomas More' thus names the figural enunciation of a man as a symbol, as a paradigm. Yet this process begins, in Hulse's analysis, with More, as he brings himself into contradiction with his self-casting in the 'theater of individuality' through his diminution of that very individuality as 'merely' symbolic. Thus the concentration of the biographers upon the exemplarity of More's life can be seen as a continuation of a process begun by More himself. Circulating for the most part in secret and in manuscript, the portraits and biographies of More act as substitute bodies, as relics in their own right.[29] The representation of the life becomes simultaneously an exhumation and a burial: the paradigm is unearthed as the singularity of the life that purportedly lies behind it is covered. Recalling the Hegelian emphasis on metaphor, symbol and interiorisation, Hulse's reading of More appears to be a continuation of a romantic aesthetic, in which subject and object come together in a unity of sense. The theatre of individuality in which More played a part during and after his lifetime is thus aligned with the narrative of modernity seen in the first part of this book.

Hulse's explanation of events is consistent, however, with the account given by Nicolas Sander, writing in 1585, who suggests that More's role was crucial in terms of public perception of the religious controversy surrounding Henry VIII's supremacy. Such importance was emphasised by More's lay status, making him, if anything, more significant than those clergy (such as John Fisher, Bishop of Rochester) who resisted the break with papal authority:

> The bishop of Rochester and Sir Thomas More were still in prison [in June 1535]: two most shining lights of all England, and towards whom men's eyes and thought were directed. Henry was well aware of this, and was therefore the more desirous of winning them over to his side, especially Sir Thomas More, who, being a layman, was more in favour with lay people, and for very good reasons, because no such layman had ever been born in England. Henry, too, liked laymen better, and was more afraid of them.[30]

More is seen in both general and singular aspects; he is a layman, and thus has a strong connection with other laymen (general), but there has never been another layman like him (singular). His significance comes both from the 'eyes and thought' directed towards him, and from the attentions of the King, who reacts to More (as he does to all laymen) with a mixture of inclination and fear. This is endorsed by Stapleton, who comments that 'The King's efforts [to get him to subscribe to the supremacy] show how much he esteemed More'.[31] More is thus exemplary before his death, as well as susceptible to exemplary exploitation after death.[32]

That the preferred method for making such an example should be public execution should not be surprising. In his essay 'On the art of conversation', Montaigne remarks upon the practice of punishing criminals, and he also draws upon notions of exemplarity:

> It is a custom of our justice to punish some as a warning to others. For to punish them for *having done* wrong would, as Plato says, be stupid: what is done cannot be undone. The intention is to stop them from repeating the same mistake or to make others avoid their error. We do not improve the man we hang: we improve others by him.[33]

To perform on the scaffold is not a matter of self-fashioning, then, but of the fashioning of others. Exemplarity overrides individuality. Montaigne's reference is to Plato's *Laws*: 'The purpose of the penalty is not to cancel the crime – what is once done can never be made undone – but to bring the criminal and all who witness his punishment in the future to complete renunciation of such criminality, or at least to recovery in great part from the dreadful state.'[34] Punishment is responsive, but this response is both to a prior transgression of the law, and to any potential repetition of that offence.[35] What both Montaigne and Plato make clear is the exemplary nature of punishment, and Plato's emphasis on witnessing marks the necessity for this example to be both communicated – made public and thus open to witnessing and interpretation – and remembered. The example is delivered to forestall the repetition of error, and is thus intended towards the future, yet it achieves this through a mobilisation of memory, which is primarily intended towards the past. This dual focus on past and future is what we might call the law of exemplarity, and it is already possible to see how the rhetorical use of examples (as explained by Puttenham) comes together with the political use.

Exemplarity formalises the intrication of the singular with law, since the example must be both unique and iterable. Thus within a given series (or law) the specific must be exchangeable through repetition. There is a curious logic at work here, since for a law to be a law it must apply to more than a single case, yet it can only ever be the sum of its actual and potential applications. Law is thus produced as a *relation* between singularities. In this, there are parallels with my earlier discussions of both literature and women's writing, in which the question of relation becomes central rather than the identification of or with subjects or objects (see pp. 62–4 and 120–2). It is this logic of exemplarity that disturbs the unity of subject and object that lies behind Hulse's reading of

More's posthumous reputation. We are brought back again to the problems associated with knowing how to read in a rhetorical mode without losing the singularity of the example. Samuel Weber has attempted to relate this logic of relation to the question of context:

> the tension inherent in this concept [exemplarity] is already tangible, legible, in the etymology of the word. What is *ex-emplary* is *taken out* of its initial context, and this in a double sense. It is taken to an *extreme* and yet, at the same time in so being transported, it appears to be *more itself* than ever before.[36]

As in Derrida's essay on the signature that was mentioned in Chapter 5, it must be possible for any particular context (initial or otherwise) to be broken with for the exemplary function to be possible. Exemplarity is thus dependent upon repetition and memory, just as these two terms imply each other without simply collapsing into one another: repetition implies the memory of something that has already happened, but also faces the potential future occurrence of an event (in memory) which will render that past present *as past*. Weber, following Kierkegaard, speaks of this 'remembering ahead', which entails a paradox more complex than a simple recollection of the past: 'As potentiality and possibility of the future, remembering "ahead" opens the way to the return of what has never been present as such and which therefore, in a certain sense, remains ever yet to come.'[37] The past precisely can never have been present *as past*, and thus falls into the future anterior – it always *will have been* – as it simultaneously reveals the necessary difference that intervenes between the moments of 'event' and 'return'. Repetition is thus iteration, in Derrida's sense. Even the writing of history (or Puttenham's historicall poesy) has to recognise that this opening to the future makes the truth of that history not relative but relational, that is, this truth has a performative and thus rhetorical dimension.

IV

At this point it seems pertinent to ask what truth a given form of exemplarity may deliver. We need to look back towards the textual tradition of More biography, in which precisely this debate about the truth of an example is staged. Ro:Ba:'s prefatory epistle 'To the Courteous Reader' stresses both More's potential for use as an example and the tradition of Christian representation within which that potential might be actualised:

> It hath bene an ancient and a commendable custome in the Church of god, and noe lesse laudable then profitable, alwaies to have had a speciall care that the lives and deaths of godes sainctes and martyrs should be with care and fidelitie registred and recorded to all faithfull posteritie.[38]

Ro:Ba: seeks to locate his *Lyfe of More* within this tradition, offering the Church as provider of both interpretative context and target audience, since it is the faithful to whom his work is addressed. This identification with institutional practice is also clear in his use of quotation, including both The Epistle of Paul the Apostle to the Hebrews 13.7 – ' "Remember your ministers or rulers who have spoken to you the word of god; beholding the end of theire conversation, imitate theire faith" ' (p. 7) – and Augustine:

> 'The consideration of the lives and deaths of godes Sainctes produceth this wholesome effect: *ut in eadem fidei regula permaneamus*, that we should continue our selves in the same rule of faith'; 'for', saith this docter in an other place, lib. 2, cap.10, *contra Iulianum*, the Pelagian, 'that which they found in the Church, that they hold fast; that which they learned they taught; that which they received of theire fathers they delivered to theire Children.' (p. 8)

These two quotations each send the reader in the same direction: the reading or hearing of the text has material effects. Language prompts repetition, becoming the spur to action, transforming the self through imitation of the virtuous life, and altering the other through the pedagogic transmission of that example.

The implicit model of a performative and transformative textuality that Ro:Ba:'s use of quotation suggests is made explicit as he attempts to describe the effects produced. Exemplarity implies repetition, and such repetition in this context must be seen as corrective, as a movement towards the form of perfection offered by texts such as *The Imitation of Christ*, which seems to be the same as that suggested by Ro:Ba:'s text:

> This ingendereth a generous emulation whereby we are sweetly entised and urged to immittate theire [those represented's] vertues.

> The example of others is very forcible, yea, it useth secret violence
> to drawe mans nature to good or evell; for an example given is, as
> it were, a table or a booke written with great Capitall letters, to be
> seene and admyred both of learned and unlerned; and in a breefe
> and compendious manner it performeth what with long instructions
> and many discourses mans witt other wise might laboure to per-
> swade. (pp. 8–9)

The force of the example, its 'secret violence', prompts consideration of the repression necessary in any process of biographical
or historical construction or reconstruction. This violence is
originary, creative in its destruction, following a certain logic of
sacrifice. In Ro:Ba:'s schema, we see that imperfection is to be
conquered, not merely to be understood through comparison with
the purity of the virtuous. The example acts as a powerful synecdoche, effectively silencing other voices (those described as 'long
instructions and many discourses'), and the generosity of emulation lies in the openness of the emulator to the violence of the
exemplary. Ro:Ba:'s recognition of the possible force of bad examples, those which may lead a man to evil, reiterates his belief in
the importance of fidelity in representation, and suggests a desire
to limit his stock of examples to those possessed of virtue. In this
suggestion we are returned once again to the problem of rhetoric's
potentially amoral force. The materiality of language is clearly
expressed in Ro:Ba:'s choice of metaphor to convey the power of
the exemplary: an example given is a book written in capital
letters. He clearly has a great investment, then, in *writing* a life of
More, and one which is shared with the emphasis on memory as
an ethical force in the rhetorical treatises.

If the importance of the exemplary figure is in its transformative
power, then this places a great deal of responsibility on the writer,
since the virtue of the figure must be projected through the representation she or he creates. In the opening quotation from the
preface above, Ro:Ba: stresses 'care' and 'fidelitie' in life-writing,
but he seems uneasy with this obligation. Although keen to emphasise the value of the labour of life-writing (p. 10), he is equally
keen to confess his unoriginality as a writer, claiming that: 'the
most part of this booke is none of my owne; I onely chalenge the
ordering and translating' (p. 14).[39] Ro:Ba:'s sense of fidelity is thus
registered in his reliance upon prior codings of More's life; his care
is expressed in the organisation of the narrative. R. W. Chambers

writes of Ro:Ba:'s work that, 'in some ways it is the best *Life of More*. The writer is more than a mere translator and compiler'.[40] Equally, both Helen White and Michael Anderegg note the contribution of Ro:Ba: to the tradition of More biography as an important but not particularly original one, suggesting that he adds little in the way of new material, but acknowledging that his rewriting is of a high quality. Anderegg offers the suggestion that this quality may in fact be the product of Ro:Ba:'s lack of originality:

> if neither Roper's nor Harpsfield's biographies were extant, Ro.Ba.'s work would have to be considered one of the most brilliant of Renaissance prose texts; but clearly, without Harpsfield, and through Harpsfield, Roper, a great part of what is best in Ro.Ba. would not exist.[41]

The text's status for Anderegg is diminished by its reliance upon earlier material; it would be brilliant, but unfortunately that quality is derivative. White is equally convinced that Ro:Ba:'s achievement is modest, but for her it is an entirely creditable one, and she notes that his biography brought valuable material from Thomas Stapleton's Latin *Life of More* to an English-speaking audience for the first time.[42] For both White and Anderegg, then, the value of the text originates in its lack of originality.

Thus Ro:Ba:'s text, which centres upon the question of imitation, is itself necessarily and avowedly imitative both of other *Lives* of More and of More's 'life'. In a dazzlingly dense passage Ro:Ba: expresses his opinion of why More is a suitable subject for commemoration:

> I intend by godes grace to write the historie of a Confessour, Doctour and Martyr, so famous, so learned, so glorious, that what in the vast Ocean of Anceant recordes may be found to pleasure or profitt, here in this one life shalbe comprehended; here we shall learne what love and feare we owe unto god, what Charitie and Justice we owe to our neighbour, what moderation and temperance to our selves. For this Saincts life is a mart where everie spirituall merchant may compendiously fraught his barke with varitie of vertues: young men may find modestie, old men wisdome, learned cunning, ignorant instruction, fathers discretion, Children obedience, Lawyers conscience, Rulers Justice, Subjetes fidelitie, Rich pittie, poore patience, and every man in his calling his dutie and devoire. It may seeme strange that so many rare gifts and vertues are seated in one brest. But knowe, his

> witt was excellent, his learning greater, but his vertues overmatched
> them both; for nature, nurture and grace eache strived to make him
> pearlesse. But the predominant must have the prize. So we may say
> he was loving, carefull, faithfull, wise, eloquent, learned, discreet,
> grave; a father, Citizen and Magistrate. But in this consisteth his
> cheefe prayse: he was a holy and a godly man, a resolute and a con-
> stant martyr, his beginning all happie, his proceedinges prosperous,
> but his end knit upp all in glorie and tryumphe. (pp. 11–12)

More's life, and by extension Ro:Ba:'s *Lyfe*, allows the reader to
comprehend the content of the entire series of Christian life histories: one exemplary life encompasses all. Thomas More is not
simply within the Christian tradition, his life is a synecdoche of that
tradition's total content. His is the truly exemplary example. The
pedagogic potential is foremost in Ro:Ba:'s description, with the
accent upon comprehension and learning. This pedagogy is
in the service of a network of institutional structures, and the
lessons are suitable for young and old, rich and poor, rulers and
subjects alike. Modesty, wisdom, cunning, instruction, discretion,
obedience, conscience, justice, fidelity, pity, patience, duty and
'devoire': these are the qualities which may be attained through a
reading of the *Lyfe of More*. Social distinction is established, since
each quality is identified as lacking in a specific grouping, but such
differentiation is dissolved in Ro:Ba:'s concluding comments: More's
chief virtue is his faith, which transcends all other distinctions.

I would like for the moment to concentrate upon two of the
terms concatenated in Ro:Ba:'s list: justice and fidelity. These are
given as the aspects lacking in rulers and subjects respectively.
Justice is also what we owe to our neighbours, and is, therefore,
a social responsibility. As we have seen, Ro:Ba: cites fidelity as one
of the necessary requisites of life-writing. A link may thus be
established between a desired form of subjecthood and the practice
of biographical representation. This relationship seems to be performative, as I have suggested, since the biographical text enacts
a violent perfection of the faithful reader. What Ro:Ba: suggests
here, as in his earlier statements on the necessity of tradition pro-
viding an interpretative context, is a structure of law. Law may be
interpreted as that force of preservation which limits violence
within a given society, justified by its own inauguration as the most
powerful force at a given moment.[43] Law uses sanctioned violence
to control unsanctioned violence, assuring its continuity by a

refusal to allow its own originary force to be used against itself. Tradition is law, but it is not justice; indeed, the persistence of tradition through repetition of an originary violence is precisely that which forestalls justice. Justice must be singular, that is, unique to each case brought before it, and cannot, therefore, take the form of a law. As Walter Benjamin comments: 'For ends that for one situation are just, universally acceptable, and valid, are so for no other situation, no matter how similar it may be in other respects.'[44] Law is performative rather than 'afformative', originarily involved in a positing of law which decays with each attempt at its conservation.[45] This law places obligations upon those subject to it, and this includes a responsibility for the writer of a life. Ro: Ba:'s desire to inflict secret violence upon his readers is thus a conscious alignment with a mechanism of law. The spiritual merchant takes his place in an economy of truth.

But law, as Ro:Ba: himself indicates, does not equal justice. Justice may be learnt, and by extension taught, from the example of More, and this is no doubt reinforced by his position as former Lord Chancellor. More's complex relationship to legal violence makes it unclear whether his exemplary power comes from his status as lawyer or as traitor.[46] If we turn to his martyrdom, there are certain difficulties created by his exemplary status. The closing words of Ro:Ba:'s preface, 'Read, imitate', express the interconnection of text and performance, identifying text as event. The importance of tradition for Ro:Ba: as a framing structure for this performance is clear in the light of what has already been identified as a defining principle for martyrdom: it is not the death but the cause that makes the martyr. The anxiety which lies behind this focus upon the cause is related to the possibility that men may die for causes other than that of the 'true' faith. Robert Southwell's statement of the problem is clear: 'if all were Martyrs that die for their Religion, then many heresies both contrary amongst themselves and repugnant to the evident Doctrines of Christ should be truthes; which is impossible'.[47] Thus it must be not simply a cause, but *the* cause, the *true* cause, which guarantees the truth of martyrdom. (This might also trouble considerations of the truth of *martyria* as a figure.) This is stated by Southwell in the form of a supplemental question: 'How is it possible, for them to have the truth of Martyrdome that want the truth of Christ?'[48] The two forms of truth are thus differentiated, but with determining authority invested in faith such that the truth of martyrdom is seen to be merely an aspect of the truth of Christ.

If we pursue Southwell's identification of the epistemological significance and complexity of martyrdom, recognising also that this is what is at stake in Ro:Ba:'s focus upon the rule of faith and upon pedagogy, we must pose questions about the truth of martyrdom and about the truth of imitation. As in the case of the reading of the Godran image, we can pursue this in two divergent directions, depending on where we locate the 'truth' of a representation. Inevitably, this raises the problematic of the relationship of truth to mimesis itself. Mimesis is central to commemoration and memory, and as Jonathan Culler, following and explicating Derrida, has argued:

> Mimesis and *mnémè* (memory) are closely related – memory is a form of mimesis or representation – and mimesis is articulated upon the concept of truth. When truth is conceived as *aletheia*, the unveiling or making present of what has been hidden, then mimesis is the representation necessary to this process, the doubling which enables something to present itself. When truth is not *aletheia* but *homoiosis*, adequation or correspondence, then mimesis is the relation between an image or representation and that to which it may truly correspond.[49]

Culler is drawing most obviously here, as he notes himself at this point, upon Derrida's *Dissemination*, in which he writes that, 'mimesis, all through the history of its interpretation, is always commanded by the process of truth', either as *aletheia* or as *homoiosis*. In the case of *aletheia*, truth is produced (literally 'unveiled') through writing, in *homoiosis* writing is true because of its correspondence with a given object, which is itself already 'known' to be 'true'. Derrida also notes that *homoiosis*, in setting up a relationship between two terms (which goes to the heart of reference and, therefore, representation), may be translated as imitation.[50] Truth as imitation must be seen in its dual significance in Ro:Ba:'s desire for exemplarity; both as principle of textual production and as intended effect. However, *aletheia* brings us closer than *homoiosis* to the essence of truth, despite the favouring of *homoiosis* in the Scholastic and Patristic philosophy, transmitted by Augustine and Aquinas, that is based on Aristotle. Simply stated, we must have access to the true object against which the 'true' statement (or representation) may be judged. The truth of martyrdom and the representation of that truth in the *lives* of martyrs double this bifurcated epistemological foundation. The relationship of truth to martyrdom is best understood by reference to *aletheia* since, as Elizabeth Hanson has suggested, it is based upon an epistemology of discovery.[51] Life-writing, on the other hand, is a matter of *homoiosis*, a discourse which pertains to a pure referentiality (fidelity) that it can never deliver.

In looking for Ro:Ba:'s sense of the truth of More's martyrdom, the representation of More's execution would seem to be an obvious point of entry, and will bring us back towards the Godran image with which we started. The actual moment of the death is described simply:

> So with one blowe of an axe his sweet soule passed out of this world unto Almightie God, the verie same daye that he most desired, and before foretold, to witt, the Octaves of Sainct Peter, the Eve of Sainct Thomas, the 6 of Julie in the yeare of our lord 1535, in the 27th yeare of the Raigne of king Henery the 8, and the yeare of his age 55 or 56, as so me say. (p. 262)[52]

Ro:Ba: gives great detail about the occasion, placing the execution in a series of parallel chronologies, but tells us little about the death itself. More's desire for death is shown but there is nothing of the pain, of the blood or the reactions of the crowd. Here, Ro:Ba: is demonstrably adhering to the tradition of representations from Roper to Stapleton which I discussed earlier in relation to the Godran illumination. Ro:Ba: repeats More's own statement (which is also to be found in Stapleton's text): 'A man may loose his head, and take no harme' (p. 263), and this quotation follows immediately on from the relation of the execution, proffering an interpretation authorised by intertextual reference. Interpretation substitutes for representation, and violence lingers behind a veil woven from the threads of Christian eschatology, political comment and classical allusion. The execution is associated with temporal markers, as part of the Christian calendar of saints, and the Julian calendar, and as an event in the reign of Henry VIII. Only finally is it an event which may be inexactly (that is, both indeterminately and inaccurately) placed by reference to More's own life. Violence, in its physical manifestation as More's execution, is communicated only as the movement of an axe through the air and the movement of a soul towards heaven. There is no edge to the executioner's axe, the blow it strikes generates a flow not of blood but of ink.[53]

V

Let us return to the image with which we began. The act of witnessing that Christian allegory demands depends upon paradox as a necessary condition of its possibility. In presenting the execution, the illuminator of the Godran manuscript offers up Thomas More to judgement. Having been judged once by the legal process, More is given as an offering, as a sacrifice, and is given to a further judgement by the observers of the picture. More witnessed or testified to his belief in the truth of the Catholic faith, and for this he was executed. We witness this execution and, in so doing, become witnesses to an act of witnessing. In this way, the illumination provokes a consideration of the act of witnessing and of judging itself. Encouraged to see the execution from the martyr's point of view (and we must remember the etymological link between 'witness' and 'martyr', from a root which also becomes 'video'), for the viewer, More figures in this picture not only as that to be judged but also as the one who judges.

In the painting, More's eyes are closed, the king's and the executioner's are averted. Each has blinded himself to the activity in which they are collectively engaged. Here, there may be an allusion to St Thomas, the sceptic whose salvation from spiritual blindness led to the invocation of his help in cases of physical blindness. More's blindness speaks: in his witnessing he dissociates himself from that which he witnesses to open up a critical, judgemental distance. The picture offers up not only More, but also his judges, to judgement. The representation of the act of judgement prompts a consideration of the criteria of judgement. Derrida proposes that blindness is a necessary part of witnessing:

> Turning into martyrdom, and thus into witnessing, blindness is often the price to pay for anyone who must finally open some eyes, his own or another's, in order to recover a natural sight or gain access to a spiritual light. The paradox stems from the fact that the blind man thus becomes the best witness, a chosen witness. In fact, a witness, as such, is always blind. Witnessing substitutes narrative for perception. The witness cannot see, show, and speak at the same

time, and the interest of the attestation, like that of the testament, stems from this dissociation. No authentification can show in the present what the most reliable of witnesses sees, or rather, has seen and now keeps in memory.[54]

Derrida thus offers us a supplementary paradox, the paradox that it is the blind who can most clearly see. The necessary absence of the object of perception, of the action witnessed, at the moment of testimony brings us again to questions of memory and representation. More's self-blinding to the world around him allows him to see the world beyond. This accords with Stapleton's later description of the execution in which he states that More covered his own eyes when on the scaffold, and explains the significance of this act: 'By binding his eyes he had just cut himself off from the sight of men, but now at once he reaches the open vision of God and the angels.'[55] His decapitation and terminal blindness allow More to bear witness to a greater spiritual light. The eyes of the king and the executioner, though they may be averted, must remain open. Their gaze is fixed on their world, however much they may look beyond the frame. By insisting on seeking a correspondence between the image and reality, Morison's reading repeats this absorption with a known and stable world, that is, with the world in which More was executed.

VI

A further and final image will help me to clarify the understanding promised by illumination. In the Caron painting, almost in the centre of the canvas and turned a little away from us, there is a shield, and on that shield the figure of the Medusa. In the figure of the Medusa we see a concatenation of sight and decapitation. To look at the Medusa face to face, to meet her eyes, is to invite petrifaction and to become as blind as a statue. Sight, a form of witnessing, may lead to blindness, but the testimony of the witness and the power of the Medusa's gaze is immortalised in stone. Witnessing itself, sight itself, is simultaneously commemorated and linked to punishment. Blindness as punishment is a common fate for witnesses. The mythological solution is decapitation. Again punishment is linked to sight, but the gaze of the Gorgon elicits a desire to dis-member rather than to re-member. Remembrance would be inappropriate, however, since, even beheaded, the Gorgon has the power to induce blindness – the gaze of the Medusa is still effective; even after decapitation the Medusa can see and be seen. The gaze that immortalizes through witnessing and the gaze that immortalizes by turning to stone are equally dangerous.

The story that the Medusa serves, the injunction to an indirect gaze, to a gaze that does not bring the witness and the witnessed face to face, recapitulates the allegorical nature of the artwork. The safety of a saying of the other, or of a witnessing of the other, is only guaranteed in this oblique approach. The forgetting of historical detail in iconographic representation, then, is not a weakness or an oversight. It is an ineluctable feature of remembering. Morison's rejection of the Godran picture on the basis of its disparity with the known details of More's execution fails to take into account the nature of testimony. The role of memory in witnessing, and the representation of that memory in the artwork, makes any rigid or simple attachment to mimesis as the representation of the real untenable. One of the clearest defintions of faith has always told us this: 'Now faith is the substance of things hoped for, the evidence of things not seen' (Hebrews 11. 1, Authorised King James Version). The icon is blind, but in its darkness it sheds light upon its allegorical otherness, and through the icon we, like Godran, may say *videbam*, 'I began to see'.

Notes

1 J. Reinhard Lupton, *Afterlives of the Saints: Hagiography, Typology, and Renaissance Literature* (Stanford: Stanford University Press, 1996).

2 Lever, *The Historie of the Defendors of the Catholique Faith* (London: 1627), pp. 67–8.

3 Lever, *Historie*, pp. 16–17. The rhetoric of blindness is pervasive, and is also to be found in the dedicatory epistle to William Cecil that prefaces Ralph Robinson's first English translation of More's *Utopia* in 1551: 'This only I say, that it is much to be lamented of all, and not only of us Englishmen, that a man of such incomparable wit, of so profound knowledge, of so absolute learning, and of so fine eloquence, was yet nevertheless so much blinded, rather with obstinacy than with ignorance, that he could not, or rather would not, see the shining light of God's holy truth in certain principal points of Christian religion.'

4 Miller, *Topographies* (Stanford: Stanford University Press, 1995), p. 239.

5 *Rhetorica ad Herennium*, trans. H. Caplan (Cambridge, MA: Harvard University Press, 1954), p. 231.

6 T. Wilson, *The Arte of Rhetorique* (London: 1553), p. cci^v.

7 Puttenham, *The Arte of English Poesie*, ed. G. D. Willcock and A. Walker (Cambridge: Cambridge University Press, 1970), p. 39.

8 T. Eagleton, *Sweet Violence: The Idea of the Tragic* (Oxford: Blackwell, 2003), p. xiv.

9 L. Wittgenstein, *The Blue and Brown Books: Preliminary Studies for the 'Philosophical Investigations'* (Oxford: Blackwell, 2003), p. 68, emphasis original. See also, among many comments worthy of more sustained investigation: 'You learned the *concept* "pain" when you learned language'. *Philosophical Investigations*, trans. G. E. M. Anscombe, 3rd edn (Oxford: Blackwell, 2001), §384.

10 E. Scarry, *The Body in Pain: The Making and Unmaking of the World* (Oxford: Oxford University Press, 1985), p. 3.

11 I am thinking here of the kind of material reproduced in J. H. Pollen (ed.), *Unpublished Documents Relating to the English Martyrs, 1584–1603* (London: Catholic Record Society, 1908).

12 The sentence, of course, continues, but the first word stands alone and is separated from the rest of the text, giving its connection to the image explicit priority. I retain this prioritisation throughout this chapter.

13 See 'Expositio Mortis Thomae Mori', MS BL Additional 28786, fol. 4^r. It is attributed to Odinet Godran, at one time President of the Parliament of Burgundy. For information on Godran, see the entry under 'Jean Godran' in *Bibliothèque des Auteurs de Bourgogne, par feu M. L'Abbé Papillon, Chanoine de la Chapelle au Riche de Dijon* (Geneva: Slatkine, 1970), pp. 259–260; and the entry for Odinet's brother, Charles Godran, in *Dictionnaire de Biographie Française* (Paris: Letouzey et Ané, 1985).

14 S. Morison, *The Likeness of Thomas More: An Iconographical Survey of Three Centuries* (London: Burns and Oates, 1963), p. 42.

15 Morison, *The Likeness of Thomas More*, p. 45.

16 P. Burke, 'How to Be a Counter-Reformation Saint', in *Religion and Society in Early Modern Europe*, ed. K. von Greyerz (London: Allen & Unwin, 1984), pp. 45–55.

17 Morison's claim is inaccurate because he is too concerned with print culture. The lives of More by Roper and Harpsfield circulated in manuscript, and the majority of surviving copies are in late sixteenth or early seventeenth-century hands, the play *Sir Thomas More* is likely to have been first written in the early 1590s, Stapleton's life is

dated to 1588, and Ro:Ba:'s to 1599. There was still sufficient interest for Cresacre More to produce another life in 1630. Outside both Rome and England there was much activity. See the entries in R. W. Gibson, *St Thomas More: A Preliminary Bibliography of his Works and of Moreana to the Year 1750* (New Haven: Yale University Press, 1961).

18 W. Roper, *The Lyfe of Sir Thomas Moore, knighte*, ed. E. V. Hitchcock (Oxford: Oxford University Press, 1958), pp. 102–3.

19 N. Harpsfield, *Life of More*, ed. E. V. Hitchcock (Oxford: Oxford University Press, 1963), p. 203. This is the source for the scene in *Sir Thomas More* that we saw in Chapter 5.

20 E. Hall, *The Union of the two noble and illustrate famelies of Lancastre & Yorke* (London: 1548), f. ccxxvii.

21 This translation appears in *Letters and Papers, Foreign and Domestic, of the Reign of Henry VIII*, ed. J. Gairdner (London: Longman, 1885), pp. 394–6. I have deleted the words 'in the other world' (indicated by the ellipsis), since I am suggesting the French account as the basis of this illumination and these words were supplied by Gairdner from a Spanish version. The French text is reproduced in Harpsfield, *Life of More*, p. 266.

22 See, for example, G. Kaftal, *Saints in Italian Art: Iconography of the Saints in Tuscan Painting* (Florence: Sensoni, 1952). See also L. Puppi, *Torment in Art: Pain, Violence and Martyrdom* (New York: Rizzoli, 1991).

23 The attribution to Caron, and its identification as a representation of More's execution, is sourced by Morison to J. Ehrmann, 'Antoine Caron', *Burlington Magazine* 92 (1950), 34–9. Ehrmann states that the connection with More was made by Mlle Souberbille, librarian of the Museum of the Castle of Blois, in 1947, and rests upon the identification of the figures in the centre foreground as More and his daughter Margaret Roper, drawing on stories of her breaking through the guards to be with him on his way to the Tower. See Roper, *Life of More*, pp. 97–9.

24 T. Stapleton, *The Life and Illustrious Martyrdom of Sir Thomas More*, ed. E. E. Reynolds and trans. P. E. Hallett (London: Burns & Oates, 1966), p. 133. This phrase – 'it is not the death but the cause that makes the martyr' – is also used by John Foxe, *Actes and Monuments of these Latter and Perillous Dayes, Touching Matters of the Church* (London: 1563), 2: 196. See J. R. Knott, *Discourses of Martyrdom in English Literature 1563–1694* (Cambridge: Cambridge University Press, 1993), p. 40.

25 Augustine, *Epistola 89. 2* and *Epistola 204. 4. Patrologia Latina Database* (Cambridge: Chadwyck-Healey, 1995).

26 The troubling of mimetic similarity, as the attempt to reproduce versions of the same, is a structural necessity since, as Melberg proposes: '*Mimesis* is inherently and always already a *repetition* – meaning that *mimesis* is always the meeting-place of two opposing but connected ways of thinking, acting and making: similarity and difference.' A. Melberg, *Theories of Mimesis* (Cambridge: Cambridge University Press, 1995), p. 1.

27 J. Derrida, *Memoirs of the Blind: The Self-Portrait and Other Ruins*, trans. P.-A. Brault and M. Naas (Chicago: University of Chicago Press, 1993), p. 13.

28 Hulse, 'Dead Man's Treasure: The Cult of Thomas More', in *The Production of English Renaissance Culture*, ed. D. L. Miller and others (Ithaca: Cornell University Press, 1994), pp. 190–225, 196. See Greenblatt, *Renaissance Self-Fashioning: From More to Shakespeare* (Chicago: University of Chicago Press, 1980), Ch. 1; and R. Marius, *Thomas More* (London: Weidenfeld, 1993).

29 An indication that these texts were treated in ways analogous to the treatment of the heretical body is revealed by the presence of Catholic biographies at Lambeth Palace. Lambeth MS 827 contains a copy of Harpsfield's *Life of More*; Lambeth MS 179 includes both Ro:Ba:'s *Life of More* and Cavendish's *Life of Wolsey*.

30 N. Sander, *Rise and Growth of the Anglican Schism*, trans. D. Lewis (London: Burns & Oates, 1877), p. 120.

31 Stapleton, *Life of More*, p. 170.

32 G. R. Elton suggests: 'the presence in the realm of so eminent a critic, however silent, was a serious embarrassment to the government who could hardly avoid remembering him when the occasion arose. After all, the rest of the world, especially abroad, always did.' *Policy and Police: The Enforcement of the Reformation in the Age of Thomas Cromwell* (Cambridge: Cambridge University Press, 1972), p. 401.

33 M. de Montaigne, *The Complete Essays*, trans. and ed. M. A. Screech (Harmondsworth: Penguin, 1991), III, 8, p. 1044.

34 See *Laws*, in *The Collected Dialogues of Plato, including the letters*, ed. E. Hamilton and H. Cairns (Princeton: Princeton University Press, 1989), 934a–b.

35 Such a treatment of violence in a religious context should not surprise us. Indeed, René Girard suggests that: 'Religion shelters us from violence just as violence seeks shelter in religion.' In Girard's account, judicial systems repress repetitive private vengeance, substituting a single decisive act of public vengeance carried out by a sovereign authority. Sovereign violence carries no threat of reprisal and enlists sacred ritual to deny the identification between one act of violence and the next in order to end the cycle of repetition. For Girard,

'Violence is the heart and secret soul of the sacred.' Girard, *Violence and the Sacred*, trans. P. Gregory (Baltimore: Johns Hopkins University Press, 1989), pp. 24, 31.

36 S. Weber, 'Upping the Ante: Deconstruction as Parodic Practice', in *Deconstruction is/in America*, ed. A. Haverkamp (New York: NYU Press, 1995), pp. 60–75, 63.

37 Weber, 'Upping the Ante', pp. 63–64.

38 Ro:Ba:, *The Lyfe of Syr Thomas More, Sometymes Lord Chancellor of England*, ed. E. V. Hitchcock, P. E. Hallett and A. W. Reed (London: Early English Text Society, 1950), p. 7. All page references are to this edition and will be given in the body of the text. I have silently regularized *u*, *v*, *i* and *j*.

39 Note also that in a passage describing the qualities which make More worthy of commemoration (which I quote and discuss below, pp. 187–8), despite emphasis on his learning, Ro:Ba: makes no mention of More's writings.

40 R. W. Chambers, *Thomas More* (London: Jonathan Cape, 1935), p. 40. Translation and imitation had a far higher (if constantly shifting) status in the early modern period than they are now accorded. See T. M. Greene, *The Light in Troy: Imitation and Discovery in Renaissance Poetry* (New Haven: Yale University Press, 1982).

41 M. Anderegg, 'The Tradition of Early More Biography', in *Essential Articles for the study of Thomas More*, ed. R. S. Sylvester and G. P. Marc'hadour (Hamden, CT: Archon Books, 1977), p. 14.

42 See H. C. White, *Tudor Books of Saints and Martyrs* (Madison: University of Wisconsin Press, 1963), pp. 129–31.

43 See W. Benjamin, 'Critique of Violence', in *Reflections: Essays, Aphorisms, Autobiographical Writings*, ed. P. Demetz and trans. E. Jephcott (New York: Schocken, 1986), pp. 277–300.

44 Benjamin, 'Critique of Violence', p. 294.

45 See W. Hamacher, 'Afformative, Strike: Benjamin's "Critique of Violence"', in *Walter Benjamin's Philosophy: Destruction and Experience*, ed. A. Benjamin and P. Osborne (London: Routledge, 1994), pp. 110–38. 'Afformation' is necessarily implicit in any performative act: 'afformations allow something to happen without making it happen'. See p. 128, n. 12.

46 See my 'Writing Limits in William Roper's *Life of Thomas More*', in *Writing the Lives of Writers*, ed. W. Gould and T. F. Staley (Basingstoke: Macmillan, 1998), pp. 79–89.

47 R. Southwell, *Epistle of comfort, to the reverend priestes* [1587] (St Omer: 1616), p. 358.

48 Southwell, *Epistle of comfort*, p. 357.

49 J. Culler, *On Deconstruction: Theory and Criticism after Structuralism* (London: Routledge, 1983), p. 186.

50 J. Derrida, *Dissemination*, trans. B. Johnson (London: Athlone Press, 1993), p. 193.

51 E. Hanson, 'Torture and Truth in Renaissance England', *Representations* 34 (1991), 53–84.

52 Since More was born in 1478, he was actually 56 or 57. Ro:Ba: is, however, closer than Stapleton, who tells us that, 'When he suffered in 1535 he was fifty-two years of age.' *Life of More*, p. 28.

53 On violence and early modern texts, see F. Barker, *The Culture of Violence: Tragedy and History* (Manchester: Manchester University Press, 1993).

54 Derrida, *Memoirs of the Blind*, pp. 102–4.

55 Stapleton, *Life of More*, p. 189.

9
Epilogue

When Aristotle comes to describe the nature of the epilogue in his *Rhetoric*, he suggests that it should contain four elements. You should make the audience think well of you, and think less well of your opponent. You should give emphasis to or minimise certain parts of the argument, according to your sense of which will help your case the most. You should arouse the appropriate emotion in your audience, selecting from pity, indignation, anger, hatred, envy, emulation or pugnacity. And you should refresh their memories, reviewing what you have said. He proposes that: 'The first step in this reviewing process is to observe that you have done what you undertook to do.'[1] It is perfectly permissible, he says, to repeat yourself at this point, to drive your message home.

Many things make me wary of following this advice. I have as little desire to write in praise of myself as, I suspect, most readers have to read words of self-aggrandisement at this point. Equally, where I have been led to criticise the works and words of others in this book, I do not see these writers as opponents. Even moments of profound disagreement make me grateful for their work and for the impulse to think that it has generated. There may be readers who will, no doubt, disagree with my own readings in this book, but I have no wish to pose their objections for them or to manipulate them into experiencing a particular emotion. And even refreshing a reader's memory is not as simple as Aristotle's scheme might suggest. I was once told that by the end of an academic discussion, no conclusion should be necessary. The work should all be there, waiting to yield up its sense to the reader, and any closing statement of what that work has added up to should be superfluous. That certainly seems to me to be an accurate account of *The sense of early modern writing.* But my sense that any final summation would be inappropriate or, at best, disappointingly inadequate, stems not from a confidence that the pages that precede can be formed like the pieces of a jigsaw into a coherent image, but rather from a conviction that the form of responsive reading that I advocate in these pages must allow a certain sense of uneasy disjunction to persist. It strikes me that the texts that I have read here exhibit a stubborn refusal to cohere, that is, to give up their singularity, in the service of a narrative or argument that would make everything 'fit'.

Part of my reluctance to go over the ground again stems from a sense that what I 'undertook' to do in this book was not to produce an overview or a historical narrative that would encompass every aspect of early modern writing, even in terms of the limited number of topics that I have been able to cover here. Such a conspectus would indeed be valuable, but I have yet to be convinced that it is possible, and certainly not within the covers of a single book. Instead, I tried to establish the significance of a concern for rhetoric, aesthetics and the senses in reading early modern texts. This was done in order to engage more explicitly than is often done with the relation between the early modern and modernity, and to demonstrate the inextricability of the two. In this respect the aesthetic as a critical category becomes a crucial area of interest, and the stakes of thinking through the aesthetic seem to me to be of the greatest significance for any attempt, formalist or historicist, to think about writing of this period. Necessarily, then, this project was also undertaken in order to reassert the necessity of a form of criticism that engaged with 'theoretical' practices of reading. My argument is not that this form of reading magically eliminates problems to which historicist readings are prone, but instead that certain problems posed by early modern writing are frequently overlooked, and that these problems cannot be wished away by any form of critical practice. This is not simply a modern or presentist imposition; it is implicit and frequently made explicit in early modern texts. As Sidney notes in his peroration to *A Defence of Poetry*, 'there are many mysteries contained in poetry, which of purpose were written darkly, lest by profane wits it should be abused'.[2] This is not a darkness that can be dissolved by a more enlightened criticism, although some forms of reading seem to me to be more illuminating than others.

Each time I return to these texts I see something else, something that I had not noticed, or that I had bracketed off as a side issue, but this does not, I think, point to a failure of my readings so much as a need to recognize that this possibility of reading differently is a necessary feature of our relation to early modern texts. Having emphasized exemplarity, repetition and performativity at several points in this book, it would make little sense for me to propose that I could provide a brief summation of the difficulties that these concepts pose to critics that would offer a suitable closing statement. The examples that I have chosen to read remain open to other possibilities, to being brought into relation with other generalities, other forms of law, other responses. Reading otherwise will always be possible, and that is as it should be. Early modern writing is not closed, completed or finished – it cannot be consigned safely to the past – and no account of it will circumscribe it to anyone's lasting satisfaction. As Thomas More comments at the end of *Utopia*, breaking off his discussion with Hythloday in order to go in to supper, 'first I said that we would find some other time for thinking of these matters more deeply, and for talking them over in more detail. And I still hope such an opportunity will present itself some day.'[3]

Notes

1 Aristotle, *Rhetoric*, in *The Complete Works of Aristotle*, ed. J. Barnes, 2 vols (Princeton: Princeton University Press, 1984), 1419b–1420a.

2 Sidney, *A Defence of Poetry*, ed. J. A. van Dorsten (Oxford: Oxford University Press, 1966), p. 75.

3 More, *Utopia*, ed. G. M. Logan and R. M. Adams (Cambridge: Cambridge University Press, 1989), p. 110.

Select bibliography

Manuscript and unpublished sources

British Library, Additional MS 28786. Odinet Godran, *Expositio Mortis Thomae Mori*
British Library, Harleian MS 7368. *The Booke of Sir Thomas More*
Leeds University Library, Brotherton Collection MS Lt q 32. Hester Pulter's Poems

Printed sources

Acheson, A., *Shakespeare, Chapman, and Sir Thomas More* (London: n.p., 1931)
Aers, D. (ed.), *Culture and History 1350–1600* (Detroit: Wayne State University Press, 1992)
Altman, J. B., ' "Preposterous Conclusions": Eros, *Enargia*, and the Composition of *Othello*', *Representations* 18 (1987), 129–57
Ameriks, K. (ed.), *The Cambridge Companion to German Idealism* (Cambridge: Cambridge University Press, 2000)
Anderson, J. H., *Biographical Truth: The Representation of Historical Persons in Tudor-Stuart Writing* (New Haven: Yale University Press, 1984)
Anderson, J. H., *Words that Matter: Linguistic Perception in Renaissance English* (Stanford: Stanford University Press, 1996)
Appignanesi, L. (ed.), *Postmodernism: ICA Documents* (London: Free Association, 1989)
Aristotle, *The Complete Works of Aristotle*, ed. J. Barnes, 2 vols (Princeton: Princeton University Press, 1984)
Aristotle, *The 'Art' of Rhetoric*, trans. J. H. Freese (Cambridge, MA: Harvard University Press, 1926)
Aristotle, *The Art of Rhetoric*, trans. H. Lawson-Tancred (Harmondsworth: Penguin, 1991)

Armstrong, P., *Shakespeare's Visual Regime: Tragedy, Psychoanalysis and the Gaze* (Basingstoke: Palgrave, 2000)

Attridge, D., *Peculiar Language: Literature as Difference from the Renaissance to James Joyce* (London: Methuen, 1988)

Attridge, D., *The Singularity of Literature* (London: Routledge, 2004)

Augustine, *Confessions*, trans. R. S. Pine-Coffin (Harmondsworth: Penguin, 1961)

Austin, J. L., *How To Do Things With Words*, 2nd edn (Oxford: Oxford University Press, 1976)

Bahti, T., *Allegories of History: Literary Historiography after Hegel* (Baltimore: Johns Hopkins University Press, 1992)

Bahti, T., *Ends of the Lyric: Direction and Consequence in Western Poetry* (Baltimore: Johns Hopkins University Press, 1996)

Banham, G., *Kant and the Ends of Aesthetics* (Basingstoke: Macmillan, 2000)

Barker, F., *The Culture of Violence: Essays on Tragedy and History* (Manchester: Manchester University Press, 1993)

Bate, J., *Shakespeare and Ovid* (Oxford: Clarendon Press, 1993)

Bate, J., *The Genius of Shakespeare* (London: Picador, 1997)

Beaumont Bissell, E. (ed.), *The Question of Literature: The Place of the Literary in Contemporary Theory* (Manchester: Manchester University Press, 2002)

Belsey, C., *The Subject of Tragedy: Identity and Difference in Renaissance Drama* (London: Methuen, 1985)

Belsey, C., 'Love as Trompe-l'oeil: Taxonomies of Desire in *Venus and Adonis*', *Shakespeare Quarterly* 46 (1995), 257–76

Bender, J. and D. E. Wellbery (eds), *The Ends of Rhetoric: History, Theory, Practice* (Stanford: Stanford University Press, 1990)

Benjamin, A. and P. Osborne (eds), *Walter Benjamin's Philosophy: Destruction and Experience* (London: Routledge, 1994)

Benjamin, W., *Reflections: Essays, Aphorisms, Autobiographical Writings*, ed. P. Demetz and trans. E. Jephcott (London: Verso, 1986)

Bennett, A. (ed.), *Readers and Reading* (London: Longman, 1995)

Bennington, G. and J. Derrida, *Jacques Derrida*, trans. G. Bennington (Chicago: University of Chicago Press, 1993)

Bernstein, J. M., *The Fate of Art: Aesthetic Alienation from Kant to Derrida and Adorno* (Cambridge: Polity, 1992)

Bernstein, J. M. (ed.), *Classic and Romantic German Aesthetics* (Cambridge: Cambridge University Press, 2003)

Berry, P., *Shakespeare's Feminine Endings: Disfiguring Death in the Tragedies* (London: Routledge, 1999)

Bibliothèque des Auteurs de Bourgogne, par feu M. L'Abbé Papillon, Chanoine de la Chapelle au Riche de Dijon (Geneva: Slatkine, 1970)

Bloom, H., *How to Read and Why* (London: Fourth Estate, 2000)

Branagh, K., *Hamlet by William Shakespeare: Screenplay, Introduction and Film Diary* (London: Chatto & Windus, 1996)

Caruth, C., *Unclaimed Experience: Trauma, Narrative, and History* (Baltimore and London: Johns Hopkins University Press, 1996)

Caruth, C. and D. Esch (eds), *Critical Encounters: Reference and Responsibility in Deconstructive Writing* (New York: Rutgers University Press, 1995)

Castiglione, B., *The Book of the Courtier*, trans. G. Bull (Harmondsworth: Penguin, 1986)

Cavallo, G. and R. Chartier (eds), *A History of Reading in the West* (Cambridge: Polity, 1999)

Cave, T., '*Enargia*: Erasmus and the Rhetoric of Presence in the Sixteenth Century', *L'Esprit Créateur* 16: 4 (1976), 5–19

Cave, T., *The Cornucopian Text: Problems of Writing in the French Renaissance* (Oxford: Oxford University Press, 1979)

Caygill, H., *Art of Judgement* (Oxford: Basil Blackwell, 1989)

Chambers, E. K., *The Elizabethan Stage*, 4 vols (Oxford: Oxford University Press, 1923)

Chambers, R. W., *Thomas More* (London: Cape, 1935)

Chapman, G., *Plays and Poems*, ed. J. Hudston (Harmondsworth: Penguin, 1998)

Charnes, L., *Notorious Identity: Materializing the Subject in Shakespeare* (Cambridge, MA: Harvard University Press, 1993)

Chase, C., *Decomposing Figures: Rhetorical Readings in the Romantic Tradition* (Baltimore: Johns Hopkins University Press, 1986)

Chedgzoy, K., M. Hansen and S. Trill (eds), *Voicing Women* (Keele: Keele University Press, 1997)

Chillington, C., 'Playwrights at Work: Henslowe's, Not Shakespeare's, Book of Sir Thomas More', *English Literary Renaissance* 10 (1980), 439–79

Clare, J., '*Art made tongue-tied by authority*': Elizabethan and Jacobean Dramatic Censorship* (Manchester: Manchester University Press, 1990)

Clark, T., *Derrida, Heidegger, Blanchot: Sources of Derrida's Notion and Practice of Literature* (Cambridge: Cambridge University Press, 1992)

Clarke, D. and E. Clarke (eds), '*This Double Voice*': Gendered Writing in Early Modern England* (Basingstoke: Macmillan, 2000)

Classen, C., *Worlds of Sense: Exploring the Senses in History and Across Cultures* (London: Routledge, 1993)

Colebrook, C., *New Literary Histories: New Historicism and Contemporary Criticism* (Manchester: Manchester University Press, 1997)

Conley, T. M., *Rhetoric in the European Tradition* (London: Longman, 1990)

Culler, J., *The Pursuit of Signs: Semiotics, Literature, Deconstruction* (London: Routledge, 1981)

Culler, J., *On Deconstruction: Theory and Criticism after Structuralism* (London: Routledge, 1983)

de Grazia, M. and P. Stallybrass, 'The Materiality of the Text', *Shakespeare Quarterly* 44 (1993), 255–83

de Grazia, M. and S. Wells (eds), *The Cambridge Companion to Shakespeare* (Cambridge: Cambridge University Press, 2001)

de Man, P., *Allegories of Reading: Figural Language in Rousseau, Nietzsche, Rilke, and Proust* (New Haven: Yale University Press, 1979)

de Man, P., *The Rhetoric of Romanticism* (New York: Columbia University Press, 1984)

de Man, P., *The Resistance to Theory* (Minneapolis: University of Minnesota Press, 1986)

de Man, P., *Critical Writings 1953–1978*, ed. and intro. L. Waters (Minneapolis: University of Minnesota Press, 1989)

de Man, P., *Aesthetic Ideology*, ed. and intro. A. Warminski (Minneapolis: University of Minnesota Press, 1996)

Derrida, J., *Speech and Phenomena, and Other Essays on Husserl's Theory of Signs*, trans. D. B. Allison (Evanston: Northwestern University Press, 1973)

Derrida, J., *Of Grammatology*, trans. G. C. Spivak (Baltimore: Johns Hopkins University Press, 1976)

Derrida, J., *Writing and Difference*, trans. A. Bass (London: Routledge, 1978)

Derrida, J., *Dissemination*, trans. B. Johnson (London: Athlone, 1981)

Derrida, J., *Margins of Philosophy*, trans. A. Bass (Hemel Hempstead: Harvester, 1982)

Derrida, J., *Signsponge/Signéponge*, trans. R. Rand (New York: Columbia Univerity Press, 1984)

Derrida, J., *The Ear of the Other: Otobiography, Transference, Translation*, trans. P. Kamuf (New York: Schocken Books, 1985)

Derrida, J., *The Truth in Painting*, trans. G. Bennington and I. McLeod (Chicago: University of Chicago Press, 1987)

Derrida, J., *Acts of Literature*, ed. D. Attridge (London: Routledge, 1992)

Derrida, J., *Memoirs of the Blind: The Self-Portrait and Other Ruins*, trans. P.-A. Brault and M. Naas (Chicago and London: University of Chicago Press, 1993)

Derrida, J., *Specters of Marx: The State of the Debt, the Work of Mourning, and the New International*, trans. P. Kamuf (London: Routledge, 1994)

Derrida, J., *Resistances of Psychoanalysis*, trans. P. Kamuf (Stanford: Stanford University Press, 1998)

Dictionnaire de Biographie Française (Paris: Letouzey et Ané, 1985)

Doherty, M. J., *The Mistress-Knowledge: Sir Philip Sidney's* Defence of Poesie *and Literary Architectonics in the English Renaissance* (Nashville: Vanderbilt University Press, 1991),

Dollimore, J., *Radical Tragedy: Religion, Ideology, and Power in the Drama of Shakespeare and his Contemporaries*, 2nd edn (Hemel Hempstead: Harvester Wheatsheaf, 1989)

Donne, J., *The Complete English Poems*, ed. A. J. Smith (Harmondsworth: Penguin, 1971)

Dubrow, H., 'The Term *Early Modern*', *PMLA* 109 (1994), 1025–6

Dunn, L. and N. Jones (eds), *Embodied Voices: Representing Female Vocality in Western Culture* (Cambridge: Cambridge University Press, 1994)

Dutton, R., *Mastering the Revels: The Regulation and Censorship of English Renaissance Drama* (Basingstoke: Macmillan, 1991)

Dutton, R., *Ben Jonson, Authority, Criticism* (Basingstoke: Macmillan, 1996)

Dutton, R., *Licensing, Censorship and Authorship in Early Modern England: Buggeswords* (Basingstoke: Palgrave, 2000)

Eagleton, T., *Sweet Violence: The Idea of the Tragic* (Oxford: Blackwell, 2003)

Ehrmann, J., 'Antoine Caron', *Burlington Magazine* 92 (1950), 34–39

Eliot, T. S., *On Poetry and Poets* (London: Faber, 1957)

Eliot, T. S., *Selected Essays* (London: Faber, 1999)

Elton, G. R., *Policy and Police: The Enforcement of the Reformation in the Age of Thomas Cromwell* (Cambridge: Cambridge University Press, 1972)

Enterline, L., *The Rhetoric of the Body from Ovid to Shakespeare* (Cambridge: Cambridge University Press, 2000)

Erasmus, *The Complete Works of Erasmus* (Toronto: Toronto University Press, 1976-)

Everson, S., *Aristotle on Perception* (Oxford: Clarendon Press, 1999)

Ezell, M. J. M., *Writing Women's Literary History* (Baltimore: Johns Hopkins University Press, 1993)

Fenves, P. D., *A Peculiar Fate: Metaphysics and World-History in Kant* (Ithaca: Cornell University Press, 1991)

Ferguson, M. W., *Trials of Desire: Renaissance Defenses of Poetry* (New Haven: Yale University Press, 1983)

Fineman, J., *Shakespeare's Perjured Eye: The Invention of Poetic Subjectivity in the Sonnets* (Berkeley: University of Calfornia Press, 1986)

Fineman, J., *The Subjectivity Effect in Western Literary Tradition: Toward the Release of Shakespeare's Will* (Cambridge, MA: MIT, 1991)

Fisher, P., *Wonder, the Rainbow, and the Aesthetics of Rare Experiences* (Cambridge, MA: Harvard University Press, 1998)

Folkerth, W., *The Sound of Shakespeare* (London: Routledge, 2002)

Forker, C. R. and J. Candido, 'Wit, Wisdom, and Theatricality in *The Book of Sir Thomas More*', *Shakespeare Studies* 13 (1980), 85–104

Foxe, J., *Actes and Monuments of these Latter and Perillous Dayes, Touching Matters of the Church* (London: 1563)

Gairdner, J. (ed.), *Letters and Papers, Foreign and Domestic, of the Reign of Henry VIII* (London: Longman, 1885)

Gallagher, C. and S. Greenblatt, *Practicing New Historicism* (Chicago: University of Chicago Press, 2000)

Galyon, L., 'Puttenham's *Enargeia* and *Energeia*: New Twists for Old Terms', *Philological Quarterly* 60 (1981), 29–40

Garber, M., *Shakespeare's Ghost Writers: Literature as Uncanny Causality* (London: Methuen, 1987)

Gasché, R., *Inventions of Difference: On Jacques Derrida* (Cambridge, MA: Harvard University Press, 1994)

Gasché, R., *The Wild Card of Reading: On Paul de Man* (Cambridge, MA: Harvard University Press, 1998)

Gasché, R., *The Idea of Form: Rethinking Kant's Aesthetics* (Stanford: Stanford University Press, 2003)

Genette, G., *Paratexts: Thresholds of Interpretation*, trans. J. E. Lewin (Cambridge: Cambridge University Press, 1997)

Gibson, R. W., *St Thomas More: A Preliminary Bibliography of his Works and of Moreana to the Year 1750* (New Haven: Yale University Press, 1961)

Girard, R., *Violence and the Sacred*, trans. P. Gregory (Baltimore: Johns Hopkins University Press, 1989)

Goldberg, J., *Voice Terminal Echo: Postmodernism and English Renaissance Texts* (London: Methuen, 1986)

Goldberg, J., *Writing Matter: From the Hands of the English Renaissance* (Stanford: Stanford University Press, 1990)

Goldberg, J., *Desiring Women Writing: English Renaissance Examples* (Stanford: Stanford University Press, 1997)

Goldberg, J., *Shakespeare's Hand* (Minneapolis: University of Minnesota Press, 2003)

Gould, W. and T. F. Staley (eds), *Writing the Lives of Writers* (Basingstoke: Macmillan, 1998)

Grady, H., *The Modernist Shakespeare: Critical Texts in a Material World* (Oxford: Oxford University Press, 1991)

Grady, H., *Shakespeare's Universal Wolf: Studies in Early Modern Reification* (Oxford: Oxford University Press, 1996)

Grady, H., 'Renewing Modernity: Changing Contexts and Contents of a Nearly Invisible Concept', *Shakespeare Quarterly* 50 (1999), 268–84

Grady, H., *Shakespeare, Machiavelli and Montaigne: Power and Subjectivity from Richard II to Hamlet* (Oxford: Oxford University Press, 2003)

Grady, H. (ed.), *Shakespeare and Modernity: Early Modern to Millennium* (London: Routledge, 2000)

Greenblatt, S., *Renaissance Self-Fashioning: From More to Shakespeare* (Chicago: University of Chicago Press, 1980)

Greenblatt, S., *Shakespearean Negotiations: The Circulation of Social Energy in Renaissance England* (Oxford: Clarendon Press, 1988)

Greenblatt, S., *Learning to Curse: Essays in Early Modern Culture* (London: Routledge, 1990)

Greenblatt, S., *Marvellous Possessions: The Wonder of the New World* (Oxford: Clarendon Press, 1991)

Greenblatt, S., *Hamlet in Purgatory* (Princeton: Princeton University Press, 2001)

Greene, T. M., *The Light in Troy: Imitation and Discovery in Renaissance Poetry* (New Haven: Yale University Press, 1982)

Greenfield, M., 'The Cultural Functions of Renaissance Elegy', *English Literary Renaissance* 28 (1998), 75–94

Greg, W. W., 'Autograph Plays by Anthony Munday', *Modern Language Review* 8 (1913), 89–90

Greg, W. W., 'Was *Sir Thomas More* Ever Acted?' *Times Literary Supplement*, 8 July 1920, 440

Greg, W. W., 'Shakespeare's Hand Once More', *Times Literary Supplement*, 24 November and 1 December 1927, pp. 871, 908

Greg, W. W., 'T. Goodal in *Sir Thomas More*', *PMLA* 46 (1931), 268–71

Greg, W. W. (ed.), *The Booke of Sir Thomas More* (Oxford: Malone Society, 1911)

Greyerz, K. von (ed.), *Religion and Society in Early Modern Europe* (London: Allen & Unwin, 1984)

Habermas, J., *The Philosophical Discourse of Modernity*, trans. F. Lawrence (Cambridge: Polity, 1987)

Hadfield, A. (ed.), *Literature and Censorship in Renaissance England* (Basingstoke: Macmillan, 2001)

Hall, E., *The union of the two noble and illustrate famelies of Lancastre & Yorke* (London: 1548)

Hall, R. (attrib.), *The Life of Fisher*, ed. R. Bayne (London: Oxford University Press, 1921)

Hamacher, W., *Premises: Essays on Philosophy and Literature from Kant to Celan* (Cambridge, MA: Harvard University Press, 1996)

Hammons, P. S., *Poetic Resistance: English Women Writers and the Early Modern Lyric* (Aldershot: Ashgate, 2002)

Hanson, E., 'Torture and Truth in Renaissance England', *Representations* 34 (1991), 53–84

Harpsfield, N., *Life of More*, ed. E. V. Hitchcock (Oxford: Oxford University Press, 1963)

Harris, J. G., *Foreign Bodies and the Body Politic: Discourses of Social Pathology in Early Modern England* (Cambridge: Cambridge University Press, 1998)

Harvey, E. D., *Ventriloquized Voices: Feminist Theory and English Renaissance Texts* (London: Routledge, 1992)

Haverkamp, A. (ed.), *Deconstruction is/in America: A New Sense of the Political* (New York: NYU Press, 1995)

Hawkes, T., *Shakespeare in the Present* (London: Routledge, 2002)

Hegel, G. W. F., *Philosophy of Mind*, trans. W. Wallace and A. V. Miller (Oxford: Clarendon Press, 1971)

Hegel, G. W. F., *Phenomenology of Spirit*, trans. A. V. Miller (Oxford: Oxford University Press, 1977)

Hegel, G. W. F., *Aesthetics: Lectures on Fine Art*, 2 vols, trans. T. M. Knox (Oxford: Clarendon Press, 1998)

Heidegger, M., *Poetry, Language, Thought*, ed. and trans. A. Hofstadter (New York: Harper & Row, 1971)

Heidegger, M., *The Principle of Reason*, trans. R. Lilly (Bloomington and Indianapolis: Indiana University Press, 1996)

Heninger, S. K., Jr, 'Sidney and Serranus' *Plato*', *English Literary Renaissance* 13 (1983), 146–61.

Heywood, E., *Il Moro: Ellis Heywood's Dialogue in Memory of Thomas More*, ed. and trans. R. L. Deakins (Cambridge, MA: Harvard University Press, 1972)

Hill, T., ' "Marked Down for Omission": Censorship and *The Booke of Sir Thomas More*', *Parergon* 17 (1999), 63–87

Hillman, D. and C. Mazzio (eds), *The Body in Parts: Fantasies of Corporeality in Early Modern Europe* (London: Routledge, 1997)

Hobbes, T., *Leviathan, with Selected Variants from the Latin Edition of 1668*, ed. E. Curley (Indianapolis: Hackett, 1994)

Honigmann, E. A. J., 'The Play of "Sir Thomas More" and Some Contemporary Events', *Shakespeare Survey* 42 (1990), 77–84

Howard-Hill, T. H. (ed.), *Shakespeare and* Sir Thomas More: *Essays on the Play and its Shakespearian Interest* (Cambridge: Cambridge University Press, 1989)

Howes, D. (ed.), *The Varieties of Sensory Experience. A Sourcebook in the Anthropology of the Senses* (Toronto: University of Toronto Press, 1991)

Jardine, L., *Erasmus, Man of Letters* (Princeton: Princeton University Press, 1993)

Jay, M., *Downcast Eyes: The Denigration of Vision in Twentieth-Century French Thought* (Berkeley: University of California Press, 1993)

Johnson, B., *A World of Difference* (Baltimore: Johns Hopkins University Press, 1987)

Jonson, B., *The Oxford Authors: Ben Jonson*, ed. I. Donaldson (Oxford: Oxford University Press, 1985)

Joughin, J. J. (ed.), *Philosophical Shakespeares* (London: Routledge, 2000)

Joughin, J. J. and S. Malpas (eds), *The New Aestheticism* (Manchester: Manchester University Press, 2003)

Kaftal, G., *Saints in Italian Art: Iconography of the Saints in Tuscan Painting* (Florence: Sensoni, 1952)

Kahn, V., *Rhetoric, Prudence and Skepticism in the Renaissance* (Ithaca: Cornell University Press, 1985)

Kamuf, P., *Signature Pieces: On the Institution of Authorship* (Ithaca: Cornell University Press, 1988)

Kant, I., *Critique of Judgment*, trans. W. S. Pluhar (Indianapolis: Hackett, 1987)

Kant, I., *Critique of Pure Reason*, trans. W. S. Pluhar (Indianapolis: Hackett, 1996)

Kastan, D. S., *Shakespeare After Theory* (London: Routledge, 2000)

Kastan, D. S., *Shakespeare and the Book* (Cambridge: Cambridge University Press, 2001)

Kastan, D. S. (ed.), *A Companion to Shakespeare* (Oxford: Blackwell, 1999)

Kennedy, G. A. (ed.), *The Cambridge History of Literary Criticism, Volume 1: Classical Criticism* (Cambridge: Cambridge University Press, 1993)

Kinney, A. F. (ed.), *The Cambridge Companion to English Literature, 1500–1600* (Cambridge: Cambridge University Press, 2000)

Kintgen, E. R., *Reading in Tudor England* (Pittsburgh: University of Pittsburgh Press, 1996)

Kolb, D., *The Critique of Pure Modernity: Hegel, Heidegger, and After* (Chicago: University of Chicago Press, 1986)

Knott, J. R., *Discourses of Martyrdom in English Literature 1563–1694* (Cambridge: Cambridge University Press, 1993)

Kraye, J. (ed.), *The Cambridge Companion to Renaissance Humanism* (Cambridge: Cambridge University Press, 1996)

Lacan, J., *The Four Fundamental Concepts of Psycho-analysis*, ed. J.-A. Miller, trans. A. Sheridan (London: Peregrine, 1986)

Lacoue-Labarthe, P., *The Subject of Philosophy*, ed. T. Tresize (Minneapolis: University of Minnesota Press, 1993)

Lacoue-Labarthe, P., *Poetry as Experience*, trans. A. Tarnowski (Stanford: Stanford University Press 1999)

Lacoue-Labarthe, P., *Poétique de l'histoire* (Paris: Galilée, 2002)

Lacoue-Labarthe, P. and J.-L. Nancy, *The Literary Absolute: The Theory of Literature in German Romanticism*, trans. P. Barnard and C. Lester (Albany: SUNY, 1988)

Lanham, R. A., *A Handlist of Rhetorical Terms*, 2nd edn (Berkeley: University of California Press, 1991)

Lanham, R. A., *The Motives of Eloquence: Literary Rhetoric in the Renaissance* (New Haven: Yale University Press, 1994)

Latour, B., *We Have Never Been Modern*, trans. C. Porter (Cambridge, MA: Harvard University Press, 1993)

Lefebvre, H., *Introduction to Modernity*, trans. J. Moore (London: Verso, 1995)

Lever, C., *The Historie of the Defendors of the Catholique Faith* (London: 1627)

Levin, D. M., *The Philosopher's Gaze* (Berkeley: University of California Press, 1999)

Levin, D. M. (ed.), *Modernity and the Hegemony of Vision* (Berkeley: University of California Press, 1993)

Lindberg, D. C., *Theories of Vision from Al-Kindi to Kepler* (Chicago: University of Chicago Press, 1976)

Lindley, D., *The Trials of Frances Howard: Fact and Fiction at the Court of King James* (London: Routledge, 1993)

Llewellyn, N., *The Art of Death: Visual Culture in the English Death Ritual c.1500–c.1800* (London: Reaktion, 1991)

Love, H., *Scribal Publication in Seventeenth-Century England* (Oxford: Clarendon Press, 1993)

Loxley, J., *Royalism and Poetry in the English Civil Wars: The Drawn Sword* (Basingstoke: Macmillan, 1997)

Lukacher, N., *Primal Scenes: Literature, Philosophy, Psychoanalysis* (Ithaca: Cornell University Press, 1986)

Lukacher, N., *Daemonic Figures: Shakespeare and the Question of Conscience* (Ithaca: Cornell University Press, 1994)

Lyotard, J.-F., *The Inhuman: Reflections on Time*, trans. G. Bennington and R. Bowlby (Stanford: Stanford University Press, 1991)

McDonald, R., *Shakespeare and the Arts of Language* (Oxford: Oxford University Press, 2001)

McGrath, L., *Subjectivity and Women's Poetry in Early Modern England: 'Why on the Ridge Should she Desire to Go?'* (Aldershot: Ashgate, 2002)

Mack, P. (ed.), *Renaissance Rhetoric* (Basingstoke: Macmillan, 1994)

McMillin, S., 'The Booke of Sir Thomas More: A Theatrical View', *Modern Philology* 68 (1970), 10–24

McMillin, S., *The Elizabethan Theatre and 'The Book of Sir Thomas More'* (Ithaca: Cornell University Press, 1987)

Mahood, M. M., *Shakespeare's Wordplay* (London: Methuen, 1957)

Marius, R., *Thomas More* (London: Weidenfeld, 1993)

Marotti, A. F., *Manuscript, Print, and the English Renaissance Lyric* (Ithaca: Cornell University Press, 1995)

Masten, J., *Textual Intercourse: Collaboration, Authorship and Sexualities in Renaissance Drama* (Cambridge: Cambridge University Press, 1997)

Matz, R., *Defending Literature in Early Modern England: Renaissance Literary Theory in Social Context* (Cambridge: Cambridge University Press, 2000)

May, S. W., 'Tudor Aristocrats and the Mythical "Stigma of Print" ', *Renaissance Papers 1980* (1981), 11–18

Melberg, A., *Theories of Mimesis* (Cambridge: Cambridge University Press, 1995)

Menke, C., *The Sovereignty of Art: Aesthetic Negativity in Adorno and Derrida*, trans. N. Solomon (Cambridge, MA: MIT, 1998)

Metz, G. H., 'The Master of the Revels and *The Booke of Sir Thomas More'*, *Shakespeare Quarterly* 33 (1982), 493–5

Miller, D. L., S. O'Dair and H. Weber (eds), *The Production of English Renaissance Culture* (Ithaca: Cornell University Press, 1994)

Miller, J. H., *The Ethics of Reading* (New York: Columbia University Press, 1987)

Miller, J. H., *Topographies* (Stanford: Stanford University Press, 1995)

Miller, J. H., *On Literature* (London: Routledge, 2002)

Miola, R. S., *Shakespeare's Reading* (Oxford: Oxford University Press, 2000)

Montaigne, M. de, *The Complete Essays*, trans. and ed. M. A. Screech (Harmondsworth: Penguin, 1991)

Montefiore, A. (ed.), *Philosophy in France Today* (Cambridge: Cambridge University Press, 1983)

Montrose, L. A., 'Renaissance Literary Studies and the Subject of History', *English Literary Renaissance* 16 (1986), 5–12

More, T., *A fruteful, and pleasaunt worke of the beste state of a publyque weale, and of the newe yle called Utopia*, trans. R. Robynson (London: 1551)

More, T., *The English Works of Sir Thomas More*, ed. W. E. Campbell, 2 vols (London: Eyre & Spottiswoode, 1931)

More, T., *The History of King Richard III and Selections from the English and Latin Poems*, ed. R. S. Sylvester (New Haven: Yale University Press, 1976)

More, T., *Utopia*, ed. G. M. Logan and R. M. Adams (Cambridge: Cambridge University Press, 1989)

Morison, S., *The Likeness of Thomas More: An Iconographical Survey of Three Centuries* (London: Burns & Oates, 1963)

Munday, A. and others, *Sir Thomas More*, ed. V. Gabrieli and G. Melchiori (Manchester: Manchester University Press, 1990)

Murphy, A. (ed.), *The Renaissance Text* (Manchester: Manchester University Press, 2000)

Nancy, J.-L., *Le Discours de la syncope: 1. Logodaedalus* (Paris: Aubier-Flammarion, 1976)

Nancy, J.-L., *The Inoperative Community*, trans. P. Connor and others (Minneapolis, Minnesota University Press, 1991)

Nancy, J.-L., *The Birth to Presence*, ed. B. Holmes (Stanford: Stanford University Press, 1993)

Nancy, J.-L., *The Muses*, trans. P. Kamuf (Stanford: Stanford University Press, 1996)

Nancy, J.-L., *The Sense of the World*, trans. J. S. Librett (Minneapolis: Minnesota University Press, 1997)

Nancy, J.-L., *Résistance de la poésie* (Bordeaux: William Blake & Co., 1997)

Nancy, J.-L., *La Communauté affrontée* (Paris, Galilée, 2001)

Nancy, J.-L., *A Finite Thinking*, ed. S. Sparks (Stanford: Stanford University Press, 2003)

Nixon, S., '"Aske me no more" and the Manuscript Verse Miscellany', *English Literary Renaissance* 29 (1999), 97–130

Norris, C., *Paul de Man: Deconstruction and the Critique of Aesthetic Ideology* (London: Routledge, 1988)

Norton, G. P. (ed.), *The Cambridge History of Literary Criticism, Volume 3: The Renaissance* (Cambridge: Cambridge University Press, 1999)

Ong, W. J., *Ramus, Method, and the Decay of Dialogue: From the Art of Discourse to the Art of Reason* (Cambridge, MA: Harvard University Press, 1958)

Ong, W. J., *Orality and Literacy: The Technologizing of the Word* (London: Methuen, 1982)

Orgel, S., *Impersonations: The Performance of Gender in Shakespeare's England* (Cambridge: Cambridge University Press, 1996)

Osborne, P. (ed.), *From an Aesthetic Point of View: Philosophy, Art and the Senses* (London: Serpent's Tail, 2000)

Parker, P., *Literary Fat Ladies: Rhetoric, Gender, Property* (London: Methuen, 1987)

Parker, P., 'On the Tongue: Cross-Gendering, Effeminacy, and the Art of Words', *Style* 23 (1989), 445–65

Parker, P., *Shakespeare from the Margins: Language, Culture, Context* (Chicago: University of Chicago Press, 1996)

Parker, P. and G. Hartman (eds), *Shakespeare and the Question of Theory* (London: Methuen, 1985)

Pascal, B., *Pensées*, trans. A. J. Krailsheimer, rev. edn (Harmondsworth: Penguin, 1995)

Peacham, H., *The Garden of Eloquence* (London: 1577)

Pepper, T., *Singularities: Extremes of Theory in the Twentieth Century* (Cambridge: Cambridge University Press, 1997)

Pieters, J., *Moments of Negotiation: The New Historicism of Stephen Greenblatt* (Amsterdam: Amsterdam University Press, 2001)

Pieters, J., (ed.), *Critical Self-Fashioning: Stephen Greenblatt and the New Historicism* (New York: Peter Lang, 1999)

Pincombe, M. (ed.), *Travels and Translations in the Sixteenth Century* (Aldershot: Ashgate, 2004)

Plato, *The Collected Dialogues of Plato, including the letters*, ed. E. Hamilton and H. Cairns (Princeton: Princeton University Press, 1989)

Pollard, A. W. and others, *Shakespeare's Hand in the Play of Sir Thomas More* (Cambridge: Cambridge University Press, 1923)

Pollen, J. H. (ed.), *Unpublished Documents Relating to the English Martyrs, 1584–1603* (London: Catholic Record Society, 1908)

Potter, L., *Secret Rites and Secret Writing: Royalist Literature, 1641–1660* (Cambridge: Cambridge University Press, 1989)

Preminger, A. and T. V. F. Brogan (eds), *The New Princeton Encyclopedia of Poetry and Poetics* (Princeton: Princeton University Press, 1993)

Pulter, H., *Poems*, ed. M. Robson (Leeds: Leeds Studies in English, 2007)

Puppi, L., *Torment in Art: Pain, Violence and Martyrdom* (New York: Rizzoli, 1991)

Puttenham, G., *The Arte of English Poesie*, ed. G. Doidge Willcock and A. Walker (Cambridge: Cambridge University Press, 1970)

Pye, C., *The Regal Phantasm: Shakespeare and the Politics of Spectacle* (London: Routledge, 1990)

Quintilian, *Institutio oratoria*, trans. H. E. Butler, 4 vols (London: William Heinemann, 1953)

Rabelais, F., *The Histories of Gargantua and Pantagruel*, trans. and intro. J. M. Cohen (Harmondsworth: Penguin, 1955)

Rainolde, R., *The Foundacion of Rhetorike*, ed. F. R. Johnson (New York: Scholars' Facsimiles and Reprints, 1945)

Rancière, J., *The Names of History: On the Poetics of Knowledge*, trans. H. Melehy, intro. H. White (Minneapolis: University of Minnesota Press, 1994)

Rancière, J., *Disagreement: Politics and Philosophy*, trans. J. Rose (Minneapolis: University of Minnesota Press, 1999)

Rancière, J., 'The Politics of Literature', *SubStance* 33 (2004), 10–24

Rancière, J., *The Politics of Aesthetics: The Distribution of the Sensible*, trans. G. Rockhill (London: Continuum, 2005)

Rebhorn, W. A., *The Emperor of Men's Minds: Literature and the Renaissance Discourse of Rhetoric* (Ithaca: Cornell University Press, 1995)

Rebhorn, W. A. (ed. and trans.), *Renaissance Debates on Rhetoric* (Ithaca: Cornell University Press, 2000)

Redfield, M., *The Politics of Aesthetics: Nationalism, Gender, Romanticism* (Stanford: Stanford University Press, 2003)

Rée, J., *I See a Voice: A Philosophical History of Language, Deafness and the Senses* (London: Flamingo, 2000)

Reinhard Lupton, J., *Afterlives of the Saints: Hagiography, Typology, and Renaissance Literature* (Stanford: Stanford University Press, 1996)

Rhetorica ad Herennium, trans. H. Caplan (Cambridge, MA: Harvard University Press, 1954)

Rhodes, N., *The Power of Eloquence and English Renaissance Literature* (London: Harvester Wheatsheaf, 1992)

Richards, I. A., *The Philosophy of Rhetoric* (Oxford: Oxford University Press, 1936)

Ro:Ba:, *The Lyfe of Syr Thomas More, Sometymes Lord Chancellor of England*, ed. E. V. Hitchcock, P. E. Hallett and A. W. Reed (London: Oxford University Press, 1950)

Robson, M., 'Shakespeare's Words of the Future: Promising *Richard III*, *Textual Practice* 19.1 (2005), 13–30

Robson, M., 'Reading Hester Pulter Reading', *Literature Compass* 2 (2005), 17C 162, 1–12

Robson, M., *Stephen Greenblatt* (London: Routledge, 2007)

Robson, M. (ed.), *Jacques Rancière: Aesthetics, Politics, Philosophy*. Special issue of *Paragraph: A Journal of Modern Critical Theory* 28.1 (2005)

Roper, W., *The Lyfe of Sir Thomas Moore, knighte*, ed. E. V. Hitchcock (Oxford: Oxford University Press, 1958)

Rothfield, P. (ed.), *Kant After Derrida* (Manchester: Clinamen Press, 2003)

Royle, N., *After Derrida* (Manchester: Manchester University Press, 1995)

Sallis, J. (ed.), *Deconstruction and Philosophy* (Chicago: University of Chicago Press, 1987)

Sallis, J. (ed.), *Reading Heidegger: Commemorations* (Bloomington and Indianapolis: Indiana University Press, 1993)

Sander, N., *Rise and Growth of the Anglican Schism*, trans. D. Lewis (London: Burns and Oates, 1877)

Saunders, J. W., 'The Stigma of Print: A Note on the Social Bases of Tudor Poetry', *Essays in Criticism* 1 (1951), 139–164

Scarry, E., *The Body in Pain: The Making and Unmaking of the World* (Oxford: Oxford University Press, 1985)

Scarry, E., *On Beauty and Being Just* (London: Duckworth, 2000)

Schiller, F., *On the Aesthetic Education of Man*, trans. and intro. E. M. Wilkinson and L. A. Willoughby (Oxford: Clarendon Press, 1967)

Schoenfeldt, M. C., *Bodies and Selves in Early Modern England: Physiology and Inwardness in Spenser, Shakespeare, Herbert, and Milton* (Cambridge: Cambridge University Press, 1999)

Schopenhauer, A., *Parerga and Paralipomena: Short Philosophical Essays*, trans. E. F. J. Payne, 2 vols (Oxford: Clarendon Press, 2000)

Shakespeare, W., *Complete Works*, ed. R. Proudfoot, A. Thompson and D. S. Kastan, Arden Shakespeare, Revised edn (London: Thomson, 2001)

The Complete Works, ed. S. Wells and G. Taylor (Oxford: Oxford University Press, 1988)

The Norton Shakespeare, ed. S. Greenblatt and others (New York: W. W. Norton, 1997)

Shakespeare, W., *Hamlet*, ed. H. Jenkins (London: Methuen, 1982)

Shakespeare, W., *Hamlet*, ed. P. Edwards (Cambridge: Cambridge University Press, 1985)

Shakespeare, W., *Hamlet*, ed. G. R. Hibbard (Oxford: Oxford University Press, 1987)

Shakespeare, W., *Julius Caesar*, ed. M. Spevack (Cambridge: Cambridge University Press, 1988)

Shakespeare, W., *Macbeth*, ed. N. Brooke (Oxford: Oxford University Press, 1990)

Shakespeare, W., *Othello*, ed. N. Sanders (Cambridge: Cambridge University Press, 1984)

Shakespeare, W., *The Poems*, ed. F. T. Prince (London: Routledge, 1990)

Shakespeare, W., *Sonnets*, ed. S. Booth (New Haven: Yale University Press, 1977)

Shakespeare, W., *Titus Andronicus*, ed. E. M. Waith (Oxford: Oxford University Press, 1984)

Shakespeare, W., *The Winter's Tale*, ed. S. Orgel (Oxford: Oxford University Press, 1996)

Sharpe, K., *Reading Revolutions: The Politics of Reading in Early Modern England* (New Haven: Yale University Press, 2000)

Sharpe, K. and S. Zwicker (eds), *Reading, Society and Politics in Early Modern England* (Cambridge: Cambridge University Press, 2003)

Sherman, W. H., *The Politics of Reading and Writing in the English Renaissance* (Amherst: University of Massachusetts Press, 1995)

Sidney, P., *A Defence of Poetry*, ed. J. A. van Dorsten (Oxford: Oxford University Press, 1966)

Silverman, K., *World Spectators* (Stanford: Stanford University Press, 2000)

Simpson, R., 'Are there any extant MSS. in Shakespeare's Handwriting?', *Notes and Queries* 183 (1871), 1–3

Skinner, Q., *Reason and Rhetoric in the Philosophy of Hobbes* (Cambridge: Cambridge University Press, 1996)

Smith, B., *The Acoustic World of Early Modern England: Attending to the O-Factor* (Chicago: University of Chicago Press, 1999)

Smith, N., *Literature and Revolution in England, 1640–1660* (New Haven: Yale University Press, 1994)

Snow, V. F., *Essex the Rebel: The Life of Robert Devereux, the Third Earl of Essex, 1591–1646* (Lincoln: University of Nebraska Press, 1970)

Southwell, R., *Epistle of comfort, to the reverend priestes* [1587] (St Omer: 1616)

Stapleton, T., *The Life and Illustrious Martyrdom of Sir Thomas More*, ed. E. E. Reynolds and trans. P. E. Hallett (London: Burns & Oates, 1966)

Stewart, S., *Poetry and the Fate of the Senses* (Chicago: University of Chicago Press, 2002)

Strier, R., *Resistant Structures: Particularity, Radicalism and Renaissance Texts* (Berkeley: University of California Press, 1995)

Summers, D., *The Judgement of Sense: Renaissance Naturalism and the Rise of Aesthetics* (Cambridge: Cambridge University Press, 1987)

Sylvester, R. S. and G. P. Marc'hadour (eds), *Essential Articles for the Study of Thomas More* (Hamden: Archon Books, 1977)

Syrotinski, M. and I. Maclachlan (eds), *Sensual Reading: New Approaches to Reading and Its Relations to the Senses* (London: Associated University Presses, 2001)

Tannenbaum, S., *The Booke of Sir Thomas More: A Bibliotic Study* (New York: 1927)

Terada, R., *Feeling in Theory: Emotion after the 'Death of the Subject'* (Cambridge, MA: Harvard University Press, 2001)

Tomkis, T., *Lingua: Or the Combat of the Tongue, and the Five Senses for Superiority. A Pleasant Comœdie.* (London: 1607)

Veeser, H. Aram (ed.), *The New Historicism* (London: Routledge, 1989)

Vendler, H., *The Art of Shakespeare's Sonnets* (Cambridge, MA: Harvard University Press, 1999)

Vickers, B., *Classical Rhetoric in English Poetry* (London: Macmillan, 1970)

Vickers, B., *In Defence of Rhetoric* (Oxford: Clarendon Press, 1988)

Vickers, B., *Shakespeare, Co-Author: A Historical Study of Five Collaborative Plays* (Oxford: Oxford University Press, 2002)

Vickers, B. (ed.), *English Renaissance Literary Criticism* (Oxford: Oxford University Press, 1999)

Vines, R., *The Hearse of the Renowned, the Right Honourable Robert, Earle of Essex* (London: 1646)

Waters, L. and W. Godzich (eds), *Reading de Man Reading* (Minneapolis: University of Minnesota Press, 1989)

Weiner, A., *Sir Philip Sidney and the Poetics of Protestantism* (Minneapolis: University of Minnesota Press, 1978)

Welsch, W., *Undoing Aesthetics*, trans. A. Inkpin (London: Sage, 1997)

White, H. C., *Tudor Books of Saints and Martyrs* (Madison: University of Wisconsin Press, 1963)

Whole Proceedings of the Barbarous and Inhuman Demolishing of the Earl of Essex Tomb on Thursday Night Last, November 26, 1646 (London: 1646)

Widdowson, P., *Literature* (London: Routledge, 1999)

Wilson, R. and R. Dutton (eds), *New Historicism and Renaissance Drama* (Harlow: Longman, 1992)

Wilson, T., *The Arte of Rhetorique* (London: 1553)

Wimsatt, W. K. (ed.), *Dr Johnson on Shakespeare* (Harmondsworth: Penguin, 1969)

Wittgenstein, L., *Philosophical Investigations*, trans G. E. M. Anscombe, 3rd edn (Oxford: Blackwell, 2001)

Wittgenstein, L., *The Blue and Brown Books: Preliminary Studies for the 'Philosophical Investigations'* (Oxford: Blackwell, 2003)

Worden, B., *The Sound of Virtue: Philip Sidney's* Arcadia *and Elizabethan Politics* (New Haven: Yale University Press, 1996)

Index

aesthetics 5, 39–59 *passim*, 65–71, 82–3, 201
aisthesis 5, 30–1, 65–6, 69, 122–4, 151, 169–71
apostrophe 137–8, 140
architectonic 70, 81–2
Aristotle 18, 22, 32, 49–50, 71–2, 74–6, 79, 81, 122–4, 200

Belsey, Catherine 44, 163–4
Bernstein, J. M. 45–7, 54

Caron, Antoine 178–80, 193–4
Chapman, George 31–3, 162
Chase, Cynthia 5–6, 48

Defence of Poetry, A see Sidney, (Sir) Philip
de Man, Paul 4, 24, 62, 64–71, 75, 82
Derrida, Jacques 49, 62–3, 95, 149, 184, 190, 192–3
Donne, John 140

ear(s) 129, 146–65
early modern 39–56
effigy 16, 27, 131–4, 139
Elyot, (Sir) Thomas 19
enargia 31–2, 80

Erasmus, Desiderius 73, 78, 126–7, 148
exemplarity 182–8
eye(s) 15, 25, 30

Ferguson, Margaret 72–5, 78–9
Fineman, Joel 3, 157–8

Gallagher, Catherine and Stephen Greenblatt 41–3
Garber, Marjorie 91–2
Gasché, Rodolphe 23–4
Godran, Odinet 174–81, 192–4
Goldberg, Jonathan 2–3, 121
Grady, Hugh 43–5
Greenblatt, Stephen 41, 44, 48
see also Gallagher, Catherine and Stephen Greenblatt

hand(s) 92–100
Harpsfield, Nicholas 177–8
Hegel, G. W. F. 20–2
Hobbes, Thomas 28–31, 33
Hoskyns, John 78
hypotyposis 23–6, 75, 80

Jonson, Ben 15–17, 21, 27–9, 139
justice 108–9, 174, 188

Kamuf, Peggy 120–2
Kant, Immanuel 5, 20, 23–6,
    45–7, 55, 69–71, 82
Kastan, David Scott 2, 97, 100

Lacoue-Labarthe, Philippe 22–3,
    61–2
Lingua (Erasmus) 126–7, 148
Lingua (Tomkis) 127–9
literature 61–4, 83
Loxley, James 134–5
Lyotard, Jean-François 122
lyric poetry 125

martyrdom 169–74, 189–93
    see also More, (Sir) Thomas
Montaigne, Michel de 182–3
More, (Sir) Thomas 107–8, 112–
    13, 169–94
    as example 182–92 *passim*
    execution 174–80, 191–4
    Works:
        The Four Last Things 107–8
        *History of King Richard
        III* 112–13
        Utopia 202
    see also Sir Thomas More (play)
Morison, Stanley 176–80, 193–4

Nancy, Jean-Luc 9–10n.10, 61–2,
    83, 120

Peacham, Henry 76–8
Plato 19, 49–50, 163, 183
prosopopeia 24, 32, 75–80
Pulter, (Lady) Hester 124–5,
    129–41
Puttenham, George 22, 25, 73,
    78, 171–2

Quintilian 18, 32–3

Rancière, Jacques 123–4
reading 3–5, 64, 92, 200–2

rhetoric 6, 18–27 *passim*, 48, 55,
    71–2, 148
Ro:Ba: 184–92
Roper, William 177–80

Sander, Nicholas 182
Shakespeare, William 43–5, 91, 93–
    4, 96–8, 100, 139, 147–65
    Coriolanus 123, 154
    Hamlet 141, 151–60 *passim*
    Henry IV, part 1 110
    Julius Caesar 147, 154
    King Lear 151
    Lucrece 140, 155
    Macbeth 94–5
    Othello 140, 147, 158
    Pericles 97
    Sonnets 139, 155–7
    Titus Andronicus 93
    Two Noble Kinsmen 97
    Venus and Adonis 152, 154,
        161–5
    The Winter's Tale 93
Sidney, (Sir) Philip 22, 51–3,
    72–82, 201
signature(s) 92, 96–7, 103–5,
    109, 113–14
Sir Thomas More (play) 91–114
    authorship 95–7, 100–2, 114
    censorship 102, 114
    naming in 106–9, 113
    wisdom in 100, 106, 109, 111–13
Southwell, Robert 189–90
Stapleton, Thomas 180, 182, 187,
    193
Syrotinski, Michael 4

Tomkis, Thomas 127–9
tongue 125–9

Vickers, Brian 2, 4, 51
voice 79, 120–9

Wilson, Thomas 18–19, 171